Myth and Reality of the Legitimacy Crisis

Myth and Reality of the Legitimacy Crisis

Explaining Trends and Cross-National Differences in Established Democracies

Edited by
Carolien van Ham, Jacques Thomassen, Kees Aarts,
and Rudy Andeweg

OXFORD
UNIVERSITY PRESS

OXFORD
UNIVERSITY PRESS

Great Clarendon Street, Oxford, OX2 6DP,
United Kingdom

Oxford University Press is a department of the University of Oxford.
It furthers the University's objective of excellence in research, scholarship,
and education by publishing worldwide. Oxford is a registered trade mark of
Oxford University Press in the UK and in certain other countries

Published in the United States of America by Oxford University Press
198 Madison Avenue, New York, NY 10016, United States of America

British Library Cataloguing in Publication Data
Data available

Library of Congress Control Number: 2017934722

ISBN 978-0-19-879371-7

Preface

As this book is going to press, there seems to be a general understanding that democracy is facing its most severe crisis since the 1930s. Brexit, the Trump presidency, and rising support for political parties on the extreme right and left of the ideological spectrum in Europe seem to indicate a decline of the legitimacy of representative democracy. Apparently people have lost their trust in the traditional political parties, the functioning of democracy, and perhaps even in democracy itself. As a consequence, observers across the Western world are deeply concerned that democracy might slide down into the abyss of either instability and chaos, or alternatively illiberal democracy and authoritarian leadership.

However, in the eye of the storm it is difficult to see present developments in perspective. In order to do so, it is helpful to take a step back and place current developments in a longer-term perspective. This is precisely what we do in this book.

It is not the first time that a general pessimism about the legitimacy and future of democracy has dominated the public and academic debate. To the contrary, ever since the Second World War there has not been a single decade without a debate on the crisis of the legitimacy of democracy. Whether it was the student revolution and its concomitant protests and new social movements that swept the Western world in the 1960s, or the overstretching of the welfare state in the 1970s, there was never a lack of arguments or theories predicting a decline of the legitimacy of democracy and the subsequent dismantling of democracy. What many of these theories have in common is their deterministic character: democracy is in decline and this is inevitable.

And yet, most established democracies still exist, suggesting that either the extent of crisis was overstated or that democracies have a remarkable capacity to adapt in response to changing circumstances.

In this book we take a step back to evaluate the empirical evidence for declining legitimacy in established democracies, going as far back in time as our empirical data allow us to. Operationalizing legitimacy as political support, we compare trends in political support in sixteen established democracies from the mid-1970s until 2015, and find no consistent evidence for declining political support. Rather than a clear-cut long-term decline in political support, we find large variation between countries both in levels and trends of support.

These findings call into question existing explanatory theories of legitimacy decline. How valid are theories of modernization, globalization, media malaise, eroding social capital, and party decline, if the predicted outcome (i.e. secular decline of political support) does not occur? And which (new) explanations can account for the empirical variation in political support in established democracies? What is the impact of institutional design and reform, of economic performance, of the quality of government, and of the popularity of public policies?

The successive chapters in this book address these questions, evaluating the empirical evidence for legitimacy decline in established democracies in Part I, critically reappraising the explanatory power of theories of legitimacy decline in Part II, and proposing alternative explanations for variation and fluctuation in legitimacy in Part III. In the final chapter of the book we reflect on the state of the art of legitimacy research, and outline a new research agenda on legitimacy.

Our long-term perspective suggests that a universal decline of political support did not occur, and that moments of declining political support are often temporary. Moreover, while political support has certainly declined in many Western democracies since the onset of the global financial crisis in 2008, these trends are far from uniform across all established democracies.

However, whether citizen support will be able to bounce back from its current low levels remains to be seen. It will depend on the degree to which political systems and leaders are able to adapt and respond to current citizen dissatisfaction. If this book illustrates anything, it is that democracy is a 'moving target', which needs to be continuously reshaped and reformed in order to keep up with social and economic change, and to continue to match citizens' expectations.

Several people have been instrumental in producing this book. The research project that made this book possible was generously funded by the Royal Netherlands Academy of Arts and Sciences (KNAW) "Over Grenzen" program. At the Royal Academy, Koen Hilberdink and Martine Wagenaar were always encouraging and provided outstanding support, in particular by helping to organize and host several conferences at the KNAW headquarters in Amsterdam.

We would also like to express our gratitude to colleagues who participated in the two international conferences held in 2012 and in 2014, and who provided excellent feedback on the research project as well as draft book chapters. In particular, we would like to thank Mark Bovens, Russell Dalton, Max Kaase, Hans-Dieter Klingemann, Hanspeter Kriesi, Tom Louwerse, José Ramón Montero, Pippa Norris, Robert Rohrschneider, Bernhard Wessels, and Anchrit Wille for their participation and feedback.

We would, of course, also like to thank our co-authors in this volume for their patience in dealing with reviewer and editorial comments and their participation in this volume.

At Oxford University Press, we would like to thank Dominic Byatt and Olivia Wells for their editorial advice and assistance, and we would like to thank the anonymous reviewers for their detailed and excellent comments on the book proposal and final manuscript.

Last but not least, Marcia Clifford at the University of Twente and Joshua Gibson at the University of New South Wales were instrumental in preparing the book manuscript: many thanks for your help and support.

Carolien van Ham, Jacques Thomassen, Kees Aarts,
and Rudy Andeweg

March 2017

Contents

Contents

List of Figures

List of Figures

List of Tables

List of Contributors

Kees Aarts is Professor of Political Institutions and Behavior and Dean of the Faculty of Behavioral and Social Sciences at the University of Groningen. He is a member of the Royal Netherlands Academy of Arts and Sciences. His research interests are in democracy, elections, and electoral behavior. He co-edited (with Andre Blais and Hermann Schmitt) *Political Leaders and Democratic Elections* (Oxford University Press 2011).

Rudy B. Andeweg is Professor of Political Science at Leiden University and a member of the Royal Netherlands Academy of Arts and Sciences. He is Chair of the European Consortium for Political Research 2015–18. His research focuses on political representation and coalition government. He recently co-authored *Governance and Politics of the Netherlands* (Palgrave 2014) and co-edited *Puzzles of Government Formation* (Routledge 2011).

Shaun Bowler is Professor of Political Science, University of California, Riverside. He works on the institutions of representative democracy and in particular the relationship between institutions and mass political behavior. His latest book (with Todd Donovan) is *The Limits of Electoral Reform* (Oxford University Press 2013) which examines the possibilities of institutional reform. Currently, Bowler is one of the co-editors of the *British Journal of Political Science*.

Peter Esaiasson is Professor of Political Science at the University of Gothenburg. His primary research interests are empirical democratic theory and the political consequences of ethnic diversity. His most recent book (co-edited with Hanne-Marthe Narud) is *Between Election-Democracy—The representative relationship after Election Day* (ECPR Press). His recent articles have appeared in many journals including *British Journal of Political Science, Electoral Studies, European Journal of Political Research; European Journal of Social Psychology, Political Research Quarterly, Journal of Ethnic and Migration Studies, Social Science Research*, and *European Political Science Review*.

David M. Farrell is Professor of Politics at University College Dublin. His research focuses on parties, elections, electoral systems, and representation, with a developing interest in the application of deliberation to debates over constitutional and institutional reform. He is a founding co-editor of *Party Politics*. His most recent book, *Political Parties and Democratic Linkage* (Oxford University Press 2011), co-authored with Russell Dalton and Ian McAllister, was awarded the GESIS Klingemann Prize for the best CSES Scholarship and the Political Studies Association of Ireland book prize. In 2012–14 he was the research director of the Irish Constitutional Convention and is currently research leader of the Irish Citizens' Assembly.

Mikael Gilljam is Professor of Political Science at the University of Gothenburg. His research interests are public opinion and democracy, political representation, local government, and election studies. Gilljam has published a variety of books and articles have appeared in *Public Opinion Quarterly, International Journal of Public Opinion Research, Journal of Theoretical Politics, European Journal of Political Research, Scandinavian Journal of Psychology, European Journal of Social Psychology, Legislative Studies Quarterly, Scandinavian Political Studies,* and *Parliamentary Affairs.* He is a member of the steering committee for the Multidisciplinary Opinion and Democracy Research center of excellence at the University of Gothenburg.

Marc Hooghe is Professor of Political Science at the University of Leuven, where he directs the Center for Citizenship and Democracy. He holds an ERC Advanced Grant to investigate the democratic linkage between citizens and the state in European democracies. He has published mainly on political participation, political trust, and democratic attitudes. His work has appeared in the *European Sociological Review,* the *British Journal of Political Science, West European Politics,* and the *European Journal of Political Research.*

Anna Kern is a postdoctoral researcher at the University of Leuven. She has written a dissertation on the effects of characteristics of the political system on political participation. She also investigates the relation between participation and trust. Previously, her articles have appeared in *Party Politics, West European Politics,* and *European Political Science.*

Pedro C. Magalhães is a Senior Research Fellow at the ICS-Lisbon. His research interests include electoral behavior, social and political attitudes, public opinion, survey research, and judicial and constitutional politics. His research has been published in journals such as *American Journal of Political Science, European Journal of Political Research, West European Politics, Public Choice, Political Research Quarterly, Experimental Economics,* and others, and in books published by Oxford University Press, Cambridge University Press, and others. He is currently coordinating SPARC, the ICS-U Lisbon research group on social attitudes and behavior.

Mikael Persson is a researcher at the Department of Political Science, University of Gothenburg and at the Department of Government, Uppsala University. His research fields are political participation and public opinion. His recent research has appeared in *British Journal of Political Science, Political Behavior,* and *Political Psychology.*

Jacques Thomassen is Professor Emeritus of Political Science at the University of Twente and a member of the Royal Netherlands Academy of Arts and Sciences. His research interests are democracy, political representation, and legitimacy. He is author and editor of numerous publications including *The European Voter* (Oxford University Press 2005), *The Legitimacy of the European Union after Enlargement* (Oxford University Press 2009), and *Elections and Representative Democracy. Representation and Accountability* (Oxford University Press 2014).

Peter Van Aelst is Professor in Political Communication at the University of Antwerp, a founding member of the research group 'Media, Movements and Politics' (www.M2P. be), and holds a VIDI research project position on Media and Politics at the University of Leiden (2011–17). His research interests are election campaigns, social movements, and (new) media and political agenda-setting. His recent work is published in journals such as *Political Communication, International Journal of Press Politics*, and *West European Politics*. He is the Chair of the International Communication Association Political Communication division.

Tom van der Meer is Professor at the Department of Political Science at the University of Amsterdam. His main research interests are (causes and consequences of) political trust, electoral volatility, and social capital. He has published on these topics in journals such as the *Annual Review of Sociology*, the *American Sociological Review, Comparative Political Studies*, and the *European Journal of Political Research*. With Sonja Zmerli he is editor of the *Handbook on Political Trust* (2015).

Carolien van Ham is a Lecturer in Comparative Politics at the University of New South Wales and an Australian Research Council Discovery Early Career Research Award recipient (2015–17). She was a postdoctoral research fellow at the University of Twente, the Netherlands, and has held research fellowships at the Electoral Integrity Project (University of Sydney) and the Varieties of Democracy Project (University of Gothenburg). Her research focuses on legitimacy and political representation, election integrity, and democratization. She has published articles on election integrity, representation and turnout in the *European Journal of Political Research, Democratization, West European Politics and Electoral Studies*.

Part I
Legitimacy and Representative Democracy

State of the Art, Concepts, and Trends

1

A Legitimacy Crisis of Representative Democracy?

Jacques Thomassen and Carolien van Ham

1.1 Introduction

Is there a legitimacy crisis of representative democracy in established democracies? In the public debate the growing disillusionment with politics seems to
be beyond dispute. Signaling widespread democratic malaise, eroding political
support, and ever-further declining trust in political leaders and politics, the
question "what's gone wrong with democracy?" is increasingly raised.[1] Among
academics as well, many publications in recent years have attempted to explain
"what's troubling" established democracies, noting "declining confidence in
politics" and "the erosion of political support," and seeking to explain "why we
don't trust government anymore" or even "why we hate politics."[2] In an era of
democracy being desired, demanded, and fought for by citizens around the
world, it seems the oldest democracies are faltering, giving rise to a worrying
paradox: everyone seems to want democracy, but once attained, very few seem
to be happy with it.[3]

If this story is true, democracy is in serious trouble indeed. There are two
reasons for this. First of all, legitimacy is important for democracy because
legitimacy ensures compliance with rules by citizens, facilitating the solution
of collective action problems and enhancing the stability of the political
system. If citizens consider political authority as legitimate, they will accept
and abide by laws even if such laws do not benefit their individual interests,
because they were passed according to legitimate procedures. Secondly, legitimacy is especially important for democracies, as the notion of legitimacy is
embedded in the concept of democracy itself. To put it briefly, a legitimate
political system is a system in which political authority rests on the consent of

its citizens. Non-democratic political systems can be legitimate, as long as citizens endorse the right of the political authority (for example, a monarch) to rule. However, while a non-democratic system can also persist without citizen consent, a democracy stops being a democracy if political authority is no longer considered legitimate by its citizens.

But is the story of a legitimacy crisis true? There are two reasons to doubt this. First of all, the story of democratic malaise and crisis is anything but new. Ever since the 1960s, crisis theories of democracy have appeared with regular intervals in media and academic analyses. Scholars such as O'Connor, Offe, and Habermas suggested that the fundamental contradictions of capitalism have resulted in a legitimacy crisis of democracy (Habermas 1973; O'Connor 1973; Offe and Keane 1984), while overload theories argued that the expansion of the welfare state and the increasing complexity of modern societies generated problems of governability that led to the declining legitimacy of democracy (Crozier, Huntington, and Watanuki 1975; Kaase and Newton 1995).

Other scholars noted that societal changes may lead to a legitimacy crisis, with scholars such as Lipset (1959) expecting that rising levels of education and affluence, as well as secularization, would dissolve existing political cleavages and lead to the "end of ideology," resulting in *disengaged* citizens. On the other hand, Inglehart (1977) noticed the emergence of new cleavages as the result of changing value orientations of citizens and wondered whether the associated *rising engagement* of citizens in new forms of political participation would challenge postindustrial democracies. Later, the end of the Cold War and the concomitant discrediting of communism as an alternative to liberal democracy, resulted in propositions about the "end of history," which, while affirming the happy end of liberal democratic supremacy—surprisingly—was foreseen to end up undermining democracy as well, as the lack of contrast with non-democratic regimes would make citizens turn their critical view toward their own political systems.[4]

More recently the political and economic consequences of globalization and the global financial crisis have been mentioned as possible causes of a legitimacy crisis.[5] Clearly, questions about the legitimacy of representative democracy have been asked time and again, as scholars and citizens alike wondered whether "real-existing democracy" matched their expectations, and speculated whether democracy would be able to adapt to changing societal and economic circumstances. Yet, despite all predictions to the contrary, a breakdown of democracy has not occurred yet in any of the older, established democracies, which might be a reason to be somewhat skeptical about successive theories predicting a crisis or even breakdown of democracy.

A second reason to doubt claims of a legitimacy crisis is that the empirical evidence regarding such a crisis is certainly not definitive. Surprisingly, despite the wealth of cross-country and over-time data now available and the soaring number of publications on the topic, empirical evidence is not at all clear about whether there is indeed a decline in the legitimacy of representative democracy in established democracies. Major comparative research projects on the topic in the past decades have come to diametrically opposite conclusions about long-term trends in legitimacy.

On the one hand, several scholars find clear support for declining legitimacy, concluding that: "By almost any measure, public confidence and trust in, and support for, politicians, political parties, and political institutions has eroded over the past generation" (Dalton 2004: 191). Referring to empirical evidence of other studies: "Today, one of the most striking features of European democracies is an apparently widespread feeling of political discontent, disaffection, skepticism, dissatisfaction and cynicism among citizens" (Schmitter and Trechsel 2004: 15).

Yet, others find scant evidence for declining legitimacy, concluding: "The citizens of West European countries have not withdrawn support from their democracies in recent decades. [...] The discourse of challenge during the 1970s and 1980s was thus presumably an élite discourse without any real mass basis" (Fuchs and Klingemann 1995: 435). "There is little evidence to support the various theories of crisis, contradiction and catastrophe. There are few signs of a general decline in trust, confidence in public institutions, political interest, or faith in democracy; nor is there much evidence of an increase in apathy, alienation or faith in democracy" (Budge and Newton et al. 1997: 132). And more recently: "Public support for the political system has not eroded consistently in established democracies, not across a wide range of countries around the world. The 'crisis' myth, while fashionable, exaggerates the extent of political dissatisfaction and too often falls into the dangers of fact free hyperbole" (Norris 2011: 241).

Hence, concerns about a legitimacy crisis appear to be a recurring theme in public and academic discourse in advanced industrial democracies. Yet, representative democracy still exists, and empirical evidence for a secular decline of legitimacy in established democracies appears to be inconclusive.

Nevertheless, most theories trying to explain a crisis of legitimacy depart from the assumption of declining legitimacy. But if no trend of secular decline were to be found, i.e. the phenomenon to be explained does not occur, how valid are theories seeking to explain such decline? And if these theories cannot explain variations in legitimacy, what new explanations can be found that *can* account for the empirical patterns found in established democracies?

This book aims to answer these questions: by (a) evaluating in a systematic fashion the empirical evidence for legitimacy decline in established democracies; (b) reappraising the validity of theories of legitimacy decline; and (c) investigating what (new) explanations can account for differences between established democracies. Before turning to these questions however, it is

5

important to discuss how legitimacy can be studied empirically and reflect on how to evaluate empirical indicators of legitimacy: i.e. what symptoms indicate crisis?

1.2 Legitimacy and Political Support

What is legitimacy? When applied to political authority, legitimacy is often defined as "the justification of authority" (*Stanford Encyclopedia of Philosophy*) or as the "rightful holding and exercising of political power" (Gilley 2006: 500).[6] Hence, legitimacy refers to the normative justification of political authority. Therefore, legitimacy judgments require a comparison of normative principles of what constitutes the "ideal, just" authority to the "real-existing" authority. If norms and reality match, authority will be considered legitimate, and if norms and reality deviate, authority will be considered to suffer from a legitimacy "gap" or "deficit" (Van Ham and Thomassen 2012).

Most contemporary scholars agree that what really matters are legitimacy judgments made by citizens and consequently legitimacy beliefs can and should be studied at the micro level of individual citizens. In empirical research on legitimacy, these individual judgments are usually operationalized and measured in terms of political support, following the seminal work of Easton (1965, 1975). Easton defines political support as "an attitude by which a person orients himself to an object either favorably or unfavorably, positively or negatively" (Easton 1975: 436). He identifies three "levels" or "objects" of political support: the political community, the political regime, and the political authorities. Easton further distinguishes "diffuse" support from "specific" support. Specific support is by definition based on short-term utility. Diffuse support refers to a more abstract and stable support for the political regime that is more or less detached from its immediate performance and forms a "reservoir of good will." Diffuse support can be based on either long-term utility, or on norms and values (Easton 1965, 1975; Fuchs 1989; Thomassen, Andeweg, and van Ham 2017). When diffuse support is based on norms and values it is referred to by Easton as legitimacy (Thomassen, Andeweg, and van Ham 2017).

While legitimacy is thus an evaluative judgment that relates to the match between ideal norms and real practices, political support is a broader evaluation that may derive from normative judgments but may also be based on instrumental considerations (Fuchs 1989; van Ham and Thomassen 2012).

Operationalizing Easton's refined and not always consistent conceptual framework has proven to be difficult. In order to operationalize the full framework we would need to distinguish between three different objects of supports (authorities, regime, and political community), between specific and diffuse support, and between three different sources of support, i.e. perceived

Most diffuse

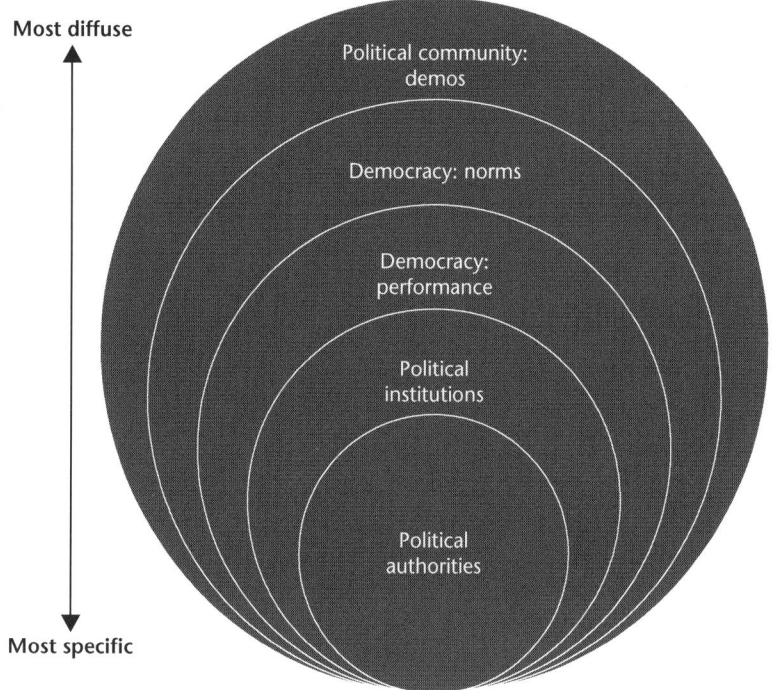

Most specific

Figure 1.1 Levels of political support
Source: Adapted from Norris 1999a.

long-term utility, moral norms or values, and perceived short-term utility (but see Thomassen, Andeweg and Van Ham 2017 for an attempt to develop such a consistent framework).

Given the complexity of Easton's conceptual framework, almost inevitably a more simplified conceptual framework that is more suitable for empirical research has been developed, as illustrated by Figure 1.1 (Norris 2011: 24). This conceptual framework differs from Easton's framework in several respects. First, whereas in Easton's conceptual framework diffuse support can refer to all three levels or objects of support, the two main dimensions of support are here reduced to a single continuum. The successive objects of support are presented as a kind of hierarchy. Moving upward in this hierarchy, political support gradually becomes more diffuse rather than specific. The often implicit assumption is that the higher up in the hierarchy we get, the more consequential political support is for the stability and eventually the survival of democracy. A lack of support for political authorities is not much of a problem. If people are dissatisfied with specific politicians or parties, or with the incumbent government, they can vote them out of office at the next elections. However, lacking support for the political system might be more problematic for the stability of democracy. Secondly, the level of the political regime has been further specified into regime principles, regime performance, and regime institutions, leaving a five-fold classification of political support. In Chapter 2 we provide an overview of the measurements most commonly used to measure citizens' political support, following this framework.

Using this conceptual framework rather than Easton's original one has several advantages. First, as we argued more extensively elsewhere (Thomassen, Andeweg, and van Ham 2017), in Easton's writings the distinction between legitimacy and political support is blurred because it is not immediately clear to what extent the sources of political support should be interpreted as the *causes* or as one of the *defining characteristics* of political support. Easton seems to opt for the latter interpretation. However, we think one should not define a phenomenon by its causes and prefer to make an operational distinction between the phenomenon we are interested in (political support) and its possible causes (in this case legitimacy and long-term utility). By making this distinction we can then consider it an empirical question to what extent political support for the political system depends on its legitimacy rather than on more utilitarian considerations. This is precisely what we do in several chapters of Part III in this volume.

Also, what are generally considered to be the most important consequences of legitimacy—compliance and stability of the political system—are mediated by diffuse support. In Easton's conceptual framework it is diffuse support, whatever its sources (i.e. not just legitimacy), that leads to compliance and political stability (Easton 1975). Therefore, it is quite understandable that diffuse support has often been interpreted as measuring the legitimacy of a political system or political institutions (Dalton 2004: 58). The underlying argument is that while the regime requires stable and high levels of support from its citizens for the objects higher up in the hierarchy to remain stable and eventually to survive, at the level of political authorities support may fluctuate more strongly, both generating and reacting to changes in the composition of incumbent political authorities. Only if citizen dissatisfaction persists over longer periods of time, such dissatisfaction may ultimately spill over to citizens' evaluations of the political regime as a whole, undermining the stability of the regime.

A final advantage of using this classification is that it has been used—with minor adaptations—in all major studies trying to answer the question to what extent there is a secular decline of legitimacy in established democracies.[7] As it is the main purpose of this volume to evaluate the empirical evidence for legitimacy decline in established democracies and to reappraise the validity of theories of legitimacy decline, it is imperative to use the same conceptual framework and data.

Concluding, using empirical data measuring citizens' political support seems to be the best strategy for an assessment of the crisis of legitimacy debate.

According to our conceptual framework a legitimacy crisis might be imminent when: (a) political support is lacking for political institutions and the political regime, rather than the (incumbent) political authorities; and (b) levels of political support follow a trend of continuous decline rather than fluctuation. In Chapter 2 we investigate to what extent these conditions are met in established democracies. Finally, as much as studying political support is relevant for the crisis of legitimacy debate, we will try to avoid mixing up the two concepts in the following chapters. Therefore, we refer to political support when discussing empirical findings based on the classification in Figure 1.1 and to legitimacy when joining the more general debate on a possible crisis of legitimacy.

1.3 Outline of the Book

This work consists of four parts: Part I evaluates in a systematic fashion the empirical evidence for legitimacy decline in established democracies; Part II reappraises the validity of theories of legitimacy decline; and Part III investigates what (new) explanations can account for differences in legitimacy between established democracies. Part IV contains the final chapter (Chapter 11), which summarizes findings and outlines questions that remain to be answered and should be part of a new research agenda.

1.3.1 Empirical Evidence for Legitimacy Decline in Established Democracies

In Chapter 2 Van Ham and Thomassen evaluate empirical trends in political support in sixteen established democracies from the mid-1970s until 2015. They find no consistent evidence for declining political support after the mid-1970s. Rather than a clear-cut long-term decline in political support that is apparent across established democracies, they find large variation between countries, both in levels of political support as well as in over time trends. Hence, despite the frequent assumption in the literature of a secular decline in support for representative democracy in advanced industrial democracies, our re-evaluation of trends in political support in established democracies seems to indicate that:

- If there has been a decline, it seems to have occurred before the mid-1970s,
- From the mid-1970s onward there is little evidence for a secular decline in political support, and
- From the mid-1970s onward there is large variation in both levels and trends of support.

These findings call for a critical reappraisal of existing theories of legitimacy decline: how valid are such theories if the predicted outcome, i.e. secular decline of political support, does not occur?

1.3.2 *Reappraising the Validity of Theories of Legitimacy Decline*

Part II addresses this question by evaluating the validity of theories "explaining" the decline of legitimacy. Chapters in this section of the book each discuss one of the major theories of legitimacy decline. Among the most prominent theories predicting a decline of the legitimacy are: (1) modernization, (2) globalization, (3) decline of social capital, (4) party decline, and (5) media malaise.[8] These theories share a common pattern. They all assume (a) a particular development in society or politics leading to (b) a decline of legitimacy, and (c) are based on an explanatory theory at the micro level explaining why *A* leads to *B*, as depicted schematically in Figure 1.2.

Therefore, knowing that *B* did not happen, the most obvious explanations why these theories are wrong are either that development *A* did not occur or that explanation *C* is invalid. In Part II we critically assess the five theories mentioned above according to this analytical scheme.

In Chapter 3, Kees Aarts, Carolien van Ham, and Jacques Thomassen test the validity of the major propositions of modernization and globalization theories. Modernization and globalization theories offer very different perspectives on legitimacy and to some extent are each other's opposites.

Modernization theory attributes legitimacy decline to the socioeconomic and cultural transformation of advanced industrial societies in the second half of the twentieth century. Societal modernization caused by economic growth, technological development, rising levels of education, and the expansion of mass communication leads to, first, a *change in value orientations*: traditional materialist values are gradually replaced by post-materialist values. Second, rising levels of education in particular lead to an increase in personal skills, to *cognitive mobilization*. Both developments have the same consequence: they lead to "critical citizens" who no longer accept the limited role citizens have in traditional representative democracy. Yet, as such a systematic decline of political support across industrial democracies did not occur, the question is where the theory of modernization might go wrong. Did a change of value

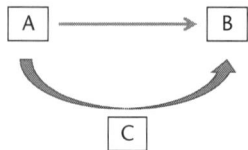

Figure 1.2 Explaining legitimacy decline

orientations and the process of cognitive mobilization really occur? And is there a relationship between value orientations and political support, and between cognitive skills and political support?

Globalization theory predicts negative consequences of globalization on political support. Globalization implies the internationalization of economic competition, which disproportionally hits lower educated and poorly skilled laborers. The work they do can easily be transferred to low-wage countries or be done by immigrants willing to do the same work for a lower wage (Kriesi et al. 2008). Therefore it is the lower classes that tend to see themselves as the main losers of globalization. As a consequence they withdraw their support for government and democracy. Again the question is, what empirical evidence is there for the two main elements in the argument: to what extent did globalization really occur; and second, is political support really declining among lower-educated citizens, i.e. the supposed losers of globalization?

In Chapter 4, Marc Hooghe and Anna Kern evaluate the claim that the decline of legitimacy is due to a decline of *social capital*. The idea that voluntary associations play an important role in establishing social cohesion and political support is a traditional insight in the field of political sociology. The basic assumption is that voluntary associations function as a learning school for democracy. Involvement in voluntary associations renders citizens more familiar with the process of democratic decision-making, which in turn would lead them to acquire democratic norms and skills that they subsequently apply in their relation with the political system in general (Newton, 2001). If this argument is correct, it could be assumed that political support is at least partly influenced by the presence of a vibrant civil society, and as a consequence, the strength of civil society and democratic legitimacy should go hand in hand. Therefore, if involvement in civil society declines we might expect political support to decline as well. As there is no convincing evidence for a secular decline in political support, the question again is where the theory might go wrong. As in Chapter 3, the authors try to answer this question in two steps: first, by evaluating to what extent there really is a downward trend with regard to civic engagement; and second, by studying the relation between civic engagement and political support.

In Chapter 5, Rudy Andeweg and David Farrell discuss the *decline of political parties* as a possible cause of the decline of legitimacy. Political parties constitute a linkage mechanism between the citizens and the political system. Therefore, it is not at all surprising that it is often assumed that a loss of support for parties could delegitimize the political system. However, the decline of political parties can only be a cause of a decline of legitimacy if such a decline does indeed occur. In light of the failing evidence for such a decline the authors debate two possible reasons why the argument might go wrong. The decline of political parties can only be a possible cause of a decline of legitimacy if political parties are indeed in decline and if there is a causal relationship between citizens' involvement in political parties and political support. The authors critically review to what extent the thesis of party decline holds in established democracies, and subsequently analyze how party decline affects political support.

In Chapter 6, Peter van Aelst analyses *media malaise* theories and their consequences for legitimacy. Media malaise theories argue that the increasing availability of information through new and old media, as well the increasingly negative and sensationalist tone of media, are to blame for a variety of political and social ills, including declining legitimacy (Newton 2006a). The increase of citizens' exposure to the media with their negative bias would lead to declining legitimacy. The chapter examines to what extent these popular views are true by providing a systematic review of the available evidence on the effects media have on political support. The chapter evaluates the two central claims of media malaise theory. The first claim is that there has been a general decline of political support because of the growing share of negative news coverage of politics. This suggests a change over time in the way politics is portrayed in the media. Second, to support this longitudinal view, scholars have suggested that a negative or cynical framing of politics has an immediate harmful effect on the political attitudes of individual news consumers. In other words, the chapter first investigates the broader development in the media sector to evaluate whether news coverage has become more negative over time, and next the micro process that might explain the link between media coverage and political support (see Figure 1.2). The chapter ends with some insights into what aspects of the news might reduce cynicism and enhance trust.

1.3.3 *What (New) Explanations Can Account for Variation in Legitimacy?*

Following the critical reappraisal of the validity of theories of legitimacy decline in Part II, Part III of the volume turns to investigating what (new) explanations can account for differences in legitimacy between established democracies. Rather than a secular decline of legitimacy, in Chapter 2 we found large differences between countries in levels and trends of political support. Chapters in this part of the book address the question of how to explain these differences. We analyze to what extent differences in macro-level factors can explain levels and trends of support in different countries, as well as analyzing to what extent contingent, idiosyncratic explanations within countries such as specific events can explain diverging trends.

In Chapter 7, Shaun Bowler analyzes to what extent variation in *political institutions* affects political support. Evaluating the relevant literature the author observes that the literature is not always clear on which institutions should produce what kind of effect, although a very general expectation is that institutional arrangements have the capacity to improve political support when they give citizens an increased sense of connection to, and regard for, the political process. In general then, we should expect institutions that strengthen the quality of representation to strengthen political support. This general expectation is specified in six hypotheses that are subsequently tested: political support is higher in more proportional electoral systems and lower in closed-list electoral systems; it is higher in political systems with multiparty governments; higher in political systems with unicameral legislatures and shorter terms; higher in political systems with more members of parliament per head of the population; and higher in more decentralized political systems. Based on these empirical analyses the chapter discusses how important institutions are for political support, compared to other macro-level factors and individual characteristics. The chapter concludes with a discussion of the prospects for institutional reform in strengthening political support.

In Chapter 8, Tom van der Meer investigates to what extent cross-national differences in political support can be explained by the *quality of government*. Whereas Chapter 7 focused on input institutions, i.e. the institutions that link citizens' policy preferences to political decision-making, this chapter examines the effect of output institutions and procedures on political support. Output institutions, as Scharpf describes them, refer to institutions that should "hinder the abuse of political power." The quality of government perspective implies that the executive ought to be bound by its own rules of impartiality and rule of law. More specifically, the chapter formulates and tests hypotheses about the expected effects of governmental impartiality, rule of law, bureaucratic professionalism, and corruption on political support. Moreover, the chapter argues that to the extent that political support is an evaluation of the regime and its institutions by citizens, any statistical effect of country-level characteristics on political support ought to be both mediated and moderated by citizens' evaluations and perceptions of these characteristics. Therefore, the analyses in this chapter examine the whole causal chain that is expected to relate quality of government to political support.

In Chapter 9, Pedro Magalhães takes the analysis one step further. He starts from the observation that both *economic outcomes* and *quality of governance* are important explanatory factors of political support. Next, he argues that the analysis should take an additional step by testing the hypothesis that the effect of economic performance is contingent on the quality of governance. This hypothesis is derived from procedural fairness theories in organizational psychology according to which procedural fairness moderates the effects of outcome favorability on support for decision-makers and authorities in organizations. The chapter examines to what extent this still applies when we move

13

from the meso level of organizations to the macro level of entire political systems. If it does, we should expect that citizens' satisfaction with the performance of democracy is most affected by economic outcomes in those countries where the quality of governance is lowest. In contrast, in contexts where institutions and policy-making adhere to high standards of quality and impartiality, political support is expected to be less sensitive to short-term fluctuations in the economy. The chapter brings this hypothesis to a test using data from the European Social Survey and aggregate level data on economic performance and the quality of government.

In Chapter 10, Peter Esaiasson, Mikael Gilljam, and Mikael Persson test to what extent variation in political support over time is influenced by *political events*. Analyzing an event within the realm of "normal politics," i.e. a policy decision in a local community to close down schools in the affluent Swedish municipality "Suburbia," the authors study changes in political support among affected citizens and non-affected citizens before decision, after decision, and after implementation. They identify four mechanisms that cause citizens to maintain political support even when faced with a policy decision that affects them negatively: procedural fairness, compromise decisions, fading memories, and constitutional arrangements for vertical division of power. The chapter explores to what extent each of these mechanisms mediates the effect of a policy decision on political support.

1.3.4 *Conclusion and Suggestions for a New Research Agenda on Legitimacy*

The final chapter of the book, Chapter 11 concludes with a reflection on the findings presented in this volume, the implications of these findings for politics and political science, and suggestions for a new research agenda on legitimacy.

In Chapter 11, Rudy Andeweg and Kees Aarts first draw conclusions from the previous chapters. What have we learned from these chapters, and which questions remain or are newly posed? On the one hand, the available (survey) data, which have provided the main empirical foundation of the previous chapters in this book as well as of earlier publications, have by now been extensively analyzed. This analysis provides promising new avenues of research to explain differences in legitimacy between countries and fluctuations in legitimacy over time within countries. At the same time, it is clear that the current data do not provide evidence of an overall legitimacy crisis. This leaves us with a puzzle, as the belief in such a legitimacy crisis is persistent, and it has proven to be quite resistant to evidence provided by political scientists on the basis of data such as analyzed in this work. This discrepancy between current data and public discourse must also prompt us to set up a mirror for political science research: what have we done so far in selecting our concepts, operationalizations, research strategies, and empirical domain, and what can and should be improved? The chapter concludes with suggestions for a new research agenda on legitimacy.

Notes

1. *Economist*, March 1, 2014.
2. Dalton 2004; Hay 2007; Nye et al. 1997; Pharr and Putnam 2000; Pharr, Putnam, and Dalton 2000.
3. *Economist*, March 1, 2014.
4. According to Fukuyama, with the victory of liberal democracy as the only remaining viable form of political organization, "there are no big issues to fight for—only possessive individualism, consumerism, materialism, self-absorption, and a life without passion or struggle, without blood or sweat or tears, and without real achievement or triumph. [...] Life will become so meaningless and so empty that there may even be a reversion to the bloody and pointless political struggles and chaos of earlier epochs." (Fukuyama 1992: 328).
5. On globalization, see Kriesi et al. 2008; on the economic crisis, see Armingeon and Guthmann 2014.
6. Where "rightful" means "in accordance with accepted standards of moral or legal behavior, justice, etc." (Gilley 2006: 500).
7. Booth and Seligson 2009; Campbell 2011; Criado and Herreros 2007; Dalton 1999; Dalton 2004; Kotzian 2011; Newton 2006a; Newton 2006b; Norris 1999a; Norris 2011, and many more. In addition, in recent years a more specific body of research has focused on explaining trust in political institutions and actors (Hardin 2002; Warren 1999; Zmerli and Hooghe 2011).
8. Of course, there are several other theories predicting a decline of legitimacy, the most prominent being *overload theories* and *theories of shifting governance and depoliticization.Overload theory* argues that governments are increasingly unable to meet citizens demands in terms of economic and welfare state policies, leading to declining legitimacy. Modern versions of overload theory argue that through processes such as globalization governments have increasingly less control over economic policies (let alone outcomes), while at the same time societal developments such as aging populations lead to increasing demands on governments (Crozier et al. 1975; Kaase and Newton 1995; Schmitter and Trechsel 2004; Newton 2006b; Kumlin 2011). *Theories of shifting governance and depoliticization* argue that traditional mechanisms of political representation are increasingly undermined by the "shift" of politics from the national political arena to supranational, subnational, and non-majoritarian arena's of decision-making. The main argument running through this literature is that due to such processes as European integration, multilevel governance and privatization, discretion over policy-making and policy implementation have increasingly shifted—vertically—from the national level to the European and

the local level, as well as—horizontally—to non-majoritarian institutions and to markets (Mair 2013; Schmitter and Trechsel 2004; Van Kersbergen and Van Waarden 2004). The consequently diminished discretion of national politicians over policy-making and implementation leaves citizens with the perception that they have little influence on politics, undermining legitimacy. The main arguments derived from these theories are very similar to those of globalization on the one hand and the decline of parties on the other hand and therefore are addressed in Chapters 3 and 5 respectively. For a concise overview of decline of legitimacy theories, see Kaase and Newton 1995; Norris 2011; Dalton 2004; and Thomassen, Van Ham, and Andeweg 2014.

2

The Myth of Legitimacy Decline

An Empirical Evaluation of Trends in Political Support in Established Democracies

Carolien van Ham and Jacques Thomassen

2.1 Introduction

Despite the wealth of data and research on political support, scholars have not been able to reach agreement on whether there is indeed a decline in the legitimacy of representative democracy in established democracies. Major comparative research projects have come to diametrically opposite conclusions about long-term trends in political support (Klingemann and Fuchs 1995; Dalton 2004; Norris 2011; Pharr and Putnam 2000; Hay 2007; Budge and Newton et al. 1997). In this chapter we review the decline of legitimacy literature and re-evaluate the empirical evidence for declining political support, comparing trends in political support in sixteen established democracies from the mid-1970s until the present.

In Section 2.2 we briefly discuss measurements of political support used in this chapter. In Section 2.3 we turn to the state of empirical research and analyze the puzzling contradictory conclusions of major comparative research projects on this topic in the past years. Section 2.4 then evaluates the empirical evidence available in three cross-national data sets (Eurobarometer, World/ European Values Survey, and European Election Studies), comparing trends in political support at the level of the political community, the political regime, the political institutions, and political authorities from the mid-1970s until the present. We find no consistent evidence for declining political support in this period. Section 2.5 concludes by summarizing the findings and discussing the implications of these findings for explanations of political support.

2.2 Measuring Political Support

Empirical research on legitimacy most often relies on measurements of political support, following the seminal work of Easton (1965, 1975). Easton defines political support as "an attitude by which a person orients himself to an object either favorably or unfavorably, positively or negatively" (Easton 1975: 436). He identified three "levels" or "objects" of political support: the political community, the political regime, and the political authorities. The level of the political regime was later further specified by Dalton (1999) and Norris (1999a) into regime principles, regime performance, and regime institutions, leaving a five-fold classification of political support (see Chapter 1, Figure 1.1).

In Chapter 1, we discussed how empirical data measuring citizens' political support can indicate a legitimacy crisis either when political support is lacking at the level of the political regime (indicating more structural dissatisfaction of citizens with their political regime rather than temporary dissatisfaction with incumbent political authorities), or when levels of political support follow a trend of continuous decline (indicating long-term and increasing dissatisfaction rather than temporary dissatisfaction). In this chapter we evaluate empirical data on political support to assess whether we find evidence for these developments in established democracies.

Table 2.1 provides an overview of the measurements most commonly used to measure citizens' political support at different levels.[1] Support for the

Table 2.1 Measuring political support: current measurements

Level of support	Indicator	Measurement
Political community	Affective attachment to political community	National pride
Political regime		
Principles	Preferred political system	Preferred: having a democratic system, democracy best political system in all circumstances
	Evaluation of democracy as a political system	Democracy may have problems but better than any other form of government
Performance	Evaluation of performance of the democratic political system	Satisfaction with way democracy works in country
Institutions	Confidence/trust in institutions	Confidence/trust in: armed forces, police, justice/legal system, parliament, political parties, civil services, local government
Political authorities	Confidence/trust in political actors and authorities	Confidence/trust in: national government/cabinet, president/prime minister, politicians, civil servants Trust the government to do what is right
	Evaluation of performance of national government	Satisfaction with the national government/cabinet Approval of government's record

political community is most commonly measured as national pride. Regarding support for the *political regime*, regime principles are often measured as support for democratic political regimes versus other regime types, or as citizens' evaluations of democracy as a political regime. Regime performance is often measured as satisfaction with the functioning of democracy. Support for *regime institutions* is most frequently measured by trust or confidence in a range of different political institutions, such as the parliament, the legal system, and political parties.[2]

Finally, support for *political authorities* is most commonly measured by trust in (incumbent) political authorities as well as evaluations of their perform- ance. Trust in political authorities often refers to trust in politicians, the president or the national government, or cabinet. Evaluations of performance tend to inquire about respondents' satisfaction with "the people in national office" or ask respondents to evaluate the governments' record or "how good (or bad) a job the government or president has done."[3] Using these data on political support, we can now turn to evaluate the empirical evidence on trends of political support.

2.3 Declining Political Support: Yes or No?

Is political support indeed declining in established democracies? Unfortu- nately, existing empirical research does not provide a conclusive answer to this question, despite the wealth of cross-country and over-time data now available. The first large-scale comparative study trying to answer this ques- tion was the *Beliefs in Government (BIG)* project, conducted in the early 1990s.[4] One of the major problems this project had to deal with was the lack of consistent measurements over time within countries, let alone longitudinal data suitable for comparisons across countries. This situation has gradually improved with the collection of data in the context of several comparative longitudinal studies such as the Eurobarometer, the European and World Values Studies, the European Election Studies, and more recently, the European Social Survey. As a consequence the number of publications seeking to answer the question of declining political support has soared.[5] However, so far this has not led to an unequivocal conclusion. On the one hand, Pharr and Putnam, Dalton, Hay and others find support for long-term decline in political support.[6] On the other hand, Fuchs and Klingemann, Budge and Newton et al., Norris, and Van de Walle et al. find no support for long-term decline.[7]

Why do these studies come to such different conclusions? The differences between the findings of the *Beliefs in Government* project and later studies can probably be explained by the longer time period and the larger number of countries covered. This, however, can hardly explain why the more recent studies come to such different conclusions. Of course, differences in conclusions reached could be due to a variety of reasons: (a) differences in conceptualization; (b) differences in measurement indicators used; (c) differences in data used; or (d) differences in sample—both in terms of countries as well as time-periods studied. As regards conceptualization and measurement, most studies use very similar conceptualizations and measurement indicators. As discussed in Section 2.2, most authors follow Easton's distinction between political objects, differentiating the political community, the political regime, and the political authorities, and use Dalton's and Norris's further distinction of three sub-elements within the political regime: regime principles, regime performance/regime norms and procedures, and regime institutions.[8] Moreover, indicators used are also very similar, with most studies relying on time series on national pride, satisfaction with democracy, and trust in institutions and political authorities for their conclusions. Differences might be due to different data used, with Dalton relying mostly on data from national election studies, while Norris and Van de Walle et al. use data from comparative data sets.[9] However, authors using national election study data have also questioned the decline of legitimacy thesis,[10] and hence this seems unlikely to be the main source of the diverging findings. Hence, it seems most likely that the different conclusions of authors are based on either the time periods analyzed (Dalton's analyses go further back in time than those of other authors), the countries studied (only European democracies or a broader sample of advanced industrial democracies including countries such as the United States, Canada, and Australia), or differences in the interpretation of trends.

When considering findings for different levels of support, the real disagreement about empirical trends appears to lie at the level of support for political institutions and political authorities. At the level of support for the political community, Klingemann, Dalton, and Norris all find that support is high and stable, and if anything increasing rather than decreasing.[11] Support for regime principles also seems to be almost universally high (and trends at this level are not studied by any of these authors due to limited over-time data measuring support for regime principles). Authors even seem to agree that support for regime performance, measured as satisfaction with the way democracy works, demonstrates no clear downward trend.[12]

At the level of support for regime institutions, however, Pharr and Putnam find declining confidence in parliament between roughly 1980 and 1995 in ten out of fourteen advanced industrial democracies and Dalton finds declining confidence in parliament between 1966 and 2001 in eleven out of seventeen countries in his sample (though for most countries the time series start in the 1970s).[13] Though Norris also finds declining confidence in parliament between 1997 and 2009 in eleven out of fifteen European democracies, only two of these over-time trends are significant, leading her to conclude there is evidence of trendless fluctuation rather than a secular decline for this level of support.[14] Looking at later data (2002–2009), a recent volume appears to confirm Norris's conclusions, arguing that trust in a wide range of political institutions, though certainly fluctuating over time and demonstrating important country differences, does not seem to follow an over-time pattern of decline.[15]

This leaves us with the level of political authorities, the level of support that Easton argued to be the least consequential for regime stability, the level of support that Kaase and Newton and many others would argue requires critical citizens, and the level of support where ups and downs are part of everyday politics.[16] While Holmberg finds strong variation in trends of trust in politicians in six European democracies (Denmark, Norway, Iceland, the Netherlands, Finland, and Sweden) from the early 1970s to mid-1990s, Hay finds declining support for political authorities in the US, France, and Sweden going further back in time (considering periods of 1958–2004, 1968–94, and 1976–2000 respectively).[17] Dalton also finds the most consistent and widespread evidence of an over-time decline in support at the level of political authorities, yet Norris only finds declining trust in national governments in half her sample and finds no evidence for declining trust in political parties.[18]

In 2012 Norris and Dalton updated their findings for trends of political support.[19] Both reiterate their earlier findings that there is scant evidence for declining levels of political support at the level of the political community and political regime. At the level of political institutions and political authorities however, Dalton argues using national election studies data from the 1960s until the present, that there is consistent evidence of declining support for parliament, political parties, and politicians in at least five established democracies (i.e. the United States, West Germany, Canada, France, and Sweden). However, his analyses also seem to show that the most significant decline took place in the 1960s and 1970s, with levels of support leveling off in the early 1980s, something also suggested in the analyses by Hay on the UK and the US.[20] The latter might explain why Norris, analyzing the later period from the mid-1990s until 2008 with Eurobarometer data, finds no evidence for declining trust in national government, political parties, or parliament in European democracies.

Hence, it seems disagreement about trends in political support is mainly located at the levels of support for political institutions and political authorities. Moreover, divergent findings appear to be driven by differences in the time period and countries analyzed, still leaving us without a conclusive answer about long-term trends in political support. In Section 2.4 we therefore analyze the available cross-national data on political support, using multiple data sets for as long as possible time period for a sample of sixteen established democracies, to evaluate the empirical evidence for declining political support in advanced industrial democracies.

2.4 Empirical Evidence of Trends

In this section we analyze the data available from three of the most commonly used cross-national data sets in research on political support: the World Values Survey and the European Values Survey (WVS/EVS), the Eurobarometer surveys (Eurobarometer), and the European Election Studies (EES).[21] These data sets vary in their coverage of countries and years, which may lead to different conclusions about trends in political support, hence we analyze them in conjunction (see Appendices: Tables 2.A and 2.B for a description of the sample covered by each data set and question wording). In addition, we use data from the American National Election Studies to complement these data for the United States. We compare trends in political support within sixteen established democracies (fifteen European democracies and the United States) at the level of the political community, the political regime, the political institutions, and political authorities.

As regards the time covered, unfortunately not all indicators of political support are measured for long periods of time in the comparative data sets. Figure 2.1 shows the time span covered for each level of political support. Support for the political community and the political regime has been measured over a longer period of time: the data on national pride start in 1980 and the data on satisfaction with democracy in 1973. As for support for political institutions, the data on trust in parliament start in 1980, however data on support for political parties start only in the mid-1990s. Finally, data on support for political authorities, i.e. trust in government, start only in the late 1980s.[22] Hence, comparative data on trends in regime-level support go back until the early 1970s, and data on trends in support for political institutions go back until the early 1980s. Comparative data on support for political authorities is only available from 1989 onward.[23]

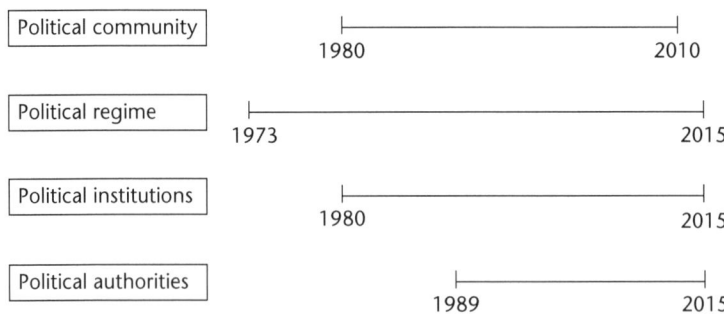

Figure 2.1 Time coverage comparative data sets

Note that the timeline for support for the political regime refers to data on political regime performance, as for support for regime principles over-time data is too limited to draw conclusions about trends.

As regards the sample of countries covered by the different data sets, fifteen European democracies and the United States are the most consistently covered, and hence we include those here. Note that since we are interested in aggregate level trends, we only include indicators and countries with a minimum of three observations in time.[24] Moreover, since in most surveys different countries were included at different points in time, to avoid the composition of the sample changing over time, we report country-level trends.[25]

2.4.1 *Support for the Political Community*

Support for the political community is measured as national pride (the proportion of respondents indicating to be very proud and quite proud of their nationality). As Figure 2.2 shows, support for the political community appears to be high, on average around eighty percent for the European democracies and over ninety percent for the United States. Support for the political community also appears to be rather stable over time. The Eurobarometer data that are collected yearly or twice a year demonstrate some fluctuation, however, here support is also rather stable. The country trend graphs also show that for most countries national pride is high and stable over time, with the exception

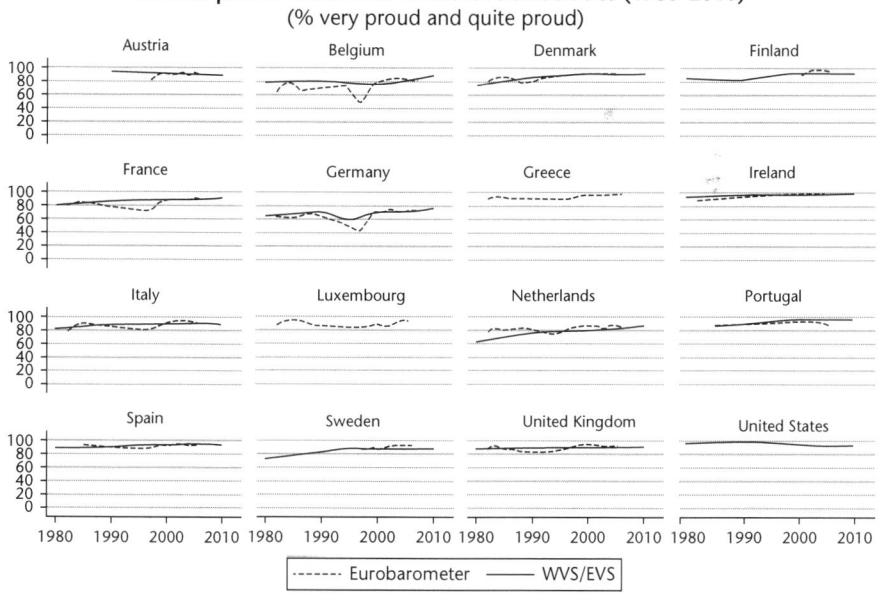

Figure 2.2 Support for the political community

Note that for Greece and Luxembourg only Eurobarometer data is reported as in the WVS/EVS data only two time points were observed. Data for the United States are only available in the WVS/EVS data.

of Germany, where levels of national pride are on average still lower than in other countries, and with some countries showing marked dips at certain points in time, such as Belgium, Germany, and to a lesser extent France. Bivariate tests of the significance of trends (see Appendices: Table 2.C) show that in thirteen out of the fifteen European democracies, national pride, in fact, increased over time, while in the US national pride appears to have declined somewhat, leaving only three out of sixteen of the established democracies to have experienced declining political support at this level. Concluding, support for the political community appears to be high and increasing in the majority of countries in our sample.

2.4.2 Support for Political Regime Principles

Support for the political regime has been measured both as support for democracy-as-an-ideal, i.e. regime principles as well as democracy-in-practice, i.e. regime performance. Support for democracy as an ideal has been measured in the data sets analyzed here with three survey questions: "having a democratic political regime" is a good way of governing this country (WVS/EVS), "democracy may have problems but is better than any other system" (WVS/EVS), and "democracy is the best political regime in all circumstances" (Eurobarometer) (see also Appendices: Table 2.B). The latter question allows citizens to choose between "democracy," or "in certain circumstances a dictatorship could be a good thing", or "no difference." Unfortunately, these questions have rarely been asked repeatedly over time, so that drawing firm conclusions about over-time trends in political support for this item is not possible (for most countries T = 2). Rather, we report the averages for the EU6, EU15,[26] and the US in Tables 2.2a and 2.2b within this chapter. Clearly, the vast majority of citizens in these established democracies support democracy as a political regime: the overall average varies between ninety-one percent

Table 2.2a Support for democracy as a political regime

Time (wave)	Having a democratic political regime (% very good and fairly good)			Democracy may have problems, but is better than other systems (% agree strongly and agree)		
	EU6	EU15	US	EU6	EU15	US
1994–1999 (3rd wave)			91			92
1999–2004 (4th wave)	93	93	89	94	93	87
2005–2007 (5th wave)			87			
2008–2010 (6th wave)	92	92		93	94	
Average	93	93	89	94	93	90

Source: WVS/EVS.

Table 2.2b Support for democracy as a political regime

Time (wave)	Democracy best political system in all circumstances (% prefers democracy)	
	EU6	EU15
1988	80	
1992	83	
1997	80	83
Average	**81**	**83**

Source: Eurobarometer.

and ninety-three percent, and country averages (not shown) range from eighty-six percent to ninety-eight percent. Also, there does not seem to be much evidence of over time change (even if our data are too limited to evaluate this). However, the Eurobarometer data demonstrate that when citizens are presented with a clear alternative system (instead of just asked to evaluate democracy), support for democracy is markedly lower: the overall average ranges from eighty-one percent to eighty-three percent, and country averages (not shown) vary from seventy percent to ninety-four percent. This underscores the need to improve measures of support for democracy by asking more specifically what citizens understand democracy to be, and contrasting democracy with alternatives, in order to avoid paying lip service to democracy.[27]

2.4.3 *Support for Political Regime Performance*

Support for democracy as it functions *in practice* has been measured by asking citizens about their satisfaction with the way democracy works or develops. For this question the Eurobarometer data provides a long-time series, starting in 1973 until 2015. Figure 2.3 shows, as could be expected, that satisfaction with the actual functioning of democracy is substantially lower than levels of support for democracy as an ideal political regime. Nevertheless, satisfaction with democracy is still quite high, on average around sixty percent. However, as the country graphs also show, there is enormous variation between countries, with average levels of satisfaction with democracy reaching a low of twenty-nine percent in Italy and a high of seventy-nine percent in Denmark. Also, trends vary widely between countries. While countries such as Denmark and Sweden, and to a lesser extent Luxembourg and the Netherlands show a clear upward trend in satisfaction with democracy over time, countries such as Portugal seem to experience a clear downward trend, while in countries such as Germany and Belgium there is strong variation over time.

Bivariate tests of the significance of trends show that, of the fifteen European democracies only four experienced declining satisfaction with democracy

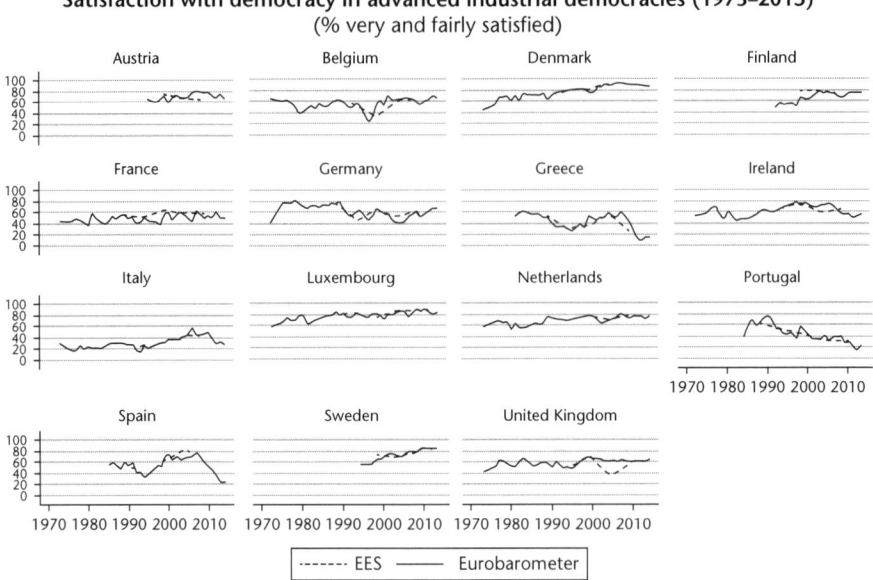

Figure 2.3 Support for the political regime

Note that data for the United States are available for only one time point in the WVS/EVS and not available in the ANES data and the US is hence not reported in this graph.

between 1973 and 2015, and eleven experienced significant increases in satisfaction with democracy in that period (Eurobarometer data). Hence, these data show no evidence for declining long-term political support for the performance of political regimes. If anything, the dominant long-term trend seems to be one of *increasing* satisfaction with democracy. However, a more accurate conclusion seems to be that there is simply no universal cross-national pattern with regard to satisfaction with democracy, rather there appears to be strong variation in over-time trends between countries.

2.4.4 *Support for Political Institutions*

As the concern with declining legitimacy refers mainly to the representative dimension of democracy, we measure support for political institutions as trust in parliament and trust in political parties. Figure 2.4 shows the trends for trust in national parliaments, from 1980 onward. Again, the data do not seem to provide much evidence for a widespread and persistent decline in political support over time, except since 2008 with the onset of the economic crisis, and in the US. The country graphs demonstrate, however, that also with respect to trust in parliament, there is strong variation between countries, both in the level of trust as well as in trends over time. Levels of trust in parliament vary

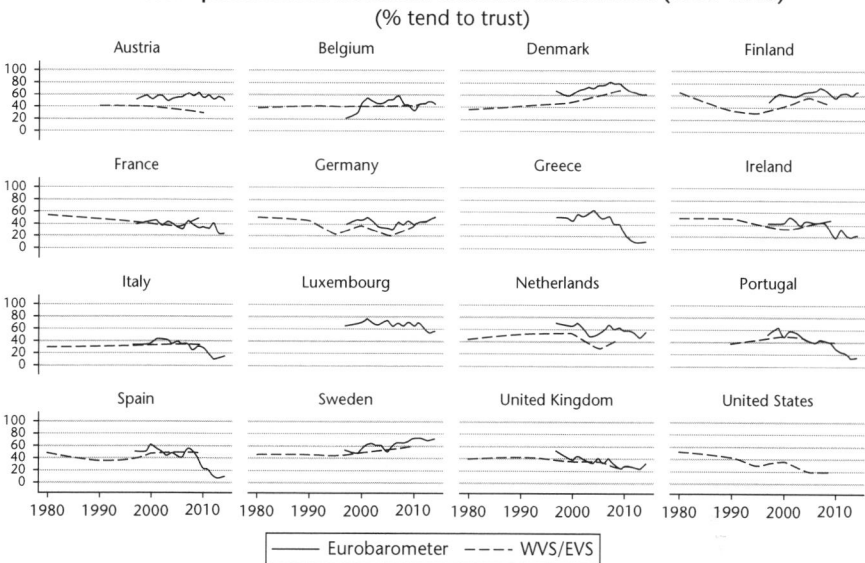

Figure 2.4 Support for political institutions—parliament

Note that for Luxembourg and Greece only Eurobarometer data are reported as in the WVS/EVS data only two time points were observed. Data for the United States are only available in the WVS/EVS data.

from country averages of thirty-one percent in Italy to sixty-nine percent in Denmark. Trends vary from clear trends of declining trust in parliament in countries such as the United States, France, and Greece, to seemingly increasing levels of trust over time in countries such as Sweden and Denmark.

Bivariate tests of the significance of trends show that trends of declining trust in parliament are more common, however. Among the sixteen established democracies in our sample, trust in parliament declined in eight out of fourteen countries between 1980 and 2010 (WVS/EVS data), and among the fifteen European democracies trust in parliament declined in nine countries between 1997 and 2015 (Eurobarometer data). Hence with respect to trust in parliament, we do confirm a negative trend in about sixty percent of the countries in our sample since the 1980s, with a stronger decline having occurred in the last decade. However, concerning as these trends certainly are, even here the data do not support a conclusion of a *universal* long-term trend of decline, as the variation between countries in Figure 2.4 shows.

Turning to trust in political parties, Figure 2.5 shows the over-time trends from 1995 onwards. Clearly, trust in political parties is very low, varying between country averages as low as thirteen percent in France to forty-three percent in Denmark. As Figure 2.5 shows, very few of the trends seem to indicate evidence of decline, however, with the data sets used here trust in

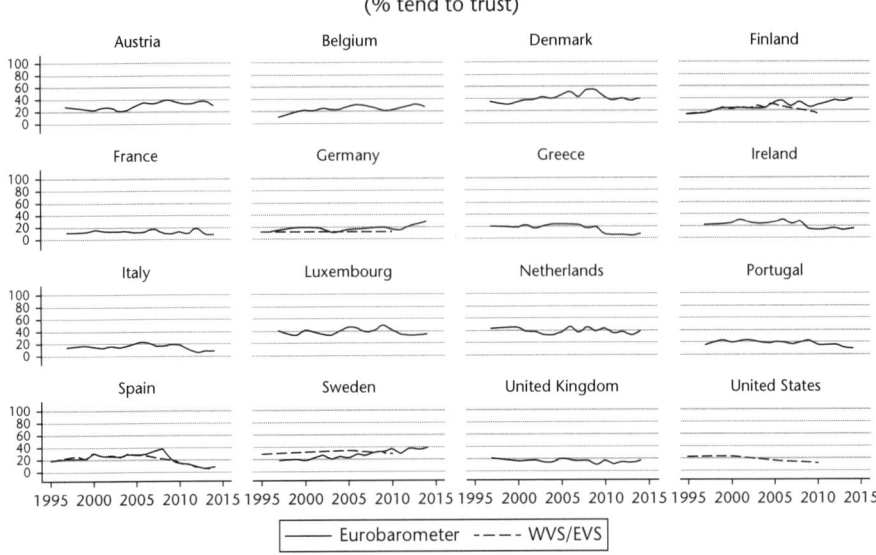

Figure 2.5 Support for political institutions—political parties

Note that for countries for which only Eurobarometer data are reported the WVS/EVS data contained only two or less time points. Eurobarometer data run until 2014, as trust in political parties was not asked in the 2015 Eurobarometer survey.

Note that data for Spain go back to 1990, but since this is the only country with data for this variable before 1995, the graph reports trends since 1995. We do use all available data for the significance tests of trends, reported in Appendices: Table 2.C.

political parties is only measured as of 1995 and hence we cannot evaluate to what extent trust in political parties might have declined in the course of the 1970s and 1980s. For the period after 1995, however, it seems clear there was no singular decline in support for political parties. The country graphs again show strong variation in trends and fluctuation over time, varying from increasing trust in political parties in Finland and Sweden, to decreasing trust in Portugal and Spain, and fluctuation in Luxembourg and the Netherlands.

Bivariate tests of significance of trends confirm the variation between countries: among the European democracies, nine out of fifteen experienced declining levels of trust in political parties, while six out of fifteen saw trust in political parties increase between 1995 and 2014 (Eurobarometer data). The WVS/EVS data indicate declining trust in political parties in the United States.

2.4.5 Support for Political Authorities

Turning to the last level of political support, we measure support for political authorities as support for the national government. This is measured with two

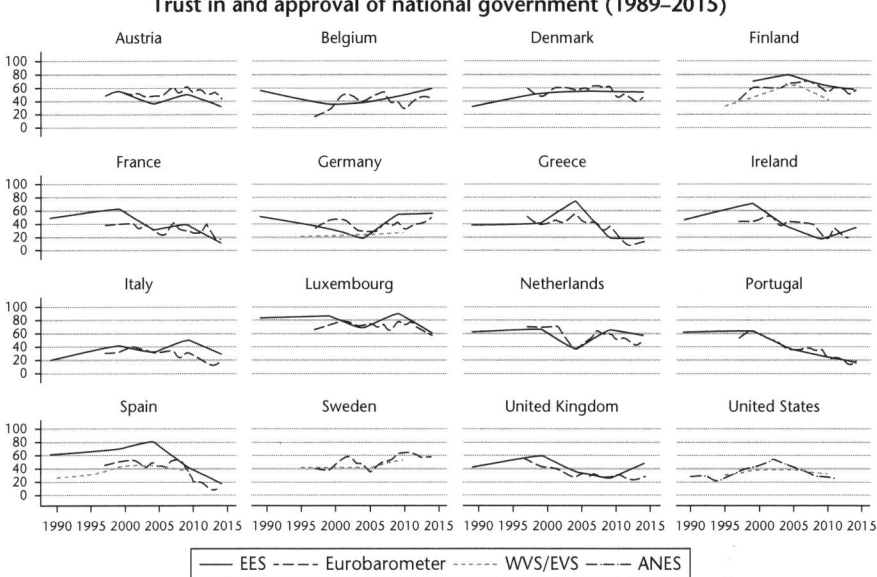

Figure 2.6 Support for political authorities

Note that for Sweden only Eurobarometer and WVS/EVS data are reported as in the EES less than two time points were observed. Note that for Italy only Eurobarometer and EES data are reported as in the WVS/EVS data only two or less time points were observed.

Note that for Austria, Belgium, Denmark, France, Greece, Ireland, Luxembourg, the Netherlands, Portugal, and the United Kingdom only Eurobarometer and EES/ANES data are reported as in the WVS/EVS data only two or less time points were observed.

Note that data for the US go back to 1958, but since this is the only country with data for this variable before 1989, the graph reports trends since 1989. We do use all available data for the significance tests of trends, reported in Appendices: Table 2.C.

indicators: trust in the national government (measured in the Eurobarometer, WVS/EVS and ANES) and approval of the national government's record or satisfaction with the national government (measured in the EES). Figure 2.6 shows the over-time trend for each data set. At this lowest level of support for political authorities, we would expect support to fluctuate more over time than more abstract support for political institutions, which appears to be borne out by the data. As the country trends in Figure 2.6 show, at this level of political support there is also significant country variation in both support levels and trends. Trust in national governments varies from averages of twenty-eight percent in Italy to seventy percent in Luxembourg, and satisfaction with the national government varies from averages of twenty-five percent in Portugal to seventy-seven percent in Luxembourg. As regards trends, support for political authorities appears to be increasing in countries such as Denmark and Sweden, decreasing in countries such as France and Portugal, and strongly fluctuating in Germany and the Netherlands.

The over-time trends also vary between countries. Bivariate tests of the significance of trends show that there was a decline in approval of the government's record from 1989 until 2014 in nine out of fourteen European democracies (EES data), yet most of these trends are not significant. Only in the more recent data gathered by the Eurobarometer (1997–2015), do we find significant decline in trust in/approval of government in about sixty percent of countries, which is most apparent in countries most strongly affected by the global economic crisis, as Figure 2.6 also showed. The ANES data show a significant decline in the United States as well. Hence our conclusion for trends in support for political authorities mirrors the trends of trust in parliament to a certain extent: we find patterns of decline in a majority of countries in our sample since 1989, with a stronger decline having occurred in the last decade (Eurobarometer data). However, the fact that there are a substantial number of countries that have not experienced decline, and that decline has become mostly apparent in the last decade, suggests that conclusions about a universal long-term trend of decline may be overstretched. Rather, support for political authorities appears to fluctuate strongly over time, and differ substantially between countries, as Figure 2.6 illustrates.

Summarizing the empirical trend data on political support presented here, there appears to be no empirical evidence for declining support for the political community between 1980 and 2010 (where WVS/EVS data provide the longest time series for this indicator). In fact in most countries in our sample we find a significant increase over time. Turning to support for the political regime, here the longest time series is provided by Eurobarometer data, ranging from 1973 to 2015. Also at this level of political support we find scant support for the thesis of secular decline in political support: in fact satisfaction with democracy has significantly increased in eleven of the fifteen European democracies between 1973 and 2015 (see Appendices: Table 2.C, which shows the significance of trends over time).

With regard to trust in parliament, here the WVS/EVS data provide the longest time series (1980–2010). In this period, declining trust in parliament was found in fifty-seven percent of our sample (though only significant in one country), while in the remaining forty-three percent trust either increased or fluctuated. Likewise, when considering trust in political parties, where the Eurobarometer data provide the longest time series (1997–2015), declining trust in parties was found in sixty percent of our sample (though only significant in five countries), while in the remaining forty percent trust either increased or fluctuated. Finally, for trust in government the EES data provide the longest time series (1989–2014), and here we find declining levels of trust in sixty-four percent of our sample (though only significant in one country), and increasing or fluctuating trust in thirty-six percent of our sample.

Concluding, our data suggest that at the level of political support for political institutions and political authorities, the majority of countries experience declining political support. Yet, in many of these countries these trends are not significant, and a substantial number of countries in our sample (about forty percent) show trends of increasing or fluctuating political support. Hence, decline is certainly not universal, rather there appears to be substantial variation between countries. Moreover, insofar as we observe decline at these lower levels of political support, the sharpest decline is observed in the last decade, coinciding with the global economic crisis. Hence, decline is certainly not long-term, but rather trends of political support at these levels seem to follow patterns of fluctuation.

2.5 Conclusion

In this chapter we have argued that despite the wealth of data and research on political support, scholars have not been able to reach agreement on whether there is indeed a decline in the legitimacy of representative democracy in established democracies. Major comparative research projects have come to diametrically opposite conclusions about long-term trends in political support. In our analysis we have sought to evaluate these diverging findings by analyzing the available cross-national data on political support, using multiple data sets with as long as possible time periods.

Overall, we find high levels of support for more abstract political objects, i.e. the political community and the political regime, and lower levels of support for more specific political objects, i.e. the political institutions and authorities. As such, we find high levels of national pride and high levels of support for democracy as an ideal political regime. Satisfaction with the actual functioning of democracy is lower, but still quite high, with the majority of citizens in established democracies indicating satisfaction with the way democracy works. Finally, support for political institutions and political authorities is lower, the majority of citizens in established democracies are critical toward parliament and their national governments, and especially political parties.

Turning to trends over time, the key point of interest of this chapter, the thesis of long-term universal decline of political support in established democracies does not seem to be supported by the data. We find that higher-level support is mostly stable: support for the political community and support for democracy as an ideal political regime do not seem to change much over time. However, we do not find similar levels of stability for democracy as it functions in practice: here support does vary over time, yet in most countries we find trends of *increasing* satisfaction with democracy from the early 1970s to the present. At the level of support for political institutions and authorities we do find more evidence for declining political support, yet even at these levels decline is not universal, nor long-term.

Summarizing, we find no consistent evidence for declining political support, at least not for the period covered by our data, i.e. the mid-1970s/early 1980s until 2015.[28] Certainly, significant trends of declining political support were found in some countries included in our sample and in specific time periods, but we also found non-linear and positive trends in quite a number of cases. Hence, rather than a clear-cut long-term decline in legitimacy that is apparent across all established democracies, we find large variation between countries, both in the levels of political support as well as in over-time trends.

These findings have several consequences for research on legitimacy. First, they call for a critical reflection on theories explaining a trend of universal secular decline of political support. What remains of their validity if the predicted secular decline of support does not occur? Second, the absence of a uniform decline of political support among advanced industrial democracies asks for the development of new explanations that can account for differences between countries in levels and trends of political support. New explanations of political support will need to address the causes of differences in levels and trends of support between countries. Are these different trends the result of composition effects, i.e. different characteristics of citizens in different countries? Or are the different levels and trends in political support driven by macro-level characteristics of countries, such as differences in economic performance, public service provision, or corruption? Or should we consider different circumstances in each country, i.e. are specific events, such as scandals or political violence, driving the different trends in political support observed? The next chapters of this book are dedicated to finding answers to these questions.

Notes

1. For a more comprehensive overview (and critique) of measures of political support see Van Ham and Thomassen (2012).
2. Note that political parties are considered as political institutions by some authors and as political authorities by others. We classify support for political parties as support for political institutions, as support refers to political parties in general, rather than only those parties that are part of the incumbent government. See also note 3.
3. Note that at the level of political authorities the object of support can be conceived of as either "the political authorities *in general*," i.e. politicians, or the political elite; or as "the *incumbent* political authorities," i.e. the particular party or coalition of

parties, and/or a particular set of politicians that are momentarily in government. This is important, because low support for the incumbents is less problematic in terms of legitimacy than low support for political authorities in general, as explained earlier.

4. Borre and Scarbrough 1995; Kaase and Newton 1995; Klingemann and Fuchs 1995; Niedermayer and Sinnott 1995; Van Deth and Scarbrough 1995. *BIG* was in its turn inspired by previous projects of comparative research, such as *The Civic Culture* (Almond and Verba 1965); *Political Action* (Barnes and Kaase 1979; Jennings and Van Deth et al. 1990); and *The Silent Revolution* (Inglehart 1971, 1977).

5. Dalton 2004; Kotzian 2011; Marien 2011a; Mishler and Rose 2001a; Newton 2006a; Newton 2006b; Norris 1999a; Norris 2011; Oskarsson 2010; Pharr and Putnam 2000; Van de Walle et al. 2008; Zmerli and Hooghe 2011.

6. Dalton 2004, 191; Hay 2007; Pharr and Putnam 2000.

7. Fuchs and Klingemann 1995, 435; Budge and Newton et al.1997; Norris 1999a; Norris 2011; Van de Walle et al. 2008.

8. Dalton 2004; Easton 1965; Norris 1999a; Norris 2011.

9. Dalton 2004; Norris 2011; Van de Walle et al. 2008.

10. Van de Walle et al. 2008; Holmberg 1999; Fuchs and Klingemann 1995; Listhaug 1995.

11. Klingemann 1999; Dalton 2004; Norris 2011. Note, however, that support for the political community is commonly measured as national pride, and hence does not include questions around multiculturalism and who should be part of the demos (van Ham and Thomassen 2012).

12. Dalton 2004; Klingemann 1999; Kumlin 2011; Marien 2011a; Norris 2011; Van de Walle et al. 2008.

13. Dalton 2004; Pharr and Putnam 2000.

14. Norris 2011.

15. Marien 2011a; Zmerli and Hooghe 2011.

16. Easton 1965; Kaase and Newton 1995.

17. Hay 2007; Holmberg 1999.

18. Dalton 2004, Norris 2011.

19. Dalton 2012; Norris 2012.

20. Hay finds "no significant decline in trust for politicians in general or government ministers in particular since the early 1980s." [...] "This suggests either that levels of trust in politicians and government ministers have always been low or, perhaps more plausibly, that the decline in levels of trust to their present (parlous) level occurred rather earlier." (Hay 2007, 36).

21. The European Social Survey (ESS) is another high-quality cross-national dataset that collects data on political support which is used in empirical analyses in later chapters in this book, however, since its time coverage is limited to the period 2002–14 we do not include it in our longitudinal analyses here.

22. Note that the data on trust in national government for the United States go much further back in time, however, in order to facilitate comparison with the European countries we limit these data to the same time period. See Figure 2.6.

23. The only way to collect data that go further back in time would be to use national election studies or other national surveys that measure political attitudes. This is the strategy Dalton (2004) pursued in his study on political support in advanced industrial democracies (Dalton 2004: 29–38). However, even when using national election studies, there are only seven countries for which data on political support in the 1960s is available, and even in those countries most national surveys start including data on political support only from 1968 and 1969 respectively (Italy and Sweden in 1968, Australia, West Germany, and Norway in 1969) (Dalton 2004). The only two countries for which data goes back further are Canada (starting in 1965) and the United States (starting in 1952). Moreover, these data only include indicators for political support for political authorities (Dalton 2004: 29), as the data on support for political institutions generally start in the 1980s (Dalton 2004: 38). Hence data that can provide a window into citizens' political support in the 1950s and 1960s is scarce, and even research based on national election studies can only provide insight into trends for very few countries.

24. For example, national pride was measured in only two of the five EES surveys analyzed here and was hence left out of the analyses.

25. Note that population and sampling weights are different in each of the comparative datasets, and hence the data reported here are unweighted.

26. EU6 refers to the six founding member states of the EU, EU15 to the fifteen member states at January 1, 1995.

27. Van Ham and Thomassen 2012. The 2012 module of the ESS in fact includes several measures on support for democracy that seek to address these concerns.

28. Certainly, it is possible that the decline in political support took place in the 1950s and 1960s, but empirical data in that period covers only a few countries and indicators, and hence we cannot evaluate whether decline was universal. Moreover, theories of legitimacy decline are based on the assumption that declining political support is universal and took place over a protracted period of time. Our findings in this chapter clearly demonstrate that those assumptions are unfounded.

Part II
What is Wrong with Theories of Legitimacy Decline?

Reappraising Existing Theories

3

Modernization, Globalization, and Satisfaction with Democracy

Kees Aarts, Carolien van Ham, and Jacques Thomassen

3.1 Introduction

In this chapter we present a critical assessment of two theories seeking to explain a secular decline of political support across advanced industrial democracies, namely modernization theory and globalization theory. We do so following the simple scheme presented in Chapter 1 (see Figure 3.1). In this scheme, which at least implicitly is at the basis of both theories of legitimacy decline, macro-level social or political developments (A) lead to a decline of political support (B) through a micro-level explanatory mechanism (C). Hence, the perceived relation between A and B at the macro level is driven by micro-level causal mechanisms that explain why A leads to B.

Figure 3.1 suggests that three successive questions need to be addressed. First, is there a secular decline of political support across established democracies? This question, which refers to the over-time variation in (B), does not really have to be answered anymore since the negative answer to it is the starting point of this chapter. The second question, which refers to the over-time variation in (A), is whether modernization and globalization respectively have actually and measurably taken place. Finally, the third question with regard to both theories refers to the validity of the micro-level theory connecting modernization and globalization respectively to a decline of political support (C). In Section 3.2 we will further elaborate questions two and three, resulting in a set of empirical hypotheses. In Section 3.3 the measurements and data are introduced. Section 3.4 reports the analyses for one set of hypotheses, namely those related to modernization theory. Section 3.5 reports the results related to another set of hypotheses, related to globalization theory. In section 3.6 we summarize and discuss our findings.

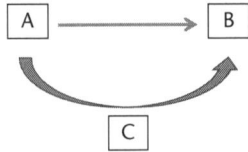

Figure 3.1 Structure of theories of legitimacy decline

3.2 Modernization and Globalization Theory

3.2.1 Modernization Theory

The central claim of modernization theory is that economic, cultural, and political changes go together in coherent patterns that are changing the world in predictable ways (Inglehart 1977: 7; Inglehart and Welzel 2005: 19). But predictable as cultural and political changes may be, they are usually only "predicted" in retrospect.

When student protests swept across North America and Western Europe in the late 1960s, social scientists were taken by surprise precisely because they were convinced of the positive relationship between socioeconomic developments and cultural and political change. In the 1960s the "end of ideology" doctrine (Bell 1960; Lipset 1960) was dominant in the social sciences. After the Second World War economic growth in the Western world had been unprecedented and the expansion of the welfare state had provided social security to a vast majority of the population. As a consequence the traditional class conflict between capital and labor had been reduced to a smoldering fire, and the polarization in politics that reflected this conflict had strongly decreased. Therefore there was a strong belief that the principles of democracy and its institutions were better grounded than ever before. From this perspective it was hardly understandable why young people, students in particular, all of a sudden were protesting against a lack of democracy in politics and in other institutions in society. Were these young people not better off and did they not have far less reason to complain than any generation before them?

It was Ronald Inglehart who first offered a possible explanation for this development, which—in the context of the decline of legitimacy debate—has been referred to as modernization theory, and inspired an impressive body of empirical research. According to Inglehart it was not *despite* the unprecedented socioeconomic developments in advanced industrial democracies that a younger generation went out on the streets to protest against the way politics and society developed but *because* of it. Economic growth, technological development, rising levels of education, and the expansion of mass communication, he argued, have two major consequences.

First, they lead to a *change in value orientations*, i.e. a change from materialist to post-materialist values, from giving top priority to physical sustenance and safety toward a stronger emphasis on belonging, self-expression, and the quality of life (Inglehart 1990: 66). This change in value orientations is brought about through socialization of new generations in a context of declining scarcity (Inglehart 1977; 1997: 33). With regard to scarcity, Inglehart argued that an individual's priorities reflect the socioeconomic environment: people place the greatest subjective value on those things that are in relatively short supply. In advanced industrial societies during the decades since the Second World War, the emergence of unprecedented high levels of prosperity, together with the relatively high levels of social security provided by the welfare state, have contributed to a decline of the prevailing sense of vulnerability (Inglehart 1997: 33). Therefore, the marginal utility of material welfare has strongly decreased in favor of more immaterial needs. The people most affected by these changes in material conditions, Inglehart argued, are young people, who grow up and are socialized in a context of relative absence of scarcity. This is because basic values reflect the conditions that prevailed during one's formative, pre-adult years. As older generations had grown up in less secure circumstances their value orientations reflect these circumstances and will continue to do so even though these circumstances have changed substantially. Therefore, a change in value orientations will first occur among younger generations and because they (just like older generations) do not easily change the value orientations developed in their formative years, generational replacement will gradually lead to a change in value orientations among the population at large.

In addition to changing value orientations, a second major consequence of rising levels of education and expanding mass communication is an *increase in cognitive skills*. These skills are politically relevant since well-educated people are better able to formulate and voice their demands to the political system, and to understand and use this system to their benefit without the intervention of traditional intermediary agents such as political parties. This development is usually referred to as *cognitive mobilization*.

Cognitive mobilization and changing value orientations are expected to lead to a more critical citizenry that is more dissatisfied with the performance of democracy, for several reasons.

First, citizens with post-materialist values and better cognitive skills are more likely to be critical of the way democracy works in practice. It is not that they don't support democratic ideals, quite the contrary: better-educated people and post-materialists are more likely to support democratic processes and institutions because they view democracy as something that is intrinsically desirable (Inglehart 1997: 211). However, the more people are inclined to support high democratic ideals, the more the actual performance of democracy will fail to meet these ideals. Therefore, they will tend to be dissatisfied with democracy, not because they do not support democracy but because democracy as it exists fails to meet their high democratic ideals.

Secondly, and related to this, both the change in value orientations and the increase in personal skills lead to new participation demands and to elites challenging forms of participation. When the traditional institutions of the political system do not provide channels for such forms of participation, this will result once more in frustration with these traditional political institutions and in dissatisfaction with the actual state of democracy. Again, dissatisfaction is not due to a lack of support for democracy but to the fact that people want a different kind of democracy, a more participatory democracy.

Thirdly, post-materialists will focus on new issue domains that are related to the quality of life, for example, environmental issues. Since established political parties poorly represent them on such issues they will become active in new political parties and in particular in new social movements, thereby turning their back not only on traditional political parties but on traditional political institutions as well. As a consequence they will be less inclined to trust traditional political institutions to represent their interests and demands. According to this argumentation a decline of political support is expected to occur if:

a. Both cognitive mobilization and a rise of post-materialist values have occurred;
b. Both cognitive mobilization and post-materialist values are negatively related to political support.

If we want to test the validity of these main arguments underlying modernization theory we should first test whether the following developments have occurred at the macro level in established democracies (A in Figure 3.1):

1. A rise of post-materialist values.
2. A process of cognitive mobilization.

Secondly, we should test the validity of the hypotheses that can be derived from the underlying micro theory (C in Figure 3.1):

3. Post-materialism is negatively related to political support.
4. Formal education is negatively related to political support.

Thirdly, if both a rise of post-materialist values and cognitive mobilization have occurred, and cognitive mobilization and post-materialist values are negatively related to political support, we should see a gradual decline of political support over time that is driven by generational replacement. Therefore, a fifth hypothesis we will test is:

5. Over time, political support decreases due to generational replacement.

3.2.2 Globalization Theory

Globalization refers to "a process that erodes national boundaries, integrating national economies, cultures, technologies and governance, producing complex relations of mutual interdependence" (Norris 2001: 155). It is primarily driven by economic developments, but its effects transcend the economic sphere. In recent years the global integration of economic markets has reached an unprecedented speed, stimulated by the fall of the Soviet empire in the 1990s, the transition of China to a market-based economy, and the acceleration of European economic integration. Technological innovations, notably the information and communication technology (ICT) revolution since the late 1970s, have further fueled this process.

The economic consequences of globalization are first and foremost a large-scale adaptation of production processes to the new reality of the world market. Labor for which no specific schooling is required, is increasingly hired where it is cheapest. As a rule, this implies that production facilities are moved from the established Western democracies to other parts of the world. Labor for which specific schooling *is* a requirement will tend to be hired where the level of education is most advanced. Currently this is often the case in the Western established democracies, but specific services such as customer services and IT services are already outsourced to countries where there is skilled and cheap labor available. In addition, capital—land, natural resources, spatial infrastructure, accumulated wealth—tends to become ever less distinguishing for one geographical location compared to another. Many forms of capital (machine equipment, raw materials) are moved across the globe in the direction of cheap labor supplies, and those forms that cannot be moved around easily (e.g. energy resources) tend to be further developed in order to enhance their accessibility. Alternatively, cheap labor follows capital. Where the interstate boundaries are relatively open, and/or the differences in life opportunities between nations are large, workers tend to migrate from the poorer toward the wealthier nations. Even when their socioeconomic position in the new homeland is low, it is often still considerably higher than their position in their country of origin.

Increasing economic interdependence, in turn, leads to increasing political interdependence. The economic fates of nations are increasingly dependent on each other, stimulating increasing internationalization of public governance through international or supranational organizations and bi- and multilateral relationships between nations.

This brief sketch of the globalization process and its consequences does not, however, explain why globalization would lead to a decline in political support, let alone which mechanism at the level of individual citizens would support the presumed connection between globalization and political support. The main argument in the literature refers to the direct consequences of economic globalization. In advanced Western democracies, the lower strata of society run an increased risk of becoming the main losers of globalization (Kriesi et al. 2008). The type of work that they do, for which formal schooling is not very important, can often be done in another country at lower costs, with cheaper labor—or by immigrants from other countries who will often accept worse labor conditions. Emigration is for these lower strata of society not a realistic option. In most destination countries they would be worse off than they are currently. Thus, they are stuck in their current position and can only hope it is sufficiently strong to weather the forces of globalization for the time being. In contrast, the higher-educated middle and upper strata possess the cognitive skills and cosmopolitan values that are needed to operate successfully in a globalizing economy and society.

This effect is strengthened by political globalization. Political globalization is characterized by a diffusion of government policies (Keohane and Nye 2000). Nation-states are losing part of their problem-solving capacity and scope of action, which means that citizens' political rights, which are mainly tied to the nation-states, are hollowed out (Kriesi et al. 2008: 7). In particular, the lower strata who were accustomed to the social protection of the national welfare state will perceive this as a negative development. Not only do they see their socioeconomic position deteriorate or at least under threat, they also see their national governments having less and less power to do something about it. Also, these lower strata tend to identify themselves more than the middle and upper classes with their national community and are more strongly attached to its political institutions. Therefore, they will perceive the weakening of this community and institutions as a loss (Kriesi et al. 2008: 8).

In summary, the consequences of globalization for the social and economic positions of lower-educated, low-skilled, low-income citizens tend to be negative. It is to be expected that the political support among this group of citizens decreases over time as globalization progresses. Globalization does not lead to precise predictions about the development of political support among the higher educated, highly skilled, high-income segments of society. Taking people's level of education as a proxy for the broader characteristics of this group, we assume that under globalization the political support among the higher educated is stable.

If we want to test the validity of these main arguments underlying globalization theory we should first test whether globalization has indeed occurred at the macro level in established democracies (A in Figure 3.1):

1. A process of globalization has occurred.

Secondly, we should test the validity of the hypotheses that can be derived from the underlying micro theory (C in Figure 3.1):

2. Formal education is positively related to political support.[1]

Thirdly, if globalization increased over time and formal education is positively related to political support, we should see a gradual decline in political support over time among the lower educated that is driven by a period effect. Therefore, a third hypothesis we will test is:

3. Over time, political support decreases among the lower educated due to a period effect.

Summing up, our discussion of modernization has resulted in five testable hypotheses and our discussion of globalization has resulted in three testable hypotheses. These hypotheses are outlined in Box 3.1.

We will test the hypotheses for modernization theory in Section 3.4 and test the hypotheses for globalization theory in Section 3.5. Before doing so, however, we discuss the data and methods used in Section 3.3.

Box 3.1 EMPIRICAL HYPOTHESES TO TEST MODERNIZATION
AND GLOBALIZATION THEORY

For modernization

At the macro level we should observe (A in Figure 3.1):

1. A rise of post-materialist values.
2. A process of cognitive mobilization.

At the micro level we should observe (C in Figure 3.1):

3. Post-materialism is negatively related to political support.
4. Formal education is negatively related to political support.
5. Over time, political support decreases due to a generation effect.

For globalization

At the macro level we should observe (A in Figure 3.1):

1. A process of globalization.

At the micro level we should observe (C in Figure 3.1):

2. Formal education is positively related to political support.
3. Over time, political support decreases among the lower educated due to a period effect.

3.3 Measurement, Data, and Methods

In order to test the above expectations, we need, for an extended period of time and for advanced (post-)industrialized countries, regularly repeated mass surveys with measurements of at least political support, education, cultural values, and age. The period of time should cover at least several decades, as the predictions of modernization and globalization theory also apply to this time frame. The surveys need to be repeated regularly, so that a distinction can be made between real change and short-term fluctuations. Finally, the indicators of political support, education, values, and age must be comparable over countries and over time. Meeting all these requirements, we decided to focus on the Eurobarometer surveys for the set of countries covered from 1973 onward, i.e. the nine EU member states in 1973: France, Germany, Italy, Belgium, Netherlands, Luxemburg, United Kingdom, Ireland, and Denmark (EU9). These countries can all be regarded as relatively wealthy Western European democracies. We use the *Mannheim Eurobarometer Trend File 1970–2002* (edition v2.0.1, Schmitt et al. 2008), and updated the trend file until 2015 with Eurobarometer data available via GESIS/ZACAT.[2] This implies that we have data covering a period of forty-three years.[3] When there have been two Eurobarometers in a single year, the surveys have been merged per year.

As indicator of political support, our dependent variable, we restrict ourselves in this chapter to *satisfaction with the way democracy works in one's own country*. This variable is available in biannual Eurobarometer surveys in the member states of the European Union since 1973. It is measured on a four-point scale, running from (1) not satisfied at all to (4) very satisfied. For our analyses, we collapsed this scale to two categories: (0) not satisfied at all/not very satisfied, and (1) fairly satisfied/very satisfied. This dichotomy between dissatisfied and satisfied citizens better fits our theoretical framework and also simplifies the presentation and interpretation of results.

Our main explanatory variables at the micro level are *post-materialist values* and the *level of education*. Post-materialism has been measured in the Eurobarometers from 1973 until 1999 with a well-known battery of four values that the respondents have to rank in order of importance. We consider the respondents who ranked "giving people more say in important government decisions" and "protecting freedom of speech" above "maintaining order in the country" and "fighting rising prices" as post-materialists. (Formal) education is notoriously difficult to measure across national educational systems, and the Eurobarometer has therefore a very crude measure of it in the form of the age up to which respondents followed full-time education. In this chapter education has been recoded into ten categories, ranging from 1 (younger than fourteen years old when full-time education ended) through to 9 (older than twenty-one years when full-time education ended), and 10 (still studying).[4] In our descriptive analyses, we group respondents who had full-time education until age sixteen as lower educated, respondents who received full time education until the ages of seventeen and twenty-one as medium educated, and respondents who received full-time education until age twenty-two or higher as higher educated.

In addition, in order to test the hypotheses regarding generational replacement and period effects, we test a model including cohort, age, and period effects. The measurement of *age* is straightforward as a person's age when the interview was conducted. As we are interested in generational replacement we recode age into cohort categories that represent generations. Following Grasso (2014) we use five cohort categories that can be considered as the relevant generations in modernization theory in the light of their formative years: pre-Second World War (born before 1926), post-Second World War (1926–45), 60s–70s (1946–57), 80s (1958–68), 90s (1969–81). We add a sixth category for the youngest generation 00s (1982–2000). Finally, period effects are measured by the year in which the survey took place.

Finally, whereas macro-level trends in post-materialist values and education levels can be evaluated by aggregating the individual level data, to evaluate the existence of a macro-level trend in globalization we need a measure of globalization. As indicated in Section 3.2, we focus here on economic globalization.[5] We use a measure of economic globalization developed by Dreher (2006), who creates an index of economic globalization based on a countries' trade, foreign direct investment, portfolio investment, income payments to foreign nationals (all in percent of GDP); hidden import barriers; mean tariff rate; taxes on international trade (in percent of current revenue); and capital account restrictions (see Dreher 2006: 1094). The indices are constructed as weighted sums of a set of variables, each rescaled to the 1–10 interval. The weights have been determined by principal components analyses in base year 2000.

In Section 3.4 we first present the results for the hypotheses related to modernization theory (hypotheses 1–4 and 5). We then continue with the tests of globalization theory in section 3.5 (hypotheses 1–2, and 3). We present descriptive results first, followed by bivariate results, and multivariate results. As for the multivariate results, we use an age–period–cohort effects model to test the generational replacement hypothesis of modernization theory (hypothesis 5). We subsequently use an age–period–cohort effects model including an interaction effect between education and period to test the period effect hypothesis of globalization theory (hypothesis 3). It should be noted that the multivariate results are based on analyses without further statistical controls. Since we are primarily interested in the global relationships between satisfaction with democracy on the one hand, and level of education, age, period, and cohort on the other hand, introducing control variables in the model would have either no effect on these global relationships, or (in the case of effects) potentially confound the relationships between our core independent variables of interest (education, age, period, and cohort) and political support (Achen 2005).[6]

Since generational (cohort) and period effects are predicted to occur, data will be analyzed with age–period–cohort methods (Grasso 2014). Age, period, and cohort effects are distinguished by including age and year as predictors in our model along with the variable measuring to which cohort respondents belong.[7] Countries may differ in their stages of both modernization and globalization, and therefore the nine countries may be regarded as a level of a multilevel model. In order to keep the presentation simple, however, we decided to present our results by country. We used logistic regression and test the robustness of our results with year-fixed effects, as well as multi-level logit, correcting standard errors for clustering within years. The results remain substantively the same in these models and are available on request from the authors.

3.4 Results for Modernization Theory

In this section the hypotheses related to modernization theory are tested. We start with hypotheses 1 and 2, which predict a rise in post-materialist values and cognitive mobilization, followed by hypotheses 3 and 4, which predict negative correlations between post-materialism and cognitive mobilization on the one hand, and political support on the other hand. Finally we address hypothesis 5 that relates a decrease in political support to a process of generational replacement.

3.4.1 Post-materialist Values and Cognitive Mobilization

Modernization theory, as elaborated in Section 3. 2, is built on two key assumptions. First, in advanced industrialized countries post-materialist values have increased in the past half-century; and secondly, a process of cognitive mobilization has occurred in the same period. In Figure 3.2, the percentage of post-materialists and materialists over time is shown for the nine countries.[8] It is clear that hypothesis 1 finds support. The proportion of materialists has declined over time in eight out of nine countries (with the exception of Belgium), and the proportion of citizens with post-materialist values has increased in seven out of nine countries. However, the increase in the proportion of post-materialists is not very strong and varies between different countries.

Turning to the question of whether a process of cognitive mobilization has occurred, Figure 3.3 shows the trends in levels of education for the nine European countries. As Figure 3.3 demonstrates, in all nine countries the

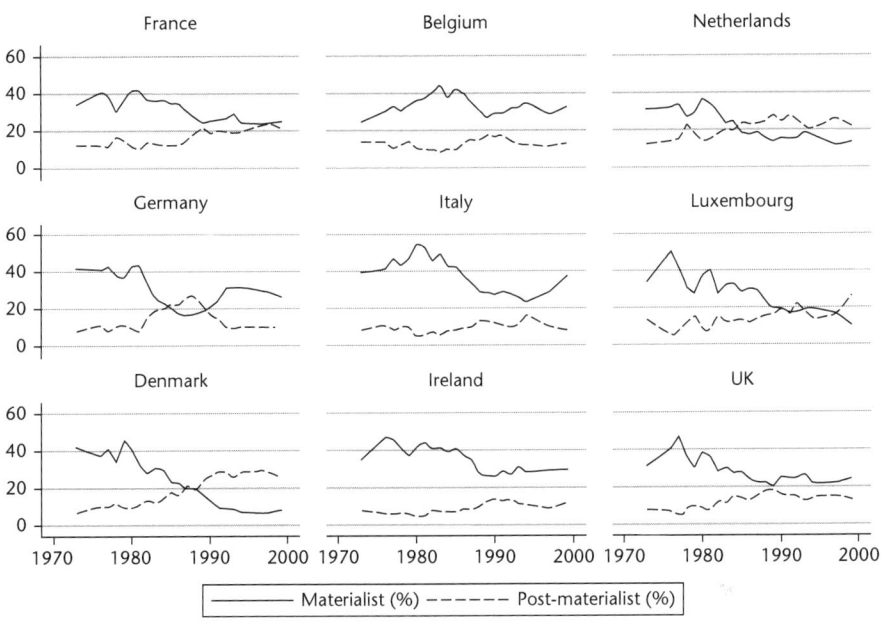

Figure 3.2 Post-materialism and materialism by country, 1973–99
Source: *Mannheim Eurobarometer Trend File* 1970–2002 (edition v2.0.1). Data unweighted.

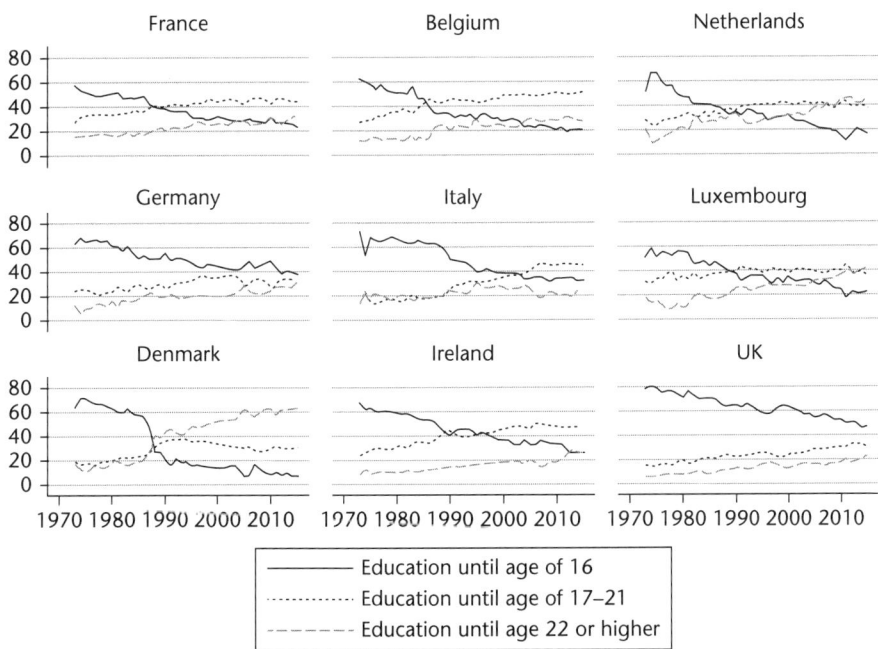

Figure 3.3 Level of education by country, 1973–2015
Source: *Mannheim Eurobarometer Trend File* 1970–2002 (edition v2.0.1). Data unweighted.

proportion of higher-educated citizens (citizens who followed full-time education until age twenty-two or older) increased, clearly supporting hypothesis 2. There are significant differences between European countries, but the trends point in the same direction in all nine countries.

3.4.2 Post-materialism, Cognitive Mobilization, and Political Support

Clearly, a rise of post-materialist values and a process of cognitive mobilization have occurred in the past decades in European democracies, supporting hypotheses 1 and 2. But to what extent are post-materialist values and education also negatively related to satisfaction with democracy, as hypotheses 3 and 4 imply? In Table 3.1 the correlations of post-materialism and level of education with satisfaction with democracy are presented per country. Interestingly, significant negative correlations between post-materialist values and satisfaction with democracy are found in seven of the nine countries, which by and large corroborates hypothesis 3: citizens with post-materialist values are indeed more critical about how democracy operates in practice. However, hypothesis 4 of modernization theory, expecting the higher educated to be more critical of the functioning of democracy, appears to be disconfirmed: in all nine countries the higher educated are significantly *more* satisfied with how democracy works in practice.[9]

Summarizing, we have now shown that aggregate-level modernization (as measured by a rise in post-materialist values and levels of education) has indeed occurred. However, we find only mixed support for the micro-level predictions of modernization theory: whereas post-materialist values are indeed negatively related to satisfaction with democracy, education is positively related to satisfaction with democracy.

Table 3.1 Satisfaction with democracy and post-materialism and level of education, by country (1973–2015)

	Post-materialism (1–3)	Education (1–10)
France	0.003	0.119***
Belgium	−0.083***	0.034***
Netherlands	0.012*	0.127***
Germany	−0.056***	0.013***
Italy	−0.050***	0.049***
Luxembourg	−0.111***	0.006
Denmark	−0.009+	0.185***
Ireland	−0.067***	0.099***
United Kingdom	−0.089***	0.080***

Source: Eurobarometer. Education data were available from 1973–2015; Post-materialism data from 1973–99. Pearsson correlation coefficients. P-values: + 0.1, * 0.05, ** 0.01, *** 0.001.

3.4.3 *Political Support and Generational Replacement*

Our final hypothesis for modernization theory posits that over time, political support decreases due to a generation effect (hypothesis 5). In order to test generation effects, multivariate analyses are needed to control for age and period effects. We analyze the main effects of age, cohort (or generation), and period on satisfaction with democracy in Table 3.2.

Table 3.2 confirms the findings presented in Chapter 2 of this book about the absence of evidence for declining political support. Looking at the effect of period (or year of survey) in Table 3.2, in eight out of nine countries satisfaction with democracy increases significantly over time (positive effects), whereas in only one of these nine countries—Germany—a marked decline in satisfaction with democracy over time occurs. In the case of Germany, the obvious explanation for this deviant development is the German reunification of 1990. From 1990 onward, Germany includes not only the former West, but also the former communist East. It is well documented (e.g. Sperling 2004) that satisfaction with democracy has been relatively low in the eastern part of Germany, and this results in the observed negative trend over time (this is also demonstrated by the sudden drop in satisfaction with democracy for Germany after 1990 in Figure 2.3 in Chapter 2).

The effect of cohort, however, appears to differ markedly between countries. In France, Germany, and Luxembourg, and to a lesser extent, Ireland and the United Kingdom, it is the post-Second World War and 1960s/1970s generations that are least satisfied. In Belgium, the Netherlands, Italy, and Denmark it seems that instead the pre-Second World War generation is the least satisfied with democracy, while more recent generations are significantly more satisfied. Yet, while generational patterns of political support thus clearly differ between countries, one finding is most common (in seven out of nine, Luxembourg and the United Kingdom excepted): the *youngest* generation is on average more satisfied with democracy than older generations. This clearly contradicts the hypothesis of modernization theory that younger cohorts are more critical towards democracy as the result of their increasingly post-materialist value orientations and higher education. If modernization has generally led to dissatisfied democrats, this seems to have applied only to the post-Second World War generation and 60s/70s generation, and to have occurred only in some of the countries in our sample.

The overall picture emerging from the age, period, and cohort effects presented in Table 3.2 is thus nuanced. In most countries the trend in satisfaction with democracy is upward (period effect), with Germany being the notable but also understandable exception (the reunification with former GDR in 1990). In most, but not all, countries people tend to be more satisfied with democracy when they get older (age effect). Finally, a clear conclusion about

Table 3.2 Modernization: testing period and cohort effects on satisfaction with democracy

	France	Belgium	Netherlands	Germany	Italy	Luxembourg	Denmark	Ireland	United Kingdom
Cohort[a]									
post-Second World War	-0.169*** (0.042)	-0.005 (0.042)	0.091* (0.046)	-0.224*** (0.036)	-0.001 (0.046)	-0.167* (0.082)	0.210*** (0.048)	-0.078+ (0.045)	-0.030 (0.036)
1960s–70s	-0.178** (0.064)	0.028 (0.065)	0.214** (0.068)	-0.242*** (0.055)	0.041 (0.071)	-0.295* (0.124)	0.398*** (0.073)	-0.100 (0.069)	-0.063 (0.055)
1980s	-0.060 (0.081)	0.139+ (0.082)	0.276** (0.087)	-0.317*** (0.069)	0.265** (0.090)	-0.307* (0.156)	0.454*** (0.094)	-0.074 (0.087)	-0.092 (0.070)
1990s	0.092 (0.099)	0.280** (0.101)	0.397*** (0.107)	-0.270** (0.085)	0.342** (0.110)	-0.273 (0.191)	0.542*** (0.115)	0.132 (0.107)	-0.014 (0.086)
2000s	0.151 (0.123)	0.626*** (0.126)	0.332* (0.135)	0.111 (0.106)	0.422** (0.137)	-0.089 (0.238)	0.130 (0.148)	0.079 (0.131)	-0.019 (0.107)
Period: year (1973–2014)	0.007*** (0.002)	0.007*** (0.002)	0.015*** (0.002)	-0.012*** (0.001)	0.015*** (0.002)	0.023*** (0.003)	0.044*** (0.002)	0.004* (0.002)	0.015*** (0.001)
Life cycle: age (1–97)	0.003 (0.002)	0.008*** (0.002)	-0.004* (0.002)	0.001 (0.001)	0.007*** (0.002)	0.004 (0.003)	0.002 (0.002)	0.002 (0.002)	-0.001 (0.001)
Constant	-0.090 (0.096)	-0.273** (0.098)	0.444*** (0.103)	0.884*** (0.083)	-1.751*** (0.108)	0.759*** (0.186)	0.015 (0.111)	0.428*** (0.104)	0.050 (0.083)
N level 1 (respondents)	66,330	65,399	67,523	99,550	69,938	28,397	66,985	63,976	85,702
N level 2 (years)	39	39	39	39	39	39	39	39	39

Logistic regression; dependent variable: not/not at all satisfied with democracy (0), very/fairly satisfied with democracy (1). P-values: + 0.1, * 0.05, ** 0.01, *** 0.001. [a]: pre-Second World War is the reference category.

satisfaction with democracy in different generational cohorts cannot be drawn as patterns vary in different countries (cohort effect). Hence, hypothesis 5 of modernization theory is not supported.

3.5 Results for Globalization Theory

3.5.1 Economic Globalization

Turning now to the arguments of globalization theory, we should first demonstrate that at the macro level a process of globalization, i.e. increasing economic interdependence between nation-states, has occurred. Using Dreher's (2006) operationalization of economic globalization discussed earlier, we present the trends in economic globalization per country in Figure 3.4. Economic globalization indeed shows the expected upward trend in practically all countries (with the possible exception of Luxembourg, which was already almost maximally globalized at the beginning of the time series). Hence, hypothesis 1 of globalization theory is corroborated.

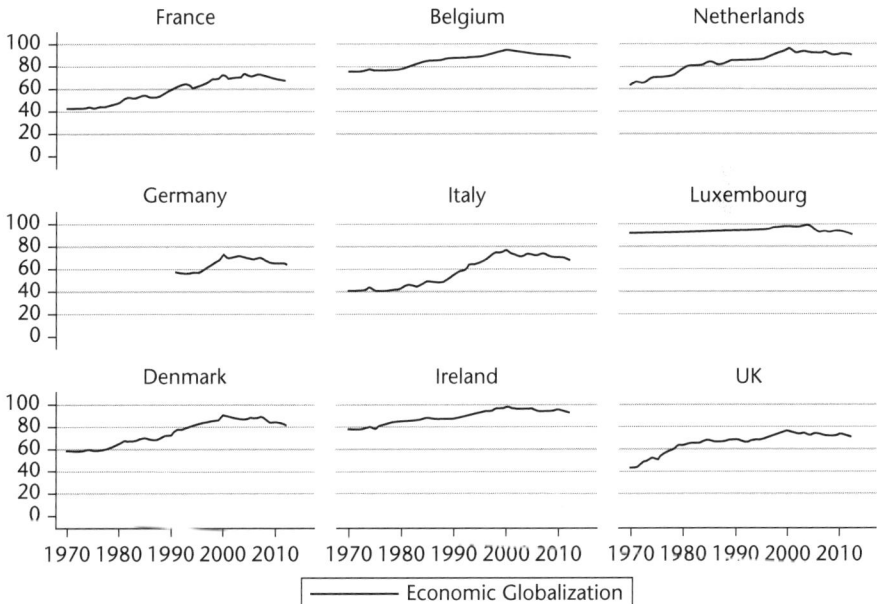

Figure 3.4 Trends in economic globalization by country, 1970–2012
Sources: KOF (Dreher 2006), as included in Quality of Government data set (Teorell et al. 2016).

3.5.2 Globalization and Political Support

Hypothesis 2 related to globalization theory proposed that at the micro level we should find that lower-educated citizens, being more vulnerable to the consequences of economic globalization, are less satisfied with democracy. The correlation coefficients presented in Table 3.1 clearly support this hypothesis: in all nine EU countries, the lower educated are less satisfied with democracy and the higher educated are more satisfied with democracy.

3.5.3 Political Support and the Effects of Period

However, in order to demonstrate that the process of globalization has affected political support, we should also find that political support decreased over time among the lower educated due to a period effect (hypothesis 3 of globalization theory). This hypothesized negative effect of increasing globalization on political support should become visible as a period effect among the lower educated in our models.

We can test this hypothesis by investigating the interaction effect between period and the level of education. The results of our analysis are reported in Table 3.3.[10] Note that due to the inclusion of an interaction effect, in Table 3.3 the main effect of "year" now stands for the period effect for the lowest educated group. In France, Belgium, and in Germany we find evidence that supports our hypothesis: the lowest educated have become significantly less satisfied with democracy over time. Yet, in three other countries the lowest educated have become significantly more satisfied with democracy over time, and in the final three there are no significant linear time trends. Thus, the empirical evidence for hypothesis 3 is anything but conclusive.

The main effect of education in Table 3.3 demonstrates the effect of education when year is at its lowest value, in this case 1973. Here we see that at the outset of the time series, in 1973, the higher educated in Belgium, Germany, Italy, and Denmark were more critical about democracy than the lower educated. The question is, however, how satisfaction with democracy has developed simultaneously over time and across levels of education. The interaction effect of period and education shows their joint development over time.

The interaction effect of period and education is consistently positive and significant in seven out of nine countries—Luxembourg and Ireland being the exceptions—suggesting that over time, the higher educated have become increasingly satisfied with democracy. Over time the lower educated tend to have become either less satisfied with democracy, or when they have become more satisfied, lag behind the higher educated. The net result is an increasing gap between lower and higher educated over time in terms of their satisfaction with democracy.

Table 3.3 Globalization: testing the interaction effect of period and education on satisfaction with democracy

	France	Belgium	Netherlands	Germany	Italy	Luxembourg	Denmark	Ireland	United Kingdom
Cohort[a]									
post-Second World War	-0.090*	0.041	0.141**	-0.178***	0.061	-0.171*	0.217***	-0.033	-0.007
	(0.043)	(0.043)	(0.046)	(0.036)	(0.046)	(0.084)	(0.049)	(0.046)	(0.037)
1960s–70s	-0.110+	0.073	0.267***	-0.191***	0.117	-0.280*	0.390***	-0.044	-0.053
	(0.065)	(0.066)	(0.069)	(0.055)	(0.072)	(0.127)	(0.074)	(0.070)	(0.056)
1980s	0.003	0.176*	0.301***	-0.260***	0.340***	-0.291+	0.441***	-0.040	-0.087
	(0.082)	(0.083)	(0.088)	(0.070)	(0.091)	(0.159)	(0.095)	(0.088)	(0.071)
1990s	0.081	0.267**	0.354**	-0.244**	0.372***	-0.266	0.486***	0.093	-0.040
	(0.101)	(0.102)	(0.108)	(0.086)	(0.111)	(0.194)	(0.116)	(0.108)	(0.087)
2000s	0.098	0.503***	0.192	0.004	0.354*	-0.082	0.054	-0.005	-0.097
	(0.125)	(0.127)	(0.137)	(0.107)	(0.139)	(0.242)	(0.151)	(0.133)	(0.109)
Period: year (1973–2014)	-0.008***	-0.008***	-0.001	-0.031***	0.004+	0.022***	0.023***	-0.001	0.010***
2014	(0.002)	(0.002)	(0.002)	(0.002)	(0.002)	(0.004)	(0.003)	(0.002)	(0.002)
Life cycle: age (1–97)	0.010***	0.009***	0.000	0.001	0.008***	0.006+	0.003+	0.006***	0.002
97	(0.002)	(0.002)	(0.002)	(0.001)	(0.002)	(0.003)	(0.002)	(0.002)	(0.001)
Education (1–10)	0.058***	-0.045***	0.008	-0.089***	-0.042***	0.018	-0.012+	0.070***	0.048***
	(0.006)	(0.006)	(0.006)	(0.006)	(0.006)	(0.012)	(0.006)	(0.007)	(0.006)
Period * Education	0.002***	0.003***	0.002***	0.004***	0.002***	-0.000	0.003***	0.000	0.001*
	(0.000)	(0.000)	(0.000)	(0.000)	(0.000)	(0.000)	(0.000)	(0.000)	(0.000)
Constant	-0.652***	-0.116	0.267*	1.197***	-1.678***	0.617**	0.092	-0.029	-0.218*
	(0.102)	(0.104)	(0.110)	(0.087)	(0.112)	(0.200)	(0.117)	(0.109)	(0.088)
N level 1 (respondents)	65,148	64,039	66,197	97,223	68,235	27,387	65,029	62,804	83,830
N level 2 (years)	38	38	38	38	38	38	38	38	38

Logistic regression. P-values: + 0.1, * 0.05, ** 0.01, *** 0.001. a. pre-Second World War is the reference category.

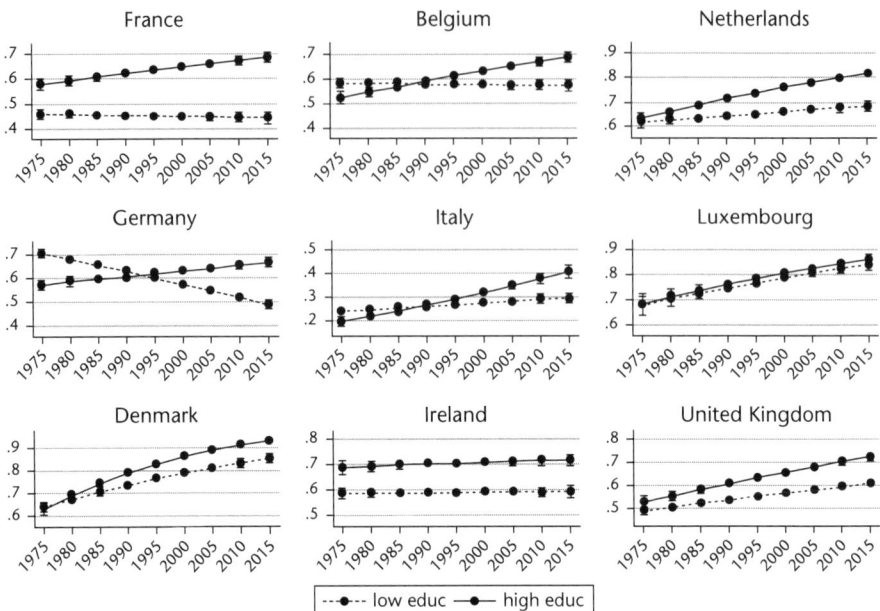

Figure 3.5 Probability of being satisfied with democracy by time and education

A more accessible and precise way to show these interaction effects is to draw marginal effects graphs, to which we now turn. Figure 3.5 shows, for each country and over time, the probability of citizens being satisfied with democracy, differentiating between the lowest-educated respondents and the highest educated respondents. We use the same classification as in Figure 3.1, i.e. the lower-educated respondents have received full-time education until age sixteen or younger, and the higher-educated respondents have received full-time education until age twenty-two or older. The middle category is not shown here.[11] Note that both groups represent a significant proportion of respondents, as on average forty-three percent of respondents are lower educated and twenty-three percent are higher educated. However, the sizes of educational groups differ significantly between countries and the effects of education on satisfaction with democracy differ significantly as well. Hence, as with the analyses presented in Tables 3.2 and 3.3, we show marginal effects for each country separately. Moreover, since coefficient sizes differ significantly between countries, the y axes indicating the probability of being fairly or very satisfied with democracy vary in their range among countries.

Figure 3.5 shows that indeed, in three out of nine countries (France, Belgium, and Germany), the lower educated have become less likely to be satisfied with democracy over time, supporting hypothesis 3.[12] Yet in five countries (Netherlands, Italy, Luxemburg, Denmark, and United Kingdom), the lower educated have become *more* likely to be satisfied with democracy over time, disconfirming hypothesis 3.

The common pattern across countries, however, appears to be a *widening gap* between educational groups over time. The gap differs in size between countries. As the y axes show (and taking the different axis scales into account), the gap between lower and higher educated has increased most sharply in France, followed by Germany and the Netherlands, Belgium, Italy, the United Kingdom, and to a lesser extent Denmark. Only in Luxembourg is there practically no trend toward a widening gap. Finally, in Ireland the gap between lower and higher educated is comparable to the other countries, but in contrast to the other countries, a substantial gap appears to have been present already in the 1970s.

3.6 Conclusion and Discussion

In Chapter 2 of this volume we observed that the often alleged decline of political support in advanced Western democracies did not occur, at least not as a general phenomenon. The implication of this finding is that theories contending to explain such a decline cannot possibly be valid. In this chapter we tried to assess possible flaws in two of these theories, modernization theory and globalization theory. In order to do so we reformulated the main arguments of both theories in the form of testable hypotheses. The first set of hypotheses refers to the socioeconomic and cultural developments these theories assume, a rise of post-materialist values, and a process of cognitive mobilization in the case of modernization theory, a process of globalization in the case of globalization theory. A second set of hypotheses refers to the micro theory explaining why these developments should lead to a decline of political support. These hypotheses and the results of our analyses for each of them are summarized in Box 3.2.

These findings clearly prove that both theories are indeed flawed. It is not because they assume developments that did not occur. There is indisputable evidence for a rise of post-materialism, an increase of the level of education, and of the process of globalization. As far as both theories got it wrong it is because they are based on a micro theory that is not unequivocally supported by our findings.

In the case of modernization theory our findings are mixed. Post-materialism is positively related to political support as the theory predicts. However, education is positively related to political support, whereas the theory predicts a negative relationship. Perhaps our most undermining finding for modernization theory is that the supposed generation effect does not occur. It is not true that political support is gradually declining because successive cohorts

---

Box 3.2 RESULTS EMPIRICAL TESTS MODERNIZATION AND GLOBALIZATION THEORY

For modernization

At the macro level we should observe (A in Figure 3.1):

1. A rise of post-materialist values. *Yes*
2. A process of cognitive mobilization. *Yes*

At the micro level we should observe (C in Figure 3.1):

3. Post-materialism is negatively related to political support. *Yes*
4. Formal education is negatively related to political support. *No*
5. Over time, political support decreases due to a generation effect. *Not generally*

For globalization

At the macro level we should observe (A in Figure 3.1):

1. A process of globalization. *Yes*

At the micro level we should observe (C in Figure 3.1):

2. Formal education is positively related to political support. *Yes*
3. Over time, political support decreases among the lower educated due to a period effect. *Not generally*

---

start their active political life with a lower level of political support than older generations did. As far as there is a generation effect it separates the baby boomers, who came of age in the 1960s and 1970s, from the younger generations. These younger generations are *more* rather than less satisfied with the functioning of democracy compared with the generation that inspired Inglehart and others in developing modernization theory. But the real development is not as clear-cut across time and across countries as this theory wants us to believe.

At first sight our findings are more supportive of globalization theory. The level of education is indeed positively related to political support as the theory predicts. However, political support does not generally decline among lower-educated people, as globalization theory predicts. Only in three out of the nine countries analyzed, the lower educated have become less satisfied with democracy over time, while in five out of the nine countries the lower educated have become *more* satisfied with democracy over time. However, an interesting trend in all countries (Luxemburg, and to some extent also Ireland excepted) is that the *gap* in satisfaction with democracy between the lower and the higher educated tends to become wider. Thus, insofar as we find empirical support for globalization theory, it is not in declining political support among the lower educated, but rather the widening gap between lower and higher educated in terms of their political support.

Our findings with regard to both theories suggest that the development of political support across time and across countries is more complex than any of these general theories of political change can explain. As both theories are a reflection of social and political developments it is quite possible that they apply to a limited time period only. This calls for further analysis. Also, the huge variation in the level and trends of political support between countries asks for a more specific analysis of these differences and of the possible system-level characteristics explaining them. This is the subject of Part 3 of this volume.

Notes

1. Note that the hypotheses on the relationship between education and political support in the two theories are each other's opposites. However, this does not apply to the assumed mechanism of change. Whereas in modernization theory the relationship between education and political support is supposed to be stable and generational replacement is the main mechanism of change, in globalization theory a *changing relationship* between education and political support, i.e. a decline of political support among lower-educated people, is the assumed mechanism of change. This is different from the mechanisms of change supposed by Dalton (2004), which are each other's opposites. He juxtaposes what he calls the *positive* and the *negative* effects thesis. According to the former a decline of political support is mainly due to a decline *among* better educated and more skilled people with higher incomes, whereas the latter assumes a decline of political support among people at the margins of the economic order: the less educated, the less skilled, and those with lower incomes. Therefore, in both cases the underlying mechanism of change is a changing relationship between education (and skills and income) and political support. For an empirical assessment of both theses, see Aarts, Thomassen, and Van Ham 2014.

2. The trend file was updated until 2015 for all variables except for the Mannheim post-materialist–materialist value orientations index, as the variables used to construct this index were not available in all Eurobarometers after 2002. The data for the post-materialist-materialist value orientations index are hence based on the Mannheim Trendfile and are available from 1973 until 1999.

3. Note that our variables were not included in Eurobarometers in the years 1974 and 1975, 1996, and 2008 hence in our multi-level models the level 2 N (years) is 39 in Table 3.1 and 38 in Table 3.2 that also includes education (data for education was missing in the year 1995).

4. To be precise, the categories are: 1—younger than fourteen when full-time education stopped, 2—fifteen years, 3—sixteen years, 4—seventeen years, 5—eighteen years, 6—nineteen years, 7—twenty years, 8—twenty-one years, 9—older than twenty-one years when full-time education stopped, and 10—still studying.

5. We do not pay attention to other dimensions of globalization, notably political and cultural globalization (Dreher 2006). These other dimensions are substantively interesting in their own right, and a specific form of political globalization can even be regarded as the driving force of European unification, by which all countries in our analysis are affected. However, satisfactory and independent indicators of political globalization are difficult to find.

6. The analyses have also been run with control variables, notably gender, marital status, and whether respondents were unemployed or not. Results are available on request from the authors.

7. Multicollinearity is not a significant problem as correlations between year and the other two variables never exceed 0.50, and correlations between age and cohort vary between -0.76 and -0.80 in all countries.

8. The middle category of mixed value patterns is not shown.

9. Note that this finding provides empirical support for hypothesis 2 of globalization theory. We will return to this in the next section when we evaluate the empirical evidence for globalization theory.

10. Note that due to the inclusion of an interaction effect, in Table 3.3 the main effect of "year" now stands for the period effect for the lowest educated group.

11. We chose to group educational categories together in the marginal effects graphs in order to improve the visual presentation of results. In order to do so, we carried out the analyses presented in Table 3.3 with the categorical educational variable used in Figure 3.1 (distinguishing low, middle, and highly educated respondents) instead of the continuous education variable. The model results are substantively similar and available on request from the authors.

12. Note again that the findings for Germany are affected by a change in composition of the target population from 1990 onward.

4

Social Capital and the Development of Political Support in Europe

Marc Hooghe and Anna Kern

4.1 Introduction

The idea that voluntary associations play an important constitutive role in establishing social cohesion and political support is a traditional insight in the field of political sociology, ranging all the way back to the work of Alexis de Tocqueville (1805–59). These associations are an important element of social capital, i.e. the whole of social networks and norms that allow for stronger ties between citizens, thus strengthening their capacity to reach collective goods (Ostrom 1990; Putnam 1993). Within social capital, both structural (i.e. associations and networks) and attitudinal components (i.e. generalized trust and reciprocity) can be distinguished (Hooghe and Stolle 2003). The basic assumption in the social capital literature is that involvement in voluntary associations renders citizens more familiar with the process of democratic decision-making, which in turn would lead them to acquire democratic norms and skills that they subsequently apply in their relation with the political system in general (Newton 2001). Traditionally, it has been stated that voluntary associations in this regard function as a training ground for democracy. If this metaphor is correct, it could be assumed that political support is at least partly influenced by the presence of a vibrant civil society. The presence of voluntary associations, and their independence from the state apparatus, allows them to have a critical look at the ways elected politicians function, and therefore they contribute to ensuring the accountability of the political system. A strong civil society, therefore, should be associated with a well-functioning political system. While this assumption is intuitively appealing, it has to be noted that this causal logic does require a number of conditions to be fulfilled (Hooghe and Stolle 2003).

To begin with, the first assumption is that within voluntary associations, democratic processes and norms prevail and that these are supported by the members of these associations. If members can have their say in the way their association is being run, this would mean that they interact with others and gain experience with the process of collective and democratic decision-making, thus allowing them to acquire more democratic skills. This assumption, however, is not always tested in a systematic manner (Wollebaek and Selle 2002). In numerous associations, decisions are not routinely jointly taken by all members, but by a more limited number of highly active members, with the result that most rank-and-file members do not get the experience of being involved in democratic decision-making. It should not be taken for granted, therefore, that membership in a voluntary association automatically means that the members gain experience with the process of democratic decision-making, or if they do, that this experience will be a positive one.

A second step in the causal chain is the assumption that in most voluntary associations, a democratic set of norms and attitudes prevails and is being strengthened by the interaction within the association. Members therefore do not just acquire democratic skills, but their democratic norms, too, are being strengthened by their interaction within associations. Again, however, it should not be assumed that this is necessarily the case in every association. In the literature, one does find a number of examples of associations that do not support democratic norms at all, and can even be considered as supporting norms that run against the generally accepted principles of democratic society. During the interwar period, for example, various extremist organizations clearly helped to undermine the democratic legitimacy of the Weimar Republic (Berman 1997). Although the social relevance of this "dark side of social capital" should not be overestimated, it is clear that at least for some associations, it is quite likely that they rather reinforce non-democratic norms than the other way around (van Deth and Zmerli 2010).

Finally, the idea is that the norms supported within the association in some way or another are being transposed toward the political system as a whole. Some research, however, also hints at the fact that voluntary engagement could also be a means to "avoid politics," as members might define their engagement as non-political, and might actually use their membership as a way to engage in their local community, without any interference from professional or institutionalized politics (Eliasoph 1998). In that case, engagement in civil society could even be negatively related to various elements of political involvement.

Furthermore, even in the original formulation of the theory by De Tocqueville, the assumption was that this process of generalization works best in local, small-scale communities. The distance between engagement in a local voluntary association and participation in, for example, a local town meeting is indeed not all that large. The question remains, however, how this insight could be applied in contemporary, large-scale democracies where there is a huge difference of scale between the small local associations and the decision-making process at the national level. Processes of globalization and the increasing power of the European Union, might even further contribute to the gap between this small-scale engagement and the increasingly complicated process of political decision-making. This, too, is a question that is not always addressed in a systematic manner in this line of research (Lichterman and Eliasoph 2014).

The question of how civil society organizations can contribute to political support is all the more relevant, given the current concern about the legitimacy of established democracies (see Chapter 1 in this volume). Despite the repeated suggestion that political support is in decline, Chapter 2 in this volume strongly suggests that there is no general downward trend in levels of political support in established democracies in Europe, so it is important to distinguish facts and myths in this discussion. If we depart from the assumption that civil society and political support are interrelated, these findings lead to a number of clear research questions on the relation between civil society involvement and political support.

First, it might imply that the level of civil society involvement has remained roughly the same, although of course with variations between countries. If civil society organizations really contribute that strongly to political support as is often suggested, one could assume that engagement levels have remained the same, despite some concerns about a declining willingness to engage in social and community life (Putnam 2002a). While it can still be assumed that especially younger age cohorts will participate in different kinds of associations than their older counterparts, the general level of participation could still be the same. A second possibility is that the research effort was misguided from the start as in reality civil society organizations do not contribute that strongly at all to political support. While members of organizations might still be characterized by higher levels of political support, it is possible that this relation is, to a large extent, the result of self-selection, as associations do not contribute in a significant manner to the formation and development of political trust (Van Ingen and Van der Meer 2016). Even if engagement levels drop, in this way this would still not have an effect on political support and developments in civil society would not matter all that much for the discussion on political support.

In this chapter we first review the literature on the relation between civic engagement and indicators of political support. Subsequently we document whether there really is a downward trend with regard to levels of civic engagement, before we investigate more closely the relation between civic engagement on the one hand, and political trust and satisfaction with democracy on the other hand.

4.2 Citizen Engagement and Political Support

In the study of determinants of political support, two opposing traditions prevail. On the one hand, some scholars depart from a top-down logic, by assuming that political support mainly reflects the functioning of political institutions. If these institutions perform in a satisfactory manner, citizens are more likely to express relatively high levels of political support for them (Rothstein and Stolle 2008). Research suggests that mainly the absence of corruption among public officials is important in this regard, as the perception of corruption has a very strong negative effect on levels of political trust (Uslaner 2008; Chapter 8 of this volume). The idea behind this reasoning is that political support is to a large extent experience-based: if citizens know from firsthand experience that most civil servants and politicians behave in a trustworthy manner, they have every reason to assume that the political system as a whole will act in a benign manner. Following this logic, it could be assumed that political support is mainly dependent on the way citizens experience the functioning of their political system. Within this line of research, political support is seen as a kind of reward for a well-functioning political system: if citizens have the perception that the political system lives up to its promises, this should result in high levels of legitimacy. As a research design, therefore, it makes sense to investigate how characteristics of the political system and its functioning have an effect on aggregate levels of political support, or, on the individual level, how specific experiences with the functioning of the political system are associated with levels of political support. As most citizens do not have contact with elected politicians on a day-to-day basis, it is assumed that especially the interactions with street-level civil servants have a powerful effect on the development of political trust.

The bottom-up approach to the development of political support, on the other hand, departs mainly from a traditional Tocquevillian perspective. It is assumed that through their engagement in voluntary associations, citizens become acquainted with the procedures of democratic decision-making and they will also internalize the norms that guide this form of interaction. If this experience is repeated frequently, the end result will be the development of a strong democratic ethos among the members. This approach to the development of democratic norms has received new academic interest following the study by Putnam (1993) demonstrating that the presence of a vibrant civil society is positively associated with the regional quality of government in Italy. Although the causal claims in this study have been heavily criticized, the idea that civic engagement could have spill-over effects on democratic governance does remain powerful and inspiring. It refers back to the Republican ideal of modern citizenship, claiming that democratic governance is not just a matter of having effective and representative institutions, but that this also calls for an active involvement of citizens. A democratic civic culture, therefore, rests on the assumption that most citizens feel sufficiently empowered to engage in political life, if they feel the need to challenge the decisions of the political elite (Jennings, Van Deth et al. 1990).

It could even be claimed that given the rising average education level of Western societies and the increasing emphasis on self-expressive values, the social demand for active involvement will have increased over the past decades (Dalton and Welzel 2014). This new generation of more assertive citizens, most likely will not join the same kind of organizations as previous generations did, but it is expected that they will have a strong preference for social and political engagement. If citizens do not take part in community life, the claim is that there will not be sufficient social support for the norms of democratic governance. While intuitively and normatively this idea might be appealing, the currently available empirical literature on this relation, however, is plagued by a number of obvious challenges, which we will discuss further. The empirical research on this claim, therefore, does not always lead to strong or clear results.

4.2.1 *Empirical Evidence*

A basic assumption in social capital research is that engagement in various networks and associations contributes to the development of more civic attitudes. To the extent that levels of participation are declining, this would also imply that this socialization function of voluntary associations would become weaker (Putnam 2000). While for the United States there seems to be compelling evidence for a decline in levels of political and social participation, this is not the case for Europe. Research on social capital indicators, such as participation in voluntary associations or levels of generalized trust and political support in general, shows a positive relationship (Dalton 2004). This by itself, however, does not suggest any form of causality, so this relation should not yet imply that civil society actually contributes to political support.

A first and very important caveat is based on the problem of endogeneity and some authors have argued this implies that it should not be assumed that associational membership has an additional socialization effect (Newton 2001). While on average, members of voluntary associations indeed have higher levels of political support, there is no guarantee at all that there is any causal relationship involved. It is just as likely that those who already have a positive evaluation of political life to start with are more likely to join voluntary associations. This form of selective recruitment is just as likely to explain the occurrence of higher trust levels among associational members, as the reverse causal logic where it is assumed that members, as a result of their engagement, gradually grow more trusting over time. While some of the available panel studies among members of civil society organizations show some impact, this is certainly not the case in all available studies (Van der Meer and Van Ingen 2009). Newton (2001) therefore concludes that there might be some relation between civil society engagement on the one hand and various indicators of political support on the other hand, but on average these relations tend to be weak, and there is not much empirical support for any causal claims.

A second important caveat is that the literature on the attitudinal consequences of civil society participation fails to acknowledge that basic value patterns tend to be rather stable once actors have reached adulthood. It is therefore rather unlikely that joining a voluntary association after adolescence would have such a strong effect on democratic attitudes. A much more likely causal chain is that engagement is especially important during the "formative" phase of one's value pattern, when democratic attitudes are still being developed. Flanagan (2013) makes the case that during adolescence, young citizens gradually develop their own perspective, both on the political system in general and on their own role within that political system. A straightforward assumption, therefore, is that civic engagement especially in the adolescent phase will have strong impact. Not only could it lead to the development of a more participatory behavioral pattern, leading to higher engagement levels later on in life, but this kind of engagement could also have a direct effect on attitudinal indicators such as political support. Panel analysis indeed suggests that especially during adolescence, there is some effect of voluntary engagement (Hooghe and Stolle 2003; Hooghe and Quintelier 2013). When following a large and representative sample of Belgian adolescents over a five-year-period, the conclusion was that especially among the members of voluntary associations that emphasize social goals, there is a clear trend with regard to trust levels. It has to be acknowledged, however, that this trend was by no means general across all kinds of associations and could not be observed among associations that have a purely leisure or entertainment purpose.

The bulk of the research on the relation between social capital and attitudes, furthermore, has focused on the effect of engagement indicators on attitudes toward society as a whole or toward specific groups of citizens. Traditionally, the notion of generalized trust here serves as a proxy variable in order to capture a broad and general assessment of the degree to which other people in society can be trusted. Other studies have focused on the feeling of hostility toward specific groups within society, e.g. by including ethnocentrism of anti-immigrant sentiments as the dependent variable in the analysis. In general, these studies show on average a limited but significant effect of participation in voluntary associations (Hooghe and Quintelier 2013). For the studies that have included attitudes toward the political system as a dependent variable, however, there are few significant results (Freitag and Ackermann forthcoming).

The idea that associational membership would lead to a more trusting attitude toward the political system, therefore, is not generally supported in the research literature. While some associations that cultivate a more positive attitude toward the political system or toward office holders might have this effect, there is no indication that this is a general phenomenon extending toward all kinds of associations. It might be remembered that in some associations, a more critical attitude toward the political system is cultivated just as well. Opposition groups, for example, might actually reinforce a more hostile attitude toward the current incumbents (Rosanvallon 2008). To conclude: while it makes sense to assume that the structural component of social capital (i.e. networks of engagement) is strongly related to a more attitudinal component of the concept (e.g. generalized trust), there is far less reason to assume it would be causally related to political trust or other indicators of political support. At first sight, therefore, there are not all that many reasons to believe in the power of voluntary associations to contribute to political support.

4.2.2 Trends Over Time

The idea that social capital might play a causal role in trends of political support does imply that social capital, too, should be caught in a downward cycle. If social capital indicators remain constant or at least do not show a systematic decline, it becomes harder to envision how this could be related to a downward trend in political support.

Unfortunately, there are very few studies available that investigate trends in social capital over time as there is no access to reliable time series. For the United States, the *Bowling Alone* study by Putnam (2000) is well known for tracing a number of indicators over a longer period of time, showing a decline in the membership rate of a large number of traditional and mass-based voluntary associations. While these trends are indeed firmly negative, it has to be remembered that Putnam only focuses on traditional associations that seem to have lost a substantial part of their popular appeal. Simultaneously, however, it is quite likely that new associations have come into existence and have gained membership. These new associations are not included in the volume, because self-evidently it is very hard to detect long-term trends in more recent voluntary associations, which are often characterized by more informal forms of organizations and a lack of strict membership criteria.

For European societies, however, there is hardly any research on trends over time with regard to levels of social capital. For the behavioral component of social capital, i.e. organizational membership, we can rely on trends with regard to membership figures. These studies, however, do not indicate a systematic decline with regard to membership levels, but rather a transition from traditional, member-based voluntary associations, toward more alternative forms of engagement (Marien, Hooghe, and Quintelier 2010). Traditional organizations, especially if they are based on one of the established cleavages within society such as associations with a religious purpose or gender-specific associations, indeed tend to lose appeal. It remains to be investigated, however, whether newly emerging forms of civic engagement have the same effect on the development of democratic attitudes as these more traditional forms of association (Sloam 2014). Some of the available research suggests that newly emerging forms of political participation, like those based on internet communication, are rapidly gaining appeal among younger groups of the population especially. To a large extent, this trend counteracts the decline of more traditional associations, while there is no indication that their relation with attitudinal components of social capital would be weaker (Boulianne 2015). This review of the literature, therefore, would suggest that civic engagement rapidly changes in the way it is being organized, but that overall, engagement levels have remained rather stable.

For the attitudinal component of social capital, i.e. generalized trust, there is no indication that trends in European societies would be downward. Although surveys show some variation on this variable, in general there is no specific trend to be observed on this crucial social capital indicator (Marien 2011a). Given the fact that a constant element cannot explain variation, it is therefore highly unlikely that social capital would play a role in explaining the alleged negative trends in political support in European societies. If there is a relation between political support and social capital, the causal logic might run the other way around, as there are indications that less trustworthy political institutions have a detrimental effect on the development of social capital within society (Rothstein and Stolle 2008). In Section 4.3 we assess empirically how civil society involvement affects political support in European democracies using data from the European Social Survey.

4.3 Data, Method, and Operationalization

For the analysis we rely on data from the European Social Survey (ESS), a representative comparative survey that has been conducted in more than twenty European countries every two years since 2002, which includes indicators on civil society involvement and political support. The question "In the past 12 months, how often did you get involved in work for voluntary or charitable organisations?" is part of the rotating module on personal and social well-being included in the questionnaires of the third wave (2006) and the sixth wave (2012). Although the survey question is not ideal for our purpose, it does offer a general measurement for a wide range of civic engagement in European societies. Given these constraints, it is not possible to construct a full time series, but the two observations are sufficiently distant from one another in order to make visible any changes over time. We pooled the data from those two waves and included in the analysis the twenty countries that participated in both waves, in order to make results comparable. Consequently, data from Belgium, Bulgaria, Cyprus, Denmark, Estonia, Finland, France, Germany, Hungary, Ireland, the Netherlands, Norway, Poland, Portugal, Slovakia, Slovenia, Spain, Sweden, Switzerland, and the United Kingdom are included in this data set. The structure of the data set is clearly hierarchical as individuals are nested within the twenty countries. Due to the hierarchical nature of the data, we make use of multi-level models for the analysis (Snijders and Bosker 1999), but given the limited number of observations on the second level we are very cautious in introducing variables at the country level. Relying on the multi-level modeling technique allows us to determine the effect of civil society engagement on both political trust and satisfaction with democracy while controlling for various other control variables. Ignoring the hierarchical nature of the data structure would result in underestimated standard errors which underlines the appropriateness of a multi-level analysis. As our dependent variables are continuous, we will use linear multi-level models, but before we proceed with the construction of the models we offer a description of the main variables in our analysis.

4.3.1 *Variable of Interest: Civil Society Involvement*

First, we focus on civil society involvement as our core variable of interest. In order to measure this variable we rely on the question "In the past 12 months, how often did you get involved in work for voluntary or charitable organisations?" which was included in the questionnaires of both the third and the sixth wave of the ESS. Respondents could answer this question using one of the following answer categories: 1) at least once a week; 2) at least once a month; 3) at least once every three months; 4) at least once every six months; 5) less often; or 6) never. The distribution of the respondents' answers in both waves is relatively similar. About seven percent of the respondents in both waves indicated that they are involved at least once a week and another seven percent at least once a month. Five percent of the respondents indicated that they are engaged at least once every three months and another six percent at least once every six months, while about twelve percent are less often involved. However, the lion's share of the respondents (63.8 percent in wave three and 63.6 percent in wave six) never engages in voluntary or charitable organizations. The obvious conclusion, therefore, is that though levels of civic engagement are rather low, levels of civic engagement are similar in 2006 and 2012 and we do not find any indications for a downward trend. This finding is in line with previous research on this topic,

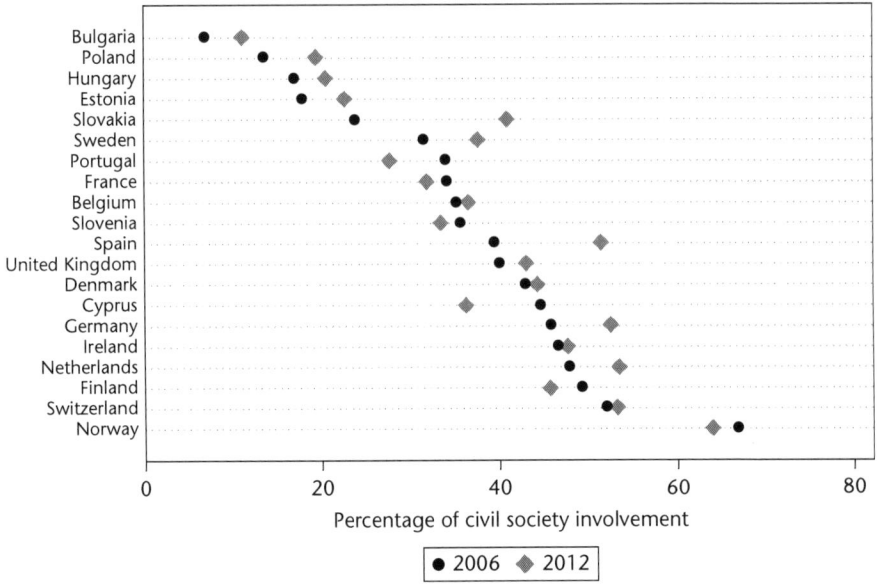

Figure 4.1 Percentage of respondents who are involved in civil society organizations, ESS, Wave 3 (2006), and Wave 6 (2012)

Note: Average percentage of respondents reporting being involved in work for voluntary or charitable organizations, in twenty European democracies that participated in both wave 3 (2006) and wave 6 (2012) of ESS.

and it confirms again that most likely there is no downward trend at all with regard to civic engagement across European societies. Given the skewed distribution of this variable, in our analysis we have decided to focus on the distinction between those who are at least somewhat engaged (about thirty-six percent of all respondents) and those that are never involved (about sixty-four percent of all respondents). The variable capturing civil society involvement is therefore recoded as a binary variable (1 = active). The average level of engagement by wave and country is illustrated in Figure 4.1.

As Figure 4.1 shows, there is quite some variance in the level of civil society engagement in Europe. While respondents in Eastern European countries such as Bulgaria, Poland, and Hungary seem to be least involved in voluntary and charitable organizations, respondents in Northern and Western Europe appear to be the frontrunners concerning civic engagement. In Norway about sixty-seven percent of the respondents in 2006 reported to be at least somewhat engaged and this percentage declined only slightly in 2012 to about sixty-four percent. Despite the fact that we have to rely on just a single item, we can observe that this pattern closely follows those found in other research on voluntary associations, thus strengthening our confidence in the reliability of these findings (Gallego 2007). Looking at the differences in engagement in the two waves, no clear trend seems to be observable, so that concerns about a declining level of civic engagement often being expressed in the United States do not seem to apply equally to the situation in Europe. While levels of engagement remained rather stable in some countries such as Switzerland, Ireland, Denmark, and Belgium, they declined in Portugal, France, Slovenia, Cyprus, Finland, and Norway, and increased in the United Kingdom, Hungary, Bulgaria, Estonia, the Netherlands, Poland, Sweden, Germany, and most notably with more than ten percentage points in Spain and Slovakia. The overall conclusion is that engagement levels in Europe do not show a clear trend of decline, but different trends in different countries.

4.3.2 Dependent Variables: Political Trust and Satisfaction with Democracy

In keeping with the operationalization of political support in Chapter 2 and throughout this volume, we measure political support with two indicators: political trust in institutions and satisfaction with democracy. For the dependent variable political trust, we rely on a battery measuring trust in political institutions. Compared to the second dependent variable, satisfaction with democracy, political trust is expected to be the most fundamental and persistent kind of support for the functioning of the political system (Easton 1965). Also, institutional trust is expected to be more stable than survey questions on satisfaction with the way democracy is functioning in the country of the respondent (Marien 2011a). Seven institutions have been included in wave three and wave six of the ESS and these seven items form a strong, one-dimensional scale on political trust (Cronbach's Alpha = 0.893, see Table 4.1). While in some previous research a distinction was made between representative institutions and law-and-order institutions (Rothstein 2011), the factor solution based on these items does not justify this distinction, as there is no indication for two different factors. A methodologically safe option, therefore, is to consider this measurement as one latent construct measuring trust in political actors and institutions.

Table 4.1 Factor analysis for political trust

Trust in country's parliament	0.871
Trust in the legal system	0.830
Trust in the police	0.724
Trust in politicians	0.896
Trust in political parties	0.879

Note: Entries are the results of a principal component analysis, ESS, wave three (2006) and wave six (2012). 1 component extracted, Eigenvalue 3.5461, 70.93 percent explained variance.

In line with previous research, we find the highest levels of political trust in Scandinavia (Denmark, followed by Finland and Norway) and the lowest levels in Eastern Europe (Bulgaria and Poland). Given the strong one-dimensional character of political trust and its internal coherence, this variable is used as a dependent variable in the analysis.

As second dependent variable, we use satisfaction with democracy, relying on respondents' answers to the question about how satisfied they are generally with the way democracy works in their country. Respondents answered using an eleven-point scale that ranges from 0 "extremely dissatisfied" to 10 "extremely satisfied." Our assumption is that this variable will be less stable, and is more strongly influenced by the view of the respondent on the current officeholders.

4.3.3 Control Variables

The impact of civil society involvement on political trust and satisfaction with democracy is investigated while controlling for other factors that have been shown to affect the level of political trust and satisfaction with democracy in the previous literature (Kern, Marien, and Hooghe 2015; Schoon and Cheng 2011; Zmerli and Hooghe 2011). First, we control for the basic demographic characteristics age and gender. Furthermore, the existing literature has consistently shown that citizens with a high level of education are more likely to trust political institutions (Anderson and Singer 2008), which is why we control for respondents' level of education. Given the ongoing concern about the effect of media use on political trust, a measurement of the time spent watching television is included in the analysis (Avery 2009; Schmitt-Beck and Wolsing 2010). As religious people are on average more trusting (Newton 2007) and more satisfied with the functioning of democracy (Zmerli et al. 2007), we also include a question on how important religion is to the respondent. Furthermore, we assume that immigrants and non-nationals have lower levels of political trust and are less satisfied with the functioning of democracy because those groups are in numerous countries being confronted with discriminatory practices.

Finally, we introduce two control variables at the country level. First, we include a dummy variable that controls for the wave of the survey in order to detect potential developments in trust and satisfaction with democracy over time, and second, we introduce a dummy for countries that have a legacy of an authoritarian regime until the early 1990s. The second control variable seems necessary because even after more than twenty years since the transition to democracy, many countries in Eastern and Central Europe are characterized by relatively low levels of political trust and democratic satisfaction (Dimitrova-Grajzl and Simon 2010).

As was already mentioned, the data underlying this analysis are clustered. Respondents are grouped within countries, which is why we construct a multi-level random intercept model in which we include characteristics of respondents as well as country-specific features as independent variables.

4.4 Results

First, we investigate the effect of civil society involvement on political trust (see Table 4.2). We start with a model that does not contain any explanatory variables (Model 0). This model can serve as a baseline to evaluate the

Table 4.2 The effect of civil society involvement on political trust

	Political Trust			
	Model 0	Model I	Model II	Model III
Intercept	−0.008	0.057	−0.041	0.474*
	(0.216)	(0.216)	(0.210)	(0.188)
Individual-level variables				
Civil society involvement (Yes = 1)			0.266***	0.115***
			(0.013)	(0.013)
Sex (Female = 1)				0.017
				(0.012)
Year of birth				0.004***
				(0.000)
Education level				0.068***
				(0.005)
Watching television				0.001
				(0.003)
Citizen of country (Yes = 1)				0.052
				(0.038)
Born in the country (Yes = 1)				−0.132***
				(0.027)
Religiousness				0.068***
				(0.002)
Political interest				0.344***
				(0.007)
Country-level variables				
Wave (2012 = 1)		−0.124***	−0.131***	−0.149***
		(0.012)	(0.012)	(0.012)
Authoritarian legacy				−1.267***
				(0.339)
Individual-level variance	2.641	2.637	2.621	2.481
Country-level variance	0.936	0.931	0.882	0.483
Deviance	265,425	265,325	264,912	261,064
N individuals	69,649	69,649	69,649	69,649
N countries	20	20	20	20

Note: Entries are parameter estimates and standard errors (in parentheses) of a multilevel linear regression. Sign: * < 0.05, ** < 0.01, *** < 0.001. Data: ESS, 2006, 2012.

explanatory power of the following models. It shows that about twenty-six percent of the variance can be found at the country level, which justifies the usage of a multilevel model. However, this model does not take into account the fact that the surveys were held at two different points in time. This is done in Model I, with the inclusion of the dummy variable that contrasts political trust in the sixth wave (2012) with political trust in the third wave (2006). The inclusion of this variable reveals there is a significant negative effect of the wave of the survey, indicating that levels of political trust are significantly lower in 2012 than in 2006. In light of the analyses of a much longer time period reported in Chapter 2, this should not be taken as evidence for a secular downward trend. It should be remembered that the year 2012 was character- ized by a very low level of economic growth and therefore also a high level of unemployment, so to some extent the low level in that specific year might be attributed to the temporary consequences of the economic crisis (Armingeon and Guthmann 2014).

When we turn to the variable of interest (Model II), we can indeed observe that engagement in a voluntary association has a significant positive effect on the level of political trust. At first sight, therefore, the optimistic assumptions about the impact of civil society on political support do receive confirmation. It has to be noted, however, that in Model II we did not include any control variables yet. When we do so (Model III) it is striking to observe that the original effect is strongly reduced in size, but it is equally important to note that the effect does remain strong and significant. So despite the fact that we included a large battery of control variables, the conclusion has to be that we do observe a significant relation between engagement in civil society and political trust, thus supporting the traditional Tocquevillian view on the social and political role of civil society. Looking at the control variables, we can observe that those who are more highly educated, have high levels of political interest, and are religiously involved, also have higher levels of political trust, which is in line with previous findings. Including all these control variables does strongly diminish the explanatory power of the voluntary engagement, indicating that self-selection mechanisms indeed play an important role in this regard. The most important finding is, however, that the initial effect of engagement on political trust remains significant, even after including such an extensive list of control variables.

Subsequently, we turn to the analysis regarding satisfaction with democracy in one's country as the dependent variable (Table 4.3). In contrast to what we observed for political trust, we note here that levels of satisfaction with democracy are, in fact, higher in 2012 than they were in 2006. Again (Model II), we find a positive relationship between engagement in civil society and levels of satisfaction. Satisfaction with democracy therefore seems to have increased and a more careful inspection of the data shows the upward trend to

Table 4.3 The effect of civil society involvement on satisfaction with democracy

	Satisfaction with democracy			
	Model 0	Model I	Model II	Model III
Intercept	5.403***	5.338***	5.273***	6.005***
	(0.258)	(0.259)	(0.255)	(0.222)
Individual-level variables				
Civil society involvement (Yes = 1)			0.176***	0.043*
			(0.018)	(0.018)
Sex (Female = 1)				−0.192***
				(0.017)
Year of birth				0.005***
				(0.000)
Education level				0.101***
				(0.007)
Watching television				0.012**
				(0.004)
Citizen of country (Yes = 1)				0.080
				(0.053)
Born in the country (Yes = 1)				−0.290***
				(0.038)
Religiousness				0.071***
				(0.003)
Political interest				0.247***
				(0.010)
Country-level variables				
Wave (2012 = 1)		0.122***	0.118***	−1.618***
		(0.017)	(0.017)	(0.397)
Authoritarian legacy				
Individual-level variance	4.858	4.854	4.848	4.722
Country-level variance	1.334	1.340	1.299	0.660
Deviance	301,037	300,986	300,889	299,085
N individuals	68,100	68,100	68,100	68,100
N coutnries	20	20	20	20

Note: Entries are parameter estimates and standard errors (in parentheses) of a multilevel linear regression. Sign: * < 0.05, ** < 0.01, *** < 0.001. Source: ESS, 2006, 2012.

be strongest in countries such as Hungary, Germany, and the United Kingdom. Considering the effect of voluntary engagement on satisfaction with democracy without control variables, Model II shows the effect to be positive and highly significant. When we subsequently take into account all the control variables, the effect of voluntary engagement stays significant, however, it is strongly reduced in size. Here, too, education level and political interest seem to have a strong effect on satisfaction with democracy and also in this case, there is an additional effect of engagement in voluntary associations. The conclusion therefore should be that civil society engagement does seem to contribute to satisfaction with democracy in one's country, although the strength of this effect is strongly reduced by including the full battery of control variables.[1]

The results of the analysis suggest that we find a significant effect of civic engagement on two crucial indicators of political support. Despite the fact that we could only rely on a very crude measurement of civil society involvement, the effects do seem to be robust. It has to be acknowledged that they are strongly reduced in size when we included a full battery of control variables, but even in the full models the observed effect does remain significant. In line with the Tocquevillian approach, therefore, in this broad analysis we observe a positive relation between civil society engagement and political support.

4.5 Conclusion and Discussion

The overall conclusion of this chapter, therefore, has to be twofold. First, the results of the analysis show that there is a significant effect of engagement in voluntary associations on the level of political trust and satisfaction with democracy. It has to be kept in mind that we find this effect, despite the fact that we had to rely on a very limited measurement of civil society engagement. So the theoretical perspective that a vibrant civil society is positively associated with citizens' political support is supported by the results of this study. It has to be noted, however, that the effect size for trust in political institutions is stronger than for satisfaction with democracy. So the idea that citizens engaging in civil society should just be seen as supporters of the political status quo obviously is not supported by this analysis. Self-evidently this does not imply that we could disregard the experience-based explanations of political trust, as these fall outside the scope of the current chapter. So while civil society engagement helps us to explain the level of political trust in European societies, it has to be noted that it seems less important for explaining the evolution in levels of political trust. As has been pointed out in the descriptive part of this chapter, there is no clear downward trend in engagement levels, and therefore an allegedly eroding civil society cannot be held responsible for trends in the level of political support in European democracies. Simultaneously, however, it is important to note that the rather skeptical view that voluntary associations do not contribute at all to a democratic political culture is not supported by our findings. Of course, we only have access to cross-sectional observations, so we cannot investigate the effect of engagement over time. The positive relation we do observe in this study, therefore, might be partly the effect of self-selection and partly the result of socialization experiences within the association. The question remains, how relevant is this discussion about causality. In the literature, voluntary associations have been described both as training grounds for democracy and as "reservoirs" of civic attitudes, indicating that membership would not have an additional learning effect. Even the "reservoir" function, however, can be important, given the ongoing concern about the legitimacy of democratic political systems. The fact that individuals with higher levels of political trust come together and can join forces implies that they will be able to play a more meaningful and effective role, both in society and in politics. To put it perhaps a bit too strongly: a democracy would also have a hard time to function if all citizens with high levels of political trust and political efficacy simply sat at home and contemplated in an isolated manner the way in which the political system of their country should function. It is exactly because they have interactions with like-minded others that they are able to contribute to the way democracy actually functions. Therefore, no matter what causal mechanism is involved, the fact that we do find such a strong positive relation highlights the role of civil society in at least maintaining a democratic culture in Europe.

Note

1. As a check of robustness, we have repeated the analysis without the inclusion of new democracies. The results in the case of political trust remain virtually the same, however, when investigating satisfaction with democracy, the effect of voluntary engagement disappears in the last model, where all control variables are included.

5

Legitimacy Decline and Party Decline

Rudy B. Andeweg and David M. Farrell

The perception that satisfaction with the functioning of democracy and trust in democratic institutions are declining is as widespread as the view that political parties are weakening, and the two diagnoses are usually seen as closely intertwined: "It is difficult therefore not to infer some link between recent party decline and the widespread feeling of cynicism, indifference and hostility towards politicians—especially in their partisan role—that has been revealed in a number of recent surveys" (Crewe et al. 1977: 188).

Any hypothesis relating a decline of political legitimacy to a decline of parties is based on the premise that political parties constitute a linkage mechanism between the citizens and the political system. When universal suffrage was introduced, many were skeptical about the feasibility of linking the enfranchised masses to political decision-making. After all, under the *régime censitaire* the electorate was still relatively small and homogeneous, restricted in terms of income and gender as it was. This small size and homogeneity at least had the advantage that they often enabled individual representatives to maintain some form of relationship with individual voters. With a much larger, and consequently also much more diverse electorate, individual political representation no longer seemed viable. It is not by accident that the interwar years saw a wave of enfranchisement in many countries, but also a wave of support for antidemocratic movements. Miraculously, whether by accident or by design, mass parties emerged or developed from preexisting cadre parties, as a new linkage mechanism between citizens and government. The importance of political parties for the functioning of mass representative democracy has been underlined by many authors since, and is epitomized in the well-known quotation from Schattschneider that "modern democracy is unthinkable save in terms of parties" (1942: 1). It is thus not surprising there should be fears that any erosion of political parties could undermine representative democracy as such, and that a loss of support for parties could delegitimize the democratic regime.

The evidence presented in Chapter 2 of this volume, however, indicates that, at least in Western Europe since the 1970s, no secular decline of political support has taken place and that we are faced rather with variation across countries and fluctuation over time. If that is so, we are left with two possibilities concerning the relationship between support for democratic institutions and party strength: either political parties have also not declined, or the relationship between parties and political support is not as tight as it is sometimes thought to be. In this chapter[1] we shall inquire into both possibilities. To determine whether there has been any decline of parties as elite–mass linkage mechanism we look at parties in the aggregate, at their strength in terms of members and supporters, and at their performance of the linkage functions that are attributed to them. And to find out whether party support is indeed related to political support, we look at the individual level, at citizens' involvement in political parties, and the effect of that partisanship on their political trust and democratic satisfaction.

5.1 Party Decline Revisited

5.1.1 *Evidence of Weakening Parties*

In the opening lines of his posthumously published work Peter Mair notes that "[t]he age of party democracy has passed" (2013: 1). He is not alone in arguing that parties are in decline, nor is he the first, but his analysis provides a useful means of framing the main points usually made about the growing threat to parties.

Table 5.1 provides summaries of the types of evidence generally used to show how parties are becoming weaker in established democracies.[2] Given that this argument on party decline has already been well rehearsed elsewhere (e.g. Dalton and Wattenberg 2000; Mair 2013) we can present the main points briefly here. The first commonly used indicator of change is decline in party membership: of all the indicators summarized in Table 5.1 this is the one that is most centered on political parties. The evidence is pretty incontrovertible: party membership is in decline to such an extent that the dues-paying party member is in danger of becoming a dying breed. In the most comprehensive study of cross-national trends Van Biezen and her colleagues contend that "party membership levels have now fallen to such a low level that membership itself no longer offers a meaningful indicator of party organisational capacity" (2012: 40). And this is a downward trend that continues unabated as shown by the most recent evidence reported in the international Political Party Database project (Poguntke et al. 2015).[3]

Table 5.1 Trend data on parties and elections

Country	Party membership as a percentage of the electorate		Turnout (VAP)		Mean aggregate electoral volatility		Party closeness (% not close to any party)	
	1980 (or as near as possible)	2008 (or as near as possible)	First two elections in 1970s	Last two elections in 2000s	1970s	2000–09	1978	2014
Austria	28.48	17.27	88.87	74.41	2.7	15.5	–	40.9
Belgium	8.97	5.52	87.16	85.32	5.3	14.5	37.3	25.8
Denmark	7.30	4.13	87.34	82.27	15.5	10.4	35.8	8.9
Finland	15.74	8.08	84.05	69.07	7.9	6.8	–	32.5
France	5.05	1.85	67.01	45.34	8.8	13.5	28.3	29.2
Germany	4.52	2.30	86.29	68.30	5.0	9.0	35.1	25.3[a]
Ireland	5.00	2.03	81.46	67.93	5.7	7.5	38.6	53.0
Italy	9.66	5.57	95.06	80.63	9.9	14.0	22.3	24.9
Netherlands	4.29	2.48	83.96	74.30	12.3	22.3	14.5	24.1
Norway	15.35	5.04	79.61	75.64	15.3	13.7	–	–
Sweden	8.41	3.87	86.56	81.61	6.3	14.9	–	15.6
Switzerland	10.66	4.76	44.32	38.53	6.0	7.9	–	–
UK	4.12	1.21	74.51	59.69	8.3	6.0	33.3[b]	49.2[b]

Notes: [a] only the Western Länder; [b] not including Northern Ireland.
Sources: Gallagher et al. 2011; van Biezen et al. 2012; <www.idea.int>; Eurobarometer 10 (1978); European Election Study 2014.

The other three indicators summarized in Table 5.1 are more outward-facing, focused on the political behavior of individual citizens and how that might relate to political parties. First there is the apparent growing indifference of citizens toward electoral politics as shown by declining electoral turnout, which is seen as a phenomenon of the last few decades in particular (e.g. Blais et al. 2004; Franklin 2004). The summary comparisons provided in Table 5.1 are consistent with more detailed analyses, showing how in most of the established democracies turnout is in decline and in some cases quite sharply. But there are exceptions: most of the Nordic countries (though not Finland) tend to somewhat buck the trend, in part perhaps reflecting lower degrees of social inequality, as does Belgium most likely due to its compulsory voting regime.

The other feature that stands out is the variation in the extent of voter abstention across all the cases: turnout is distinctly (and notoriously) lowest in Switzerland and France (the regularity of elections and referendums in the former and the semi-presidential nature of the latter being partially to blame); but in five of the cases (Belgium, Denmark, Italy, Norway, and Sweden) more than three-quarters of voters are still turning out in recent elections, and in two others (Austria and the Netherlands) the proportion is averaging more than seventy-four percent. As Franklin has suggested: "Perhaps, in the light [of such evidence] the question that we should be asking is not why is turnout declining, but why is turnout so stable?" (2004: 11). Nevertheless, having said that, the trend in voter turnout is downward and most especially so in recent decades, suggesting, as Mair puts it, a growing sense of indifference toward the electoral process.

An additional indicator of change relates to the extent to which those who still vote are becoming more fluid or inconsistent in their voting behavior, as shown by average trends in aggregate electoral volatility. As is well known, this is an imperfect measure—it doesn't allow for individual-level switching in countervailing directions, nor does it allow for demographic changes among the electorate, and it is prone to dramatic shifts due to particular national circumstances—but as the summary trends in Table 5.1 show, aggregate electoral volatility is on the rise: in most of the countries it is in double-digit territory in the 2000s compared to just three instances in the 1970s. Again according to Mair (2013: 29), volatility points to citizen withdrawal: "Hand in hand with indifference goes inconsistency."

Finally, there is the well-known individual-level measure of partisan attachment. In his detailed analysis of cross-national trends through to the end of the 1990s, Dalton finds striking uniformity in the downward trajectory of party identification. As he notes: "[s]eldom is the public opinion evidence from such a diverse group of nations so consistent in following a general trend" (2004: 33). Schmitt, however, who includes the early years of the new century for some countries, is somewhat more nuanced: "Taken together, [there is] compelling evidence of a decline of partisanship. However, this decline is neither uniform nor universal" (2009: 81). And Hooghe and Kern (2015: 9), looking at the most recent decade note that "current trends are stable." It is hard to find data that are truly comparable over time and the summary data provided in Table 5.1 should be interpreted cautiously (we return to this issue later in this chapter). Nevertheless, of the eight countries for which we can compare over time, three show lower percentages of voters who do not feel close to any party in 2014 than in 1978 (i.e. where party attachment increased rather than declined). The erosion of party loyalty to which Dalton (2004) and others (e.g. Mair 2013) refer as additional evidence of a threat to parties is no longer a uniform and consistent phenomenon.

The trends summarized in Table 5.1 are not the only indicators used to make the case that parties are in decline. Other indicators commonly cited include: the emergence of alternative actors in the electoral process, such as interest groups, candidate-support organizations (e.g. US political action committees), or independent candidates with their own electoral machines (Farrell and Schmitt-Beck 2008), the rise of candidate-centered, presidentialized politics (e.g. Poguntke and Webb 2005; Wattenberg 1991), the impact of globalization and of non-majoritarian institutions on party control over the policy process (e.g. Majone 2001).

In combination it seems the omens are not good: the future for parties does not seem too bright. Fewer of us are party members; fewer of us vote in elections; of those of us who do vote we are more inconsistent in our voting behavior—though curiously perhaps we are still inclined to show some loyalty in our attachment to particular parties.

5.1.2 Reinterpreting the Evidence

But before we write the obituary for political parties as a species, it is worth reflecting on a few things, the first of these being the fact that we've been here before. The refrain of political parties in decline is by no means a new one. Scholars have been warning about this for generations in the US, perhaps most notably in the influential "responsible parties" report issued by the American Political Science Association's Committee on Political Parties published in the 1950s. By the early 1980s Crotty and Jacobson were warning that "a partyless era, with implications still uncertain, may be settling on us" (1980: 255; see also Kirkpatrick 1978; Wattenberg 1998). Outside the US the suggestion that parties may be "failing" is relatively more recent, but it still dates back over three decades. As Lawson and Merkl note in the introduction to their influential comparative study: "The phenomenon of major party decline, often remarked in the context of the American political system, is becoming increasingly apparent in other political systems as well" (1988: 3; also Reiter 1989).

One explanation for the long-term persistence of the "party decline" discourse is that this decline is not comparing the current empirical situation of parties with a historical empirical situation. We should not overestimate the degree to which the parties ever enjoyed the supposed Golden Age of "mass party" politics personified by Duverger's classic account (1964). Scarrow's careful analysis shows how Duverger's model was more an ideal type than a widespread political reality. As she notes: "democratic parties with large individual memberships have been relatively rare" (2015: 67).

A second observation about the decline of parties and about the downward trends in party membership in particular, relates to the meaning of "party membership" in the modern age. As we have seen, most parties have experienced a drop in dues-paying members over the past two decades, but at least some of this could reflect a reconfiguring by citizens as well as by parties of what it means to be a party supporter. In her recent study, Scarrow refers to a growing tendency for parties to pursue "a multi-speed approach to party membership" (2015: 128) in which the traditional paid-up membership is supplemented by alternative ways of showing support such as by donating to parties without joining them or signing up to party's e-newsletters, engaging in parties' policy forums, and so on. Scarrow's analysis indicates that many parties have been experimenting with ways of making "it easier for their supporters to connect with them" (p. 151)—perhaps one factor that might help to explain the leveling off of party identification trends in recent years.

A third qualification of the party decline thesis is that the analyses tend to downplay other dimensions of party activity. While it may be argued—as we have suggested—that those who contend that parties are in decline perhaps over-fixate on features of party design that are of a bygone age, equally we might suggest that insufficient attention is paid to some of the classic functions of parties (e.g. Almond 1960)—functions that, in many respects parties are still fulfilling. To borrow Kay Lawson's terminology (1980) we can refer to the "linkage" role of parties that distinguishes them from other organizations, marking them out as the primary representative agents between citizens and the state.

In many respects, parties still provide key linkage functions in our representative system of government.[4] To this day parties continue to play a key role in the election campaign process. They control the selection of candidates for election (with few exceptions, the vast bulk of candidates are nominated by political parties; e.g. Hazan and Rahat 2010) and dominate the political discourse of campaigns (Farrell 2006). They also play a key role in turning out the vote at elections (e.g. Karp et al. 2008; Karp and Banducci 2011). Even in an age of declining voter turnout, most citizens still continue to vote in election after election, and studies provide clear evidence that parties play an important role in this regard.

Parties also help voters determine who to vote for in an election. Analysis reported in Dalton et al. (2011) shows that many voters still view their political preferences through the lens of the left–right policy continuum, even in a time when some differences between the major parties may be becoming less noticeable. Without denying the rise of new issues and parties that are less clearly linked to the left–right continuum, it is important to note that voters as a collective can still correctly identify most parties' locations on that continuum. And having done so, for the most part the voters use this information to make informed choices between the parties. In short, the ideological or policy congruence between voters and parties (e.g. Huber and Powell 1994) continues to be an important determinant of voter choice.

Finally, there is substantial evidence that parties provide a meaningful policy linkage between citizens and the state, supporting the perspective that it "matters" which party or coalition of parties are in office (Castles 1982). Voters seek out parties for their policy goals and for the most part, parties implement those goals when they gain office (e.g. Klingemann et al. 1994; Benoit and Laver 2006). In short, the policy outputs of governments are broadly consistent with the ideological profiles of the parties that form them.

In many respects, therefore, it could be argued that the classic notion of democracy as "party democracy" (Castles and Wildenmann 1986) still applies. In a typically forthright piece on the fate of parties, Philippe Schmitter (hardly a fan of the genre) opined that "parties are not what they once were" (2001). That may well be true, but does it inevitably lead to the conclusion that parties are in jeopardy as a consequence? As Michael Saward has observed: that parties may not be what they once were "does not necessarily mean that they are *less* than they once were" (2010: 133 emphasis in the original).

Finally, we should point out that even those aspects of party decline that are not in dispute need not necessarily indicate that "citizens are heading for the exits of the national political arena" (Mair 2013:43). Clearly the decline in party membership in recent decades is an important change in the dynamic of party politics, but whether blame for this should be attached to the parties is questionable. As Richard Katz has observed: "there are good grounds to believe that . . . the decline has been a by-product of social changes that neither can— nor in most cases should—be reversed" (2013: 63). Certainly, the party membership trends need to be considered in the wider context of societal change that has affected institutions beyond political parties: societal change has contributed to a breakdown of collective identities as citizens become increasingly individualized (Andeweg 2003; Putnam 2000).

Other indicators of party decline may even point to increased political engagement rather than disengagement. Electoral volatility, for example, unquestionably has made individual political parties more vulnerable, but at the same time it could be argued that it has made party democracy as a whole stronger. After all, liberated from their subcultural shackles, voters are finally beginning to choose (Rose and McAllister 1986), as they are expected to in a mature democracy.

There is also some evidence of ongoing adaptations to our democratic institutions to suit new styles of political participation by our citizens that may compensate for any party decline that has taken place. For instance, as Russell Dalton and his colleagues observe: "Although electoral participation is generally declining, participation is expanding into new forms of action" (2003: 1) as more of us engage in new, less conventional (sometimes even unconventional) forms of political action, as more of us become "good" (Dalton 2009) or even "critical" citizens (Norris 1999a), seeking a more active (less passive) role in the political system, prepared to challenge (and thereby engage with) existing systems and norms. In short, even if it may be the case that citizens are turning away from some forms of conventional politics (including party politics) that does not mean that they're giving up on all forms of political activity.

5.2 Partisanship and Political Support

5.2.1 *Party Membership and Party Closeness*

These observations question the correlation between partisanship and political support at the individual level, and we now look more closely at that correlation. To the extent that involvement in a political party socializes citizens into politics, helps them identify with the political system, and assists them in making sense of politics, the weakening appeal of party involvement is likely to negatively affect political support. As such, the undisputed decline of formal party membership is an indicator of eroding partisanship, but the proportion of dues-paying party members in the electorate was never very high in most countries. Formal membership is likely to underestimate partisanship. For that reason, we include a less formal type of partisanship: party closeness. Here the longitudinal data are murky, but we cautiously concluded that the more recent measurements show a leveling off, or even a recovery, in many countries. We should state at the outset, however, that party closeness is not only less formal, but also more ambiguous in its meaning. It is often interpreted as a form of party attachment or even identification—a kind of psychological membership, but it can also be regarded as a different dimension of partisanship—of ideological proximity to a particular political party. We return to this point in our discussion of the data analysis later in the chapter.

To investigate the impact of these two variables, we make use of the first five rounds of the European Social Survey, covering the 2002–10 period, including all sixteen countries for which data are available from all five points in time.[5] Rounds six and seven (2012, 2014) were not used because they do not contain a question about party membership. Although all analyses were done on all sixteen countries and on the thirteen Western European democracies alone, we present the results only for the latter as the focus of this volume is on well-established democracies. However, the differences between the analyses including and excluding Hungary, Poland, and Slovenia are negligible. All analyses were also done for each individual country, and for each individual ESS round, separately, and reported whenever noteworthy.

As indicators of legitimacy, we use the degree of satisfaction with the way national democracy works (political support at the level of the regime), and trust in parliament (political support for democratic institutions), both measured on an eleven-point scale. We did not use satisfaction with the national government as it is likely to be affected by one's sympathy for a governing or opposition party. We also did not use trust in politicians and trust in political parties because they refer to whole categories of political actors of which some members are likely to be trusted more than others (Andeweg 2014: 184–5).

Our two main independent variables are party membership and party close-ness. Party closeness is measured by two survey questions: whether there is a particular political party to which the respondent feels closer than to any other party, and if so, how close the respondent feels to that party. We combined the answers to these two questions into a five-point scale ranging from "there is no party closer than any other party," to "one party is very close to me."

To mitigate the risk that we are measuring spurious relations we also include some of the "usual suspects" in explanations of individual variation in polit-ical support. Whether one is interested in politics or not (four-point scale) is such an important predictor at the attitudinal level. Economic satisfaction (i.e. satisfaction with the present state of the national economy, eleven-point scale) is also frequently mentioned as such (but see Chapter 9). Social back-ground factors that may play a role are gender, age (in years), and level of education (five-point scale). Finally, we also include the disposition to trust or to distrust, measured by a question whether the respondent feels that most people can be trusted, or that you can't be too careful in dealing with people—usually called "generalized trust" or "social trust" (eleven-point scale). There is evidence that a trustworthy government may not only generate political trust, but also facilitate the development of social trust, resulting in a spurious correlation between social and political trust (Levi and Stoker 2000: 493–5; Newton 2007; Zmerli and Newton 2011). The inclusion of generalized trust in the final model assumes that its role as an independent variable is dominant, but doubtful readers can simply ignore Model IV in our tables.

Tables 5.2a and 5.2b show the results of a multilevel regression analysis in which the clusters are added stepwise from Model 0 which only includes individual-level, country-level, and ESS round-level variation to Model IV which includes partisanship, political interest, and economic satisfaction, social back-ground, and generalized trust.

The overall patterns are quite similar for both democratic satisfaction and trust in parliament. That nearly all coefficients are statistically significant need not surprise us given the huge number of respondents in the pooled data set of five rounds of surveys in thirteen countries. The decline of the AICs from one model to the next shows that adding variables does increase the models' fit. However, comparing Model 0 to Model I—the most important step for our purposes—the contribution of party membership and party closeness to the fit can only be described as modest. It is definitely more substantial than the negligible contribution of social background to the fit, but the inclusion of political interest and economic satisfaction improve the model's fit much more. It would seem that the assumption that the role of political parties as a linkage mechanism between individual citizens and the political system should translate into a correlation between partisanship and political support finds only modest support in the data.

Table 5.2a The effect of partisanship on satisfaction with the way national democracy works

	Model 0	Model I	Model II	Model III	Model IV
Party membership (yes = 1)		0.079*	−0.035	−0.018	−0.022
		(0.035)	(0.031)	(0.031)	(0.031)
Party closeness		0.188***	0.109***	0.116***	0.108***
		(0.005)	(0.004)	(0.004)	(0.004)
Political interest			0.176***	0.175***	0.142***
			(0.007)	(0.007)	(0.007)
Economic satisfaction			0.452***	0.451***	0.424***
			(0.003)	(0.003)	(0.003)
Gender (male = 1)				0.015	0.021
				(0.012)	(0.012)
Age				−0.003***	−0.003***
				(0.000)	(0.000)
Education level				0.007***	0.004*
				(0.002)	(0.002)
Generalized trust					0.128***
					(0.003)
Intercept	5.729***	5.252***	2.780***	2.906***	2.413***
	(0.269)	(0.260)	(0.144)	(0.145)	(0.133)
Individual-level variance	2.492	2.466	1.962	1.961	1.914
Country-level variance	0.903	0.837	0.200	0.200	0.161
ESS round-level variance	0.015	0.013	0.024	0.024	0.023
AIC[1]	670,007	667,877	635,942	635,764	633,260
N	124,563	118,555	117,078	116,371	116,202

Notes: The entries are parameter estimates and standard errors in parentheses of a multilevel linear regression. All models include random intercepts for individual respondents on the first level, thirteen Western European countries (Belgium, Denmark, Finland, France, Germany, Ireland, the Netherlands, Norway, Portugal, Spain, Sweden, Switzerland, and the United Kingdom) on the second level, and five ESS rounds (2002, 2004, 2006, 2008, and 2010) on the third level. The data are weighted using ESS post-stratification and population size weights.

[1] To allow for comparison between the Akaike Information Criterion (AIC) of the various models, they have been calculated including only the 116,202 respondents for whom information on all variables is available.

The separate analyses by country and by ESS round (not presented) confirm this finding. Although the R^2s are slightly higher in 2010 than in 2002 there is not a linear trend between the first and last round of ESS. The patterns do not vary much across countries, but the variation that is explained by the models does: they perform worst in explaining trust in parliament and democratic satisfaction in Switzerland, and this seems largely due to a different role of partisanship there: Model I, for example, produces an R^2 of only 0.005 for trust in parliament and 0.008 for satisfaction with the functioning of democracy in Switzerland. Factors most likely accounting for this finding include the fact that the Swiss *Zauberformel* for coalition formation weakens the impact of electoral choice on the government's composition, and the regular use of the referendum which offers a non-partisan linkage between citizens and public policy. Model I performs best in Germany, with R^2s of 0.027 and 0.038 for trust and satisfaction respectively. Adding variables does not change

Table 5.2b The effect of partisanship on trust in parliament

	Model 0	Model I	Model II	Model III	Model IV
Party membership (yes = 1)		0.329***	0.133***	0.158***	0.154***
		(0.035)	(0.032)	(0.032)	(0.032)
Party closeness		0.247***	0.125***	0.134***	0.122***
		(0.005)	(0.005)	(0.005)	(0.004)
Political interest			0.408***	0.409***	0.360***
			(0.007)	(0.007)	(0.007)
Economic satisfaction			0.396***	0.395***	0.357***
			(0.003)	(0.003)	(0.003)
Gender (male = 1)				−0.045***	−0.038**
				(0.012)	(0.019)
Age				−0.005***	−0.005***
				(0.000)	(0.000)
Education level				0.010***	0.006***
				(0.002)	(0.002)
Generalized trust					0.184***
					(0.003)
Intercept	4.972***	4.338***	1.690***	1.909***	1.206***
	(0.230)	(0.214)	(0.130)	(0.131)	(0.121)
Individual-level variance	2.335	2.285	1.883	1.877	1.796
Country-level variance	0.624	0.532	0.108	0.108	0.080
ESS round-level variance	0.024	0.022	0.040	0.040	0.038
AIC[1]	661,448	657,868	632,979	632,692	628,065
N	125,193	119,159	117,336	116,634	116,478

Notes: The entries are parameter estimates and standard errors in parentheses of a multilevel linear regression. All models include random intercepts for individual respondents on the first level, thirteen Western European countries (Belgium, Denmark, Finland, France, Germany, Ireland, the Netherlands, Norway, Portugal, Spain, Sweden, Switzerland, and the United Kingdom) on the second level, and five ESS rounds (2002, 2004, 2006, 2008, and 2010) on the third level. The data are weighted using ESS post-stratification and population size weights.

the conclusion with regard to Switzerland, but Germany shows average results for Model IV. For that Model, R^2 is highest in Hungary (0.347 for democratic satisfaction and 0.261 for trust in parliament).

5.2.2 *The Meaning of Party Closeness*

So far, we have not distinguished between party membership and party closeness. However, whereas the parameter estimates for party closeness are significant and positive in all models for both dependent variables, party membership is no longer significantly related to democratic satisfaction in three of the four models and the sign changes to negative, indicating that, if anything, party members are less rather than more satisfied with the way democracy works. The part correlation coefficients in a multivariate analysis confirm that of these two variables, it is party closeness, not party membership that has the stronger (positive) impact (see Table 5.3).

Table 5.3 Relative impact of party membership, party closeness, and other variables on democratic satisfaction and trust in parliament (part correlation coefficients)

	Satisfaction with working democracy	Trust in parliament
Party membership	−0.001	0.014
Party closeness	0.069	0.097
Political interest	0.049	0.103
Economic satisfaction	0.418	0.327
Gender	0.002	−0.007
Age	−0.027	−0.034
Education level	−0.005	−0.004
Generalized trust	0.131	0.184

The part correlation coefficients indicate how much each independent variable contributes to the overall explained variance. The importance of economic satisfaction and generalized trust is reaffirmed, as is the weak impact of the social background variables. Party closeness is the third- (for satisfaction) or fourth- (for trust) strongest independent variable, with party membership having but a marginal impact on the two measures of political support (and a negative effect on democratic satisfaction). The separate analyses by country and by ESS round show that this difference between the two party variables is present in all countries, and in each individual round of the European Social Survey. Hooghe and Kern (2015), using the same data but a different country selection, a differently constructed dependent variable, and a different selection of independent variables, have reached the same conclusion: the perception that one political party is clearly closer to you than the others is much more important for one's political trust than being a member of a party.

This warrants a closer look at the variable of party closeness. We already mentioned that there are two interpretations possible. The most common interpretation sees survey questions about party closeness as measuring an informal party attachment or identification. As originally developed by the Michigan School, party identification refers to a strong psychological bond, with belonging to a party as part of an individual's self-reported identity: "Generally speaking, do you usually think of yourself as a Republican, a Democrat, or what?" As such, party identification did not travel well beyond the US (and to some extent the UK) context and it was reconceptualized as a positive attitude toward a political party, more as a summary measure of ideological preferences and long-term experiences than as part of one's identity (Bartle and Bellucci 2009). As a term, party identification continues to be used, but within this attitudinal approach we can see a convergence, at least in Europe, on a different measurement: whether there is a party that one feels close to (and how close). However, the question wording has not always been identical. The Eurobarometer surveys, for example, asked the question "Do you consider yourself to be close to any political party" and if the answer was affirmative, the respondent was asked whether (s)he felt "very close, fairly close, or merely a sympathizer." That last answering category refers to a feeling of attachment, rather than to perceived distance. This is even clearer in some of the translations that were used in other languages: in the French version "very/fairly close" was translated as "tres/assez attaché," in German the word "verbunden" was used, and so on. In Table 5.1 we compared answers to the Eurobarometer question from the 1970s to European Election Studies from 2009 and 2014, because the Eurobarometer ceased asking about party closeness in 1994 and the European Election Study uses virtually identical questions and answering categories. The questions asked in the various rounds of the European Social Survey that we used in the other tables in this chapter have the advantage that they do not combine a question about perceived closeness with answering categories that indicate strength of attachment. The questions are exclusively about the degree of closeness, also in the translated versions of the questionnaire.

This is not the place for a lengthy methodological discussion of the pros and cons of different question wordings (for that see Sinnott 1998), but the substantive point to make is that there is considerable reason to doubt that questions about party closeness measure party identification or even party attachment, as is usually assumed. To the extent that the question wording also uses terms that refer to attachment, it may still be interpreted in that way albeit cautiously. But when the question wording is only about the (degree of) closeness to a party ("Is there any particular party you feel closer to than all other parties? Very close, quite close, not close, not at all close") we prefer to take the question literally: as a question about perceived proximity in terms of ideological position of one party compared to other parties, rather than about party identification. In that sense it is similar to questions used in national election studies about the feeling that one's views are represented by a particular party (see Holmberg 2014). This implies that party closeness refers to a different linkage mechanism than party membership. It is not a measurement of informal membership of a party, but of the perception that the supply of political parties collectively facilitates one in making a meaningful political choice (Wessels and Schmitt 2014). To the extent that all parties are seen as equidistant or very close to each other, the party system cannot perform its function to link a citizen to the political system. It is in this sense that also Hooghe and Kern (2015) interpret the question about party closeness. The fact that we did not find a marked decline of party closeness, and that the impact of party closeness on legitimacy is stronger than that of party membership, which has declined significantly, points to the importance of differentiating between the ways in which parties can link citizens to the state.

5.2.3 *Populist Party Support and Political Support*

Before we conclude that the very linkage function of political parties that shows fewest signs of erosion—offering citizens a meaningful choice—is also the linkage function that contributes most (in relative terms) to political support, we should note that we have not distinguished between political parties. We have assumed that feeling closer to any political party than to other parties provides the citizen with a linkage to the political system and contributes to that citizen's belief that the political system is legitimate. A counterargument would be that this reasoning does not apply to antisystem parties. After all, such parties seek to convince citizens that the system is not legitimate and they do not aspire to act as a linkage between that system and the citizen. Citizens who are members of or voters for an antisystem party are unlikely to be satisfied with the way democracy works or to trust political institutions.

Traditional antisystem parties such as communist or (neo-)fascist parties have become rare while populist parties are in ascendance. Beyond the Manichean distinction between the "pure" people and the "corrupt" elite (Mudde 2004), populist parties do not have much in common, but most of them do not seem to be as opposed to the democratic political system as traditional antisystem parties once were. They prefer a different, more "populist," and less "constitutional" democracy (Mény and Surel 2002), but they do not seek to abolish democracy. Nevertheless, they are generally opposed to the intermediary role between the people and the formulation of public policy that political parties are supposed to play—"populist democracy vs. party democracy" in the words of Peter Mair (2002). In that sense populist parties are sufficiently "anti" to expect their supporters to lack satisfaction with and trust in contemporary party democracy (but see Fieschi and Heywood 2004 for a more nuanced view).

The pluriformity of the populist party family has prevented a consensus on the classification of political parties as being populist parties or not. Here we follow one of the most recent attempts at identifying populist parties in European party systems (Van Kessel 2015: 33–73, 144–68), even though some of his classifications must remain open to discussion (such as the exclusion of the Socialist Party in the Netherlands).[6] We confine the analysis to countries in which populist parties had significant electoral support, which means that we had to exclude Spain and Portugal from the selection of countries, leaving fourteen countries in the analysis. Again, the data presented in Table 5.4 refer only to the eleven established Western European democracies.

Table 5.4 first repeats Model IV from Tables 5.2a and 5.2b. Because the analysis is now based on eleven rather than thirteen countries, the coefficients are slightly different from those in Tables 5.2., but the patterns are quite similar. Models V in Table 5.4 add having voted for a populist party or not, and this variable indeed is strongly and negatively related to satisfaction with the

Table 5.4 The contribution of a populist vote to satisfaction with the way national democracy works and trust in parliament

	Democratic Satisfaction	Democratic Satisfaction	Trust in Parliament	Trust in Parliament
	Model IV	Model V	Model IV	Model V
Party membership (yes = 1)	−0.066*	0.059	0.190***	0.196***
	(0.032)	(0.032)	(0.032)	(0.032)
Party closeness	0.114***	0.117***	0.136***	0.139***
	(0.005)	(0.005)	(0.005)	(0.005)
Political interest	0.161***	0.162***	0.353***	0.355***
	(0.008)	(0.008)	(0.008)	(0.008)
Economic satisfaction	0.431***	0.428***	0.349***	0.346***
	(0.003)	(0.003)	(0.003)	(0.003)
Gender (male = 1)	0.035**	0.048***	−0.020	−0.007
	(0.013)	(0.013)	(0.013)	(0.013)
Age	−0.004***	−0.004***	−0.007***	−0.007***
	(0.000)	(0.000)	(0.000)	(0.000)
Education level	−0.006**	0.005**	0.007***	0.007***
	(0.002)	(0.002)	(0.002)	(0.002)
Generalized trust	0.137***	0.134***	0.192***	0.189***
	(0.003)	(0.003)	(0.003)	(0.003)
Voted for populist party (yes = 1)		−0.766***		−0.754***
		(0.031)		(0.031)
Intercept	2.329***	2.378***	1.255***	1.304***
	(0.129)	(0.134)	(0.127)	(0.128)
Individual-level variance	2.151	2.134	2.033	2.026
Country-level variance	0.127	0.141	0.080	0.082
ESS round-level variance	0.021	0.021	0.040	0.039
AIC	452,217	446,905	447,475	446,905
N	99,590		99,985	

Notes: The entries are parameter estimates and standard errors in parentheses of a multilevel linear regression. All models include random intercepts for individual respondents on the first level, eleven Western European countries (Belgium, Denmark, Finland, France, Germany, Ireland, the Netherlands, Norway, Sweden, Switzerland, and the United Kingdom) on the second level, and five ESS rounds (2002, 2004, 2006, 2008, and 2010) on the third level. The data are weighted using ESS post-stratification and population size weights.

working of democracy and trust in parliament. However, the separate analyses for each country show considerable variation in this respect, with some countries showing an insignificant relation between a populist vote and democratic satisfaction or trust in parliament (e.g. Denmark and the UK). Apparently, the heterogeneity of populist parties also translates into a less than uniform relationship between voting for such a party and political support.

5.2.4 *The Direction of Causality*

What is also striking in Table 5.4 is that the inclusion of a populist vote does not improve the fit of the model by much. For trust in parliament in

SMA

ike N...

particular, the decrease of the AIC for Model V compared to Model IV is insubstantial. This is also visible in each ESS round and in each individual country. The effect of a populist vote on political support appears to overlap substantially with the combined effect of the other independent variables in the model.

This raises questions about the causal relationship between populism and political support. Populism may lead to lower political support and directly or indirectly also reduce partisanship, political interest, economic satisfaction, and generalized trust. Or low partisanship, low interest, low economic satisfaction, and low generalized trust reduce political support, which in turn increases the probability of a populist vote. Both causal directions are plausible, but they are difficult to disentangle. Van der Brug, for example, explains the sudden emergence of the populist List Pim Fortuyn (LPF) in the Netherlands in 2002 by suggesting that:

> preferences for the LPF are *not* caused by discontent, but the effect is reversed. It is plausible that someone acquires a preference for the LPF, because he/she agrees with the party on some of the main issues. The LPF consistently proclaimed that the political elite had lost touch with the feelings and ideas of the common man and that this elite could not be trusted. It seems a logical possibility therefore that this consistent message made the LPF supporters more cynical (Van der Brug 2003: 100).

Van der Zwan, on the other hand, argues that political cynicism and in particular political inefficacy (also seen to be affected by a vote for the LPF by Van der Brug) are basic attitudes that are unlikely to be endogenous to a change in opinion such as a decision to vote for a populist party (Van der Zwan 2004; rejoinder by Van der Brug 2004). Finally, Bélanger and Aarts (2006) use panel data covering but also predating the 2002 elections to show that voters who were already "discontented" (inefficacious and cynical) in 1998 were more likely to vote LPF in 2002. The level of cynicism and discontent did increase in 2002, but among all voters, not just among LPF supporters. This implies that it is discontent that is the cause and the populist vote is the consequence.

The debate on the rise of the LPF in the Netherlands as cause or consequence of low political trust or democratic satisfaction does not stand alone. Paskeviciute (2009) examines data from the United States, seven established European democracies, and five new European democracies, linking parties' support for the constitutional order as expressed in these parties' manifestos to the democratic satisfaction and external political efficacy of the parties' voters, and calling this a party persuasion effect. Similarly, Anderson and Just (2013) use data covering fifteen countries and find that office-seeking parties express more positive attitudes toward the political system than policy-seeking parties do, and that this difference corresponds to different levels of democratic satisfaction and external political efficacy among supporters of these parties. They conclude that political parties communicate their attitude toward the system to their supporters, and that the political support of these supporters is therefore endogenous. On the other hand, Bélanger (2004) uses data from three countries (Canada, the United Kingdom, and Australia) and finds that general antiparty feelings (as opposed to negative feelings towards a specific party) contribute to absenteeism unless a political party channels such feelings. If we may generalize from antiparty to antisystem feelings, political support is thus treated as exogenous to the existence of such third parties by Bélanger. Similarly, Denmark and Bowler (2002) compare the electoral appeal of populist and other minor parties in Australia and New Zealand. Finding correlations between a vote for minor parties and political disaffection, they conclude that such parties "represent," "reflect," or "tap into" disillusionment with the political system. In summary, we see that authors interpret similar correlations between voting for a populist party and expressing low political trust and satisfaction in opposite ways. Without the kind of individual before–after design that Bélanger and Aarts (2006) were able to use in the Dutch case, it will be impossible to settle this dispute in general.

This is unfortunate, because the direction of causality affects not only the relationship between populism and political support. It goes to the heart of the relationship between partisanship and political support in general. Throughout this chapter we have assumed that parties contribute to political support by acting as a linkage mechanism between individual citizens and the political system. Hence we have treated party membership and party closeness as independent variables, and satisfaction with the working of democracy and trust in parliament as dependent variables. But it could just as easily be viewed the other way around: citizens may no longer see the political system or its institutions as legitimate for other reasons (economic adversity, media malaise, etc.) discussed in other chapters in this volume, and that loss of confidence then leads them to resign their party membership and to see all political parties as Tweedledum–Tweedledee. This is the perspective taken by Dalton (2000: 34–5), when he discusses a "performance model" to explain party dealignment. He uses satisfaction with the working of democracy as an indicator of how well political parties are perceived to perform, and analyzes its impact on strength of partisanship on the basis of the 1976 and 1992 Eurobarometer surveys. The fact that democratic satisfaction is a rather distant proxy of satisfaction with the performance of parties, and the fact that Dalton found only a weak and inconsistent relationship at the time do not mean that the direction of causality cannot plausibly be seen in two ways.

5.3 Conclusion

"[W]hile Schattschneider's proposition is usually taken to mean that the survival of democracy will guarantee the survival of parties...we can also read it the other way around, suggesting that the failure of parties might indeed imply the failure of democracy" (Mair 2013: 14–15).

As we discussed earlier, Peter Mair was not alone in arguing that political parties are in decline and with them representative democracy as we know it. But the evidence presented in this chapter suggests otherwise. In the first instance, there are doubts over whether political parties are actually in decline. There is certainly evidence of change (fewer members, fewer voters, more volatile voters), but not in all respects (in many countries large proportions of voters still vote; the supposed erosion of party loyalty is far from uniform), the trends are not unique to parties (erosion of memberships is widespread across society), the parties are proving to be quite adaptive (not least in how they treat the notion of "membership;" see Scarrow 2015), and they continue to play a central role as linkage agents for citizens in our representative system of government (Dalton et al. 2011).

Not only do we not find much evidence of a decline of parties in terms of their elite–mass linkage roles, there are also important questions to be raised over the degree to which support for parties is related to political support. What relationship there is seems pretty slight and relates more to measures of party closeness than to party membership. If our interpretation of party closeness as an indication of the degree to which the party system allows the voter to choose among the parties, rather than as a measure of commitment to an individual party, is correct, our findings suggest that political parties continue to contribute to support for the democratic system and its institutions not by individually engaging citizens in party activities, but by collectively offering citizens a meaningful choice.

It is not just the weakness of the relationship that is at issue; so, too, is the direction of causality. There is already discussion over whether the rise of populism is a cause or a consequence of declining political support, but this debate can be extended easily to the relationship between partisanship and political support in general. With the type of cross-sectional data that are available, it is not possible to decide whether a decline in partisanship leads to a weakening of political support or the other way around. But it is at least plausible that political distrust and dissatisfaction make people turn away from political parties, rather than that resigning one's party membership causes a drop in trust and satisfaction. Contrary to Mair who wondered whether the failure of parties, that he believed was happening, might "imply the failure of democracy" (2013: 15), it would seem that, if anything, it is democracy's failings that might, in time, detrimentally impact on the parties. In that sense, at least, Schattschneider's "unthinkable" could yet come to pass.

Notes

1. We are grateful to Tim Mickler for his assistance and to the anonymous reviewer for helpful feedback on an earlier draft. The usual disclaimer applies.
2. While Table 5.1 provides a useful summary of trends we are aware that the two time period presentation over-simplifies things and may mask important time-related or country-specific features.
3. See also <http://www.politicalpartydb.org>. In her recent book-length study of the subject, Kölln (2014) finds evidence of cases that buck the trends of membership decline, but on the whole her evidence also points to a general downward tendency in overall party membership.
4. The following paragraphs briefly summarize the key findings of Dalton et al. (2011).
5. Belgium, Denmark, Finland, France, Germany, Hungary, Ireland, the Netherlands, Norway, Poland, Portugal, Slovenia, Spain, Sweden, Switzerland, and the United Kingdom.
6. The following parties are classified as populist: Belgium (Vlaams Blok/Vlaams Belang; Front National; Lijst Dedecker); Switzerland (Schweizerische Volkspartei; Lega dei Ticinesi; Schweizer Demokraten; NB: the populist Mouvement Citoyens Genevois was not coded separately in the ESS Survey); Germany (Republikaner; Partei des Demokratischen Sozialismus; Die Linke; Nationaldemokratische Partei Deutschlands; Deutsche Volksunion); Denmark (Dansk Folkeparti; Fremskridtspartiet); Finland (Perussuomalaiset: "True Finns"); France (Front National); Hungary ("Justice and Life;" "Movement for a Better Hungary;" FIDESZ (after 2006)); United Kingdom (British National Party; UK Independence Party); Ireland (Sinn Féin); the Netherlands (Lijst Pim Fortuyn; Leefbaar Nederland; Partij voor de Vrijheid; Trots op Nederland); Norway (Fremskrittspartiet); Poland ("Self Defence;" "Law and Justice"); Slovenia (Slovenian National Party); and Sweden (Sverigedemokraterna).

6

Media Malaise and the Decline of Legitimacy

Any Room for Good News?

Peter Van Aelst

6.1 Introduction

When things go wrong in society, the news media are in the front row to get the blame. This is also the case when dealing with falling levels of political trust and rising political cynicism. There are, of course, good reasons for that; for ordinary citizens, the news media are the dominant way to learn about most issues, actors, and policies. Or as Strömbäck and Shehata (2010: 575) put it: "The media constitute the most important source of political information and channel of communication between the governors and the governed." Most people have little direct contact with politicians and learn about political actors and public policy via the news media. Not having any other sources or lacking direct experiences, for some issues (e.g. foreign events), the media sometimes even have a monopoly on information provision. In short, politics is highly mediated (Bennett and Entman 2001), and if politics is losing some (or most) of its prestige, it is not unlikely that the mass media are part of the problem. This media-is-bad-for-democracy forms the core argument of the media malaise theory.

The claims that the media might have damaging influences on (perceptions of) politics are almost as old as the media itself, or at least go back to the first studies on media and politics. For instance, pioneers in political communication such as Kurt and Gladys Lang (Lang and Lang 1959), even before the 1960s, referred to the potentially damaging effects of election coverage on how voters perceived politics. Later on Robert Dahl (1967) linked the growing "political malaise" among younger parts of the population, in particular, to the role of television. It was, however, only in the mid-1970s that Robinson (1976) more systematically studied the potentially negative effect of television on its audience and labeled it as "video malaise." Robinson showed in an experimental design that a current affairs program about the Pentagon could have negative effects on the public perception of the US military. He argued that the mechanism works via the large inadvertent audience that lacks the political sophistication to resist the interpretative, conflictual, and "anti-institutional" coverage. The result is "more cynical, more frustrated, and more despairing" citizens (1976: 426). Since then, many scholars have built on the work of Robinson, broadening it to include more types of media outlets such as newspapers and more recently also new media. The often-cited study of Capella and Jamieson (1997), also using experiments, showed a significant effect of strategic coverage on cynicism. The more politics was presented as a strategic game the more cynical people perceived politics, and politicians in particular. This spiral of cynicism has found some (partial) confirmation in different contexts (e.g. Pedersen 2012; Valentino, Beckmann, and Buhr 2001; De Vreese and Elenbaas 2008).

In the US, in particular, the number of studies focusing on the negative effects of media coverage on politics has grown steadily. The titles of some of these studies leave little doubt on their findings: *Good intentions make bad news. Why Americans hate campaign journalism* (Lichter and Noyes 1996); *The nightly news nightmare: Television's coverage of US presidential elections* (Farnsworth and Lichter 2007); "Breaking the news: How the media undermine American democracy" (Fallows 1996); "Bad news, bad governance" (Patterson 1996). Thomas Patterson is one of the loudest and most pessimistic voices when talking about the impact of the media on audiences and ultimately trust in democracy. In his study on campaign coverage of the late 1970s he concluded that "In its coverage of a presidential campaign, the press concentrates on the strategic game played by the candidates in their pursuit of the presidency, thereby de-emphasizing questions of national policy and leadership" (Patterson 1980: 21). In his later work the lists of complaints at the address of the media has become longer and more diverse. It is not only about television, but about all types of media outlets, and not only about the strategic, cynical reporting style, but also about too much soft news and infotainment (Patterson 1993, 1996, 2002).

The media malaise thesis has not been left unchallenged. Scholars such as Pippa Norris, Kenneth Newton, and others claim rather the opposite effect: in contrast with media consumption in general, news consumption is correlated with higher political knowledge, higher political trust, and more political participation (Holz-Bacha and Norris 2001; Newton 1999; Norris 2000). Norris talks in this respect of a "virtuous circle" of positive attitudes toward politics and media use. People who are interested and knowledgeable about politics, are more inclined to watch the news and in turn learn more about politics, become gradually less cynical and more inclined to participate (Norris 2011). These optimistic accounts of the media have found ample confirmation across time and countries. Scholars found positive relationships between media use and political variables, such as political knowledge (e.g. Aarts and Semetko 2003), political interest (e.g. Strömbäck and Shehata 2010), political partici-pation (e.g. Schuck, Vliegenthart, and De Vreese 2016) and also political trust (e.g. Adriaansen, Van Praag, and De Vreese 2010).

Although the debate on "media malaise" versus "virtuous circle" has been linked to a variety of political effects, ranging from political knowledge to political participation, we restrict our discussion, in line with the central query of this book, to measures of political support, in particular political trust and political cynicism. The concept of cynicism, which is used extensively in the media effects literature, refers to opinions about (the morality and motiv-ations of) individual politicians and leaders, while trust is mostly related to political institutions and support for the political system in general. We will focus on the role of traditional news media such as newspapers and television news, but end with some thoughts on the growing role of social media.

This chapter aims to provide a systematic review of the available evidence on the effect media have on political support. We deal with the two central claims of the media malaise theory. First, that there has been a general decline of political support because of the growing share of negative news coverage of politics. This suggests a change over time in the way politics is portrayed in the media. Second, to support this longitudinal view, scholars have suggested that a negative or cynical framing of politics has an immediate harmful effect on the political attitudes of individual news consumers. In other words, we first investigate the broader development in the media sector, and next the micro process that might explain the link between citizens' media use and exposure and political support (see also Figure 1.2 in Chapter 1). We end the chapter with some insights in to what aspects of the news might reduce cynicism and enhance trust.

6.2 Studying the Political Media Environment in Longitudinal and Comparative Perspective

In Chapter 2 of this book Van Ham and Thomassen conclude that there is no overall structural decline of political support since the mid-1970s, but that there is large variation in levels of support across time and space. To link some of these developments to the role of the media, we need to first have a closer look at the available evidence about levels of trust and political journalism in longitudinal and comparative perspectives.

The most explicit criticisms of the media have been voiced in the US. Patterson and others have explicitly linked the increasing amount of strategic news coverage and "bad news" to declining support for politicians and political institutions. The origin of the changing attitudes of journalists toward politics is situated at the end of the 1960s and strongly influenced by dramatic events such as Watergate and the contested Vietnam War. Since then US journalists see it as their main task to bring forward the "real" story that played behind the scenes. It is argued that the original skepticism has been replaced by a cynical view on politics. Politicians are driven by their own personal interests, and it is up to journalists to reveal that. This has led to more interpretative journalism with a focus on the strategic motivations of politicians, more "bad news," and a focus on conflicts. According to Patterson (1993) the share of negative news coverage at election times has risen from twenty-five percent in 1960 to sixty percent at the beginning of the 1990s.[1] In 2000 he notes: "The real bias of the press today is not a partisan one, but a pronounced tendency to report what is wrong with politics and politicians rather than what is right" (Patterson 2000: 14).

Can the growing negativity of the news be held responsible for the decline in political support witnessed in the US at the end of the 1960s and most of the 1970s (Dalton 2004; see also Chapter 2 in this volume)? At least two concerns preclude a direct link. First, there is no empirical proof for a causal relationship between this change in journalistic style and the steady decline of political support in the US at the end of the 1960s and most of the 1970s. So it might be that the more critical and less respectful attitude of the media toward political institutions and actors is rather a reflection of a broader trend of declining respect for authority than the cause of it (Norris 1999a). Studies that tried to find a causal link between media coverage and political attitudes over time have remained scarce and results mixed. Norris (2011), for instance, combines news content, and more particularly, the amount of scandal coverage, with aggregate public opinion data over the last decade (2000–10). Using time series analyses she shows that this specific type of coverage does not affect public attitudes in the United Kingdom, but it does slightly negatively affect satisfaction with the goverment in the US. This different impact of scandal news on political trust might be caused by the type of scandal that is reported on, as Kumlin and Esaiasson (2012) show that only scandals that involve multiple parties are negatively effecting people's satisfaction with democracy.

A second reason to be careful when making a link between media coverage and political trust is that the claims of Patterson and others mostly focus on election coverage. The campaign period might be rather atypical and not representative of routine political coverage (Van Aelst and De Swert 2009). A recent comparative study of political news in routine times showed relatively low levels of negativity in US news coverage (Esser, Engesser, Matthes, and Berganza 2016). Furthermore, election campaigns run by US candidates have always been negative, and this has merely further increased during the post-war era (Soroka 2014: 18). Although the effect of negative campaigning on political attitudes is open for discussion, it seems that the negativity of US campaigns is also the responsibility of the political candidates (Ansolabehere and Iyengar 1995). We will come back to this point in the discussion.

In short, there is no proof of a causal link, but still the decline of political support starting at the end of the 1960s in the US has gone together with a steady increase of more strategic and negative news coverage at election times (but not in "routine" times between elections). Can we make similar comparisons about the trends in other countries? The available evidence is very limited. A notable exception is the study by Kepplinger (2000) who analyzed political reporting in the German press over a period of forty-five years (1951–95) and public opinion data about the declining image of politicians. He finds that statements about German political elites have become gradually more negative over time and that this seems related to the less positive perceptions of the morality and capabilities of politicians. However, again, these descriptive findings should be treated with caution, as a causal analysis is lacking. Furthermore, Kepplinger shows that after a steady increase of negativity between the end of the 1960s and the mid-1980s, statements in the press became less negative again, while public trust in individual politicians further declined. The author also notes that the increase in negative statements about politicians is mainly caused by other politicians. Reinemann and Wilke (2007) come to similar findings in their longitudinal analysis of the main candidates for the chancellorship in the election coverage by the German press. After an increase of negativity, between 1949 and 1980, a negative tone toward both incumbent and chancellor has become the norm (see also Magin 2015).

More European studies have been conducted about changes in political reporting since the 1990s. In general, the coverage has *not* become more strategic or negative. Zeh and Hopmann (2013) show that in Germany and Denmark there is no significant increase in negativity toward candidates between 1990 and 2010. Vliegenthart et al. (2010) come to similar conclusions about the UK and the Netherlands, and rather find an opposite trend, with a slight increase in positivity toward politicians. A finding that is confirmed for the Netherlands, where since the turn of the century, election news is less focused on the contest and less negative (Takens, Van Atteveldt, Van Hoof, and Kleinnijenhuis 2013). In sum, we can conclude that over time political news has become more strategic, critical toward political actors, but that this trend has mainly occurred before the 1990s, and since then did not persist.

Most European countries seem to have followed the US trend toward more critical news coverage, but at a slower pace and, certainly less systematically at election times. The central role of public broadcasting in most European countries might be part of the explanation. For instance, in the beginning of the 1980s the BBC coverage of the campaign was much more guided by a respectful "sacerdotal approach" toward politics, while US media were already much more guided by their own news values (Semetko, Blumler, Gurevitch, and Weaver 1991). In many European countries, public broadcasters at that time devoted relatively little attention to politics during election times as they were afraid to be seen as biased or offending politicians in power. Since then public broadcasters have broadened their range of news programming (Aalberg, Van Aelst, and Curran 2010). Also outside election time the supply of information in most European countries has grown rather than diminished over the last decades. In a comparative study of thirteen European democracies, Esser and colleagues (2012) showed that the amount of attention given to news and current affairs has risen significantly since the late 1970s. The introduction of commercial broadcasting has not led to less, but rather to more news as some of them also presented news and public affairs in lengthy and prominent time slots (see Figure 6.1). At the same time, the political news coverage of the public broadcasters has become less cautious, with journalists

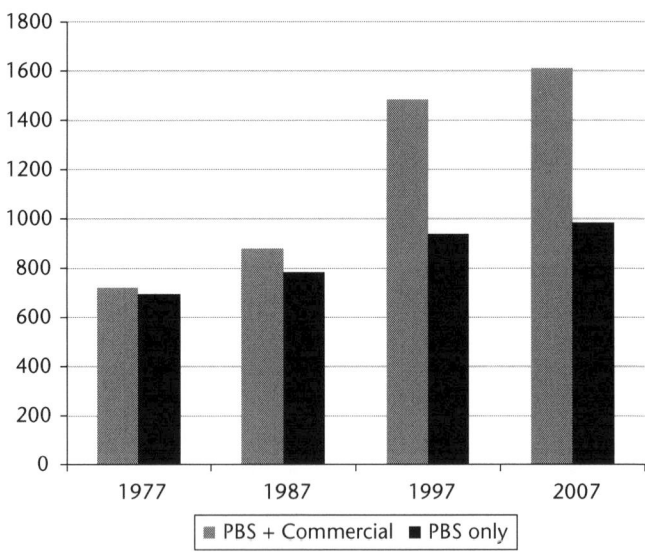

Figure 6.1 Number of minutes for news and current affairs per week on the two most important commercial and public TV channels in thirteen European countries (1977–2007)

Source: Esser et al. (2012).

being more active and intervening. In contrast to the US, this interpretative style of reporting has, however, not gone hand in hand with an outspoken cynical or negative view on politics (Brants and Van Kempen 2002; Goddard, Scammell, and Semetko 1998; McNair 2002; Van Aelst 2007).

Thus, empirical evidence at the macro level of a growing share of negative news coverage of politics is at best mixed. Nevertheless, there is certainly evidence of long-term changes in political journalism. Can we see these changes as (partial) causes of changes in political support over time? This remains largely an open question as strong proof is lacking. In an attempt to answer this question, we will look at the micro process connecting media use and political support in Section 6.3.

6.3 Individual Media Use and Political Support

If negative news coverage in the media undermines political support, we should expect to find a negative association between citizens' exposure to media and their levels of political support. In this section we investigate to what extent there is indeed a negative association between media use and political support. We also take a long-term perspective to evaluate to what extent this relationship has changed in the past decades. We used the Mannheim Eurobarometer Trend File 1970–2002 (edition v2.0.1, Schmitt et al. 2008), and updated the trend file until 2014 with Eurobarometer data available via GESIS/ZACAT.[2] As not all Eurobarometer surveys ask questions about media use, the resulting data set covers the period from 1983 to 2014, a period of thirty years, with data on media use being collected for nineteen years in that period.

As an indicator of political support, our dependent variable, we restrict ourselves in this chapter to *satisfaction with the way democracy works in one's own country*. This variable is measured on a four-point scale, running from (1) not satisfied at all, to (4) very satisfied. For our analyses, we collapsed this scale to two categories: (0) not satisfied at all/not very satisfied, and (1) fairly satisfied/very satisfied.

Our main explanatory variable at the micro level is media use. Here we rely on the media use index variable available in the Mannheim Eurobarometer Trend File 1970–2002 (edition v2.0.1, Schmitt et al. 2008), and update it until 2014. The media use index variable combines three variables measuring respondents' frequency of usage of different news media, namely television, newspapers, and radio.[3] The index is a four-point categorical variable ranging from very low to very high.[4] The index is constructed as follows: if television, radio, and newspapers are all used several times a week or more, overall media use is classified as very high. If two out of three media types are used several times a week or more, overall media use is classified as high. If only one medium is used several times a week or more, overall media use is classified as low, and if all three media are used less than several times a week, overall media use is coded as very low (see *Codebook Trend File* 2005).

As control variables we include a number of variables that have been found to affect political support in previous research (Dalton 2004; Norris 2011), namely, the level of education, age, gender, marital status, and whether respondents were unemployed. As we seek to analyze as long a time period as possible, we include the set of countries where media use questions have been asked by the Eurobarometer from 1983 onwards, i.e. the nine EU member states at 1973: France, Germany, Italy, Belgium, Netherlands, Luxemburg, United Kingdom, Ireland, and Denmark (EU9). In order to keep the presentation of results simple, we present our results by country.

We use logistic regression, and test the robustness of our results with multi-level logistic regression, correcting standard errors for clustering within years. The results remain substantively the same in these models and are available on request from the author.[5] We model change in the effect of media use on satisfaction with democracy over time by including an interaction term of media use and year in all models. Table 6.1 presents the results of models testing only the main effect of media use on satisfaction with democracy, and Table 6.2 presents results of models including the interaction effect with year.

The results in Table 6.1 demonstrate that, contrary to what media malaise theories would predict, media use has a consistent and significant positive effect on political support in all nine European democracies in our sample. The strength of the effects differs considerably between countries, with media use being most strongly associated with high levels of satisfaction with democracy in the Netherlands and Denmark, and the weakest associations in the United Kingdom, Belgium, and Ireland. However, these findings are based on pooled data from 1983 until 2014, so it is entirely possible that the relationship between media use and political support changed over time. Table 6.2 therefore shows how the effect of media use on satisfaction with democracy has changed in this time period.

The main effect of media use now shows the effect of media use in the first year for which we have data, 1983. In that year we do find some evidence for a negative association between media use and satisfaction with democracy: in Belgium and in Germany those respondents who used more media were also more dissatisfied with democracy. However, in the other seven European democracies the association between media use and satisfaction with democracy was positive (though only significant in four countries). Interestingly, it is in Belgium and Germany (and Denmark) where the interaction effect with year is significant, suggesting an increasingly positive association between media use and satisfaction with democracy over time. In the other countries

Table 6.1 The effect of media use on political support in nine European democracies (1983–2014)

	France	Belgium	Netherlands	Germany	Italy	Luxembourg	Denmark	Ireland	United Kingdom
Independent variables									
Media use (1–4)	0.123***	0.071***	0.223***	0.110***	0.127***	0.093**	0.199***	0.077***	0.068***
	(0.016)	(0.015)	(0.020)	(0.014)	(0.018)	(0.030)	(0.025)	(0.018)	(0.015)
Control variables									
Education (1–10)	0.105***	0.033***	0.077***	0.016***	0.027***	0.013	0.100***	0.062***	0.062***
	(0.005)	(0.005)	(0.005)	(0.004)	(0.005)	(0.008)	(0.006)	(0.006)	(0.005)
Age (15–97)	0.004***	0.004***	−0.008***	0.001	0.002*	0.008***	−0.004***	−0.000	0.003***
	(0.001)	(0.001)	(0.001)	(0.001)	(0.001)	(0.002)	(0.001)	(0.001)	(0.001)
Gender—female (0–1)	−0.111***	0.081**	0.041	−0.041*	−0.033	0.090+	−0.106**	−0.077**	−0.028
	(0.027)	(0.027)	(0.030)	(0.020)	(0.030)	(0.046)	(0.035)	(0.029)	(0.024)
Marital status—married (0–1)	−0.007	0.055*	0.072*	0.022	−0.005	0.061	0.105**	−0.071*	0.042+
	(0.028)	(0.028)	(0.032)	(0.021)	(0.032)	(0.050)	(0.036)	(0.031)	(0.025)
Unemployed (0–1)	−0.343***	−0.429***	−0.508***	−0.939***	−0.302***	−0.277+	−0.399***	−0.793***	−0.394***
	(0.056)	(0.050)	(0.066)	(0.037)	(0.070)	(0.155)	(0.065)	(0.053)	(0.045)
Constant	−0.934***	−0.380***	0.067	−0.271***	−1.505***	0.504***	0.390***	0.309***	−0.200**
	(0.070)	(0.075)	(0.090)	(0.059)	(0.079)	(0.131)	(0.102)	(0.082)	(0.065)
N level 1 (respondents)	23,105	23,199	23,500	41,918	23,525	11,393	23,297	22,420	29,770
N level 2 (years)	19	19	19	19	19	19	19	19	19

Source: Eurobarometer. Logistic regression; dependent variable: not/not at all satisfied with democracy (0), very/fairly satisfied with democracy (1). P-values: + 0.1, * 0.05, ** 0.01, *** 0.001.

Table 6.2 The effect of media use on political support over time in nine European democracies (1983–2014)

	France	Belgium	Netherlands	Germany	Italy	Luxembourgrg	Denmark	Ireland	United Kingdom
Independent variables									
Media use (1–4)	0.095+	−0.133**	0.131*	−0.217***	0.134*	0.166	0.028	0.183**	0.046
	(0.051)	(0.050)	(0.066)	(0.049)	(0.057)	(0.107)	(0.079)	(0.060)	(0.049)
Year (1983–2014)	−0.002	−0.006	0.003	−0.033***	0.033***	0.030*	0.014	0.015+	0.008
	(0.006)	(0.006)	(0.009)	(0.006)	(0.006)	(0.014)	(0.011)	(0.008)	(0.006)
Media use *Year	0.001	0.008***	0.004	0.013***	−0.001	−0.003	0.009**	−0.004+	0.001
	(0.002)	(0.002)	(0.002)	(0.002)	(0.002)	(0.004)	(0.003)	(0.002)	(0.002)
Control variables									
Education (1–10)	0.104***	0.019***	0.066***	0.011**	0.010*	0.000	0.057***	0.061***	0.053***
	(0.005)	(0.005)	(0.006)	(0.004)	(0.005)	(0.009)	(0.006)	(0.006)	(0.005)
Age (15–97)	0.004***	0.001+	−0.010***	−0.000	−0.000	0.006***	−0.010***	−0.000	0.001*
	(0.001)	(0.001)	(0.001)	(0.001)	(0.001)	(0.002)	(0.001)	(0.001)	(0.001)
Gender—female (0–1)	−0.112***	0.074**	0.030	−0.045*	−0.066*	0.071	−0.117***	−0.078**	−0.031
	(0.027)	(0.027)	(0.030)	(0.020)	(0.030)	(0.047)	(0.035)	(0.029)	(0.024)
Marital status—married (0–1)	−0.006	0.047+	0.079*	0.021	−0.039	0.041	0.117**	−0.073*	0.053*
	(0.028)	(0.028)	(0.032)	(0.021)	(0.032)	(0.050)	(0.036)	(0.031)	(0.025)
Unemployed (0–1)	−0.346***	−0.470***	−0.521***	−0.938***	−0.386***	−0.388*	−0.410***	−0.793***	−0.413***
	(0.056)	(0.050)	(0.067)	(0.037)	(0.071)	(0.157)	(0.065)	(0.054)	(0.045)
Constant	−0.877***	−0.030	0.133	0.636***	−2.081***	−0.111	0.411	−0.061	−0.329*
	(0.163)	(0.169)	(0.233)	(0.178)	(0.176)	(0.384)	(0.282)	(0.213)	(0.165)
N level 1 (respondents)	23,105	23,199	23,500	41,918	23,525	11,393	23,297	22,420	29,770
N level 2 (years)	19	19	19	19	19	19	19	19	19

Source: Eurobarometer. Logistic regression, dependent variable: not/not at all satisfied with democracy (0), very/fairly satisfied with democracy (1). P-values: + 0.1, * 0.05, ** 0.01, *** 0.001.

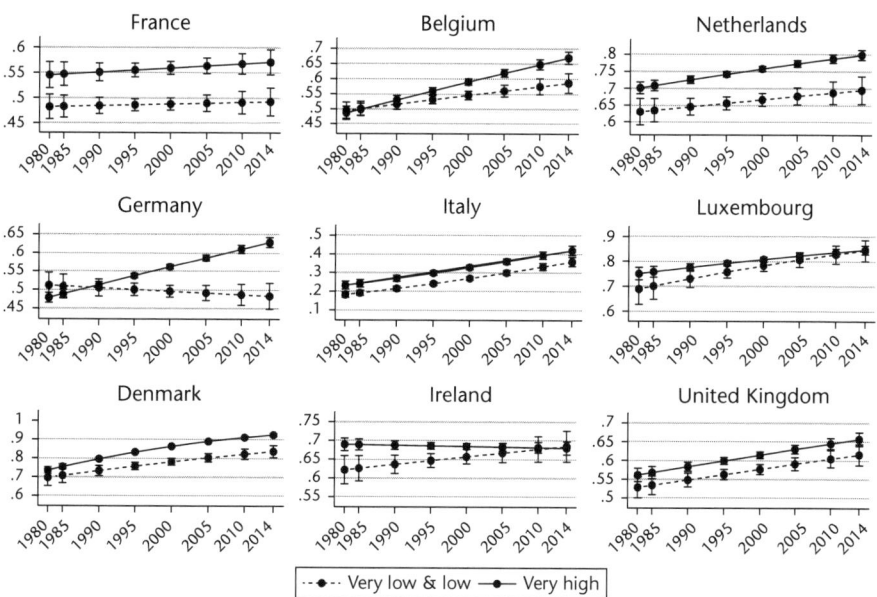

Figure 6.2 Probability of being satisfied with democracy by time and media use in nine European democracies (1983–2014)

the interaction effect does not appear to be significant, though the trend is positive in six out of nine countries.

However, a more accurate way to interpret interaction effects is to present predicted probabilities of being satisfied with democracy by different levels of media use. These are presented in Figure 6.2. To improve readability the figure contrasts respondents with very high media use to respondents with low media use.[6]

As Figure 6.2 shows, with the exception of Belgium and Germany in the early 1980s, in all other time periods and in the other seven established European democracies, respondents with higher levels of media use are more satisfied with democracy, and levels of satisfaction with democracy appear to go up over time in all nine European democracies except Ireland. Hence if anything, exposure to news media increases political support, rather than decreasing it as media malaise theory suggests. Moreover, the differences in political support between low and high media users are not large in most countries, suggesting that the media have only weak effects on political support (Newton 2006a).

However, a problem with analyses such as the ones presented here is that it is unclear what the exact content was of the media that citizens' were exposed to, and hence this might include both negative news coverage as well as other news coverage, potentially diluting media effects on political support. Moreover, an even more serious concern is the direction of the causal relationship: is media use shaping citizens' political support or are citizens with high political support using more media? Therefore, in Section 6.4 we will focus on short-term effects studies that can make much stronger claims on the causal relationship between media consumption and measures of political trust and political cynicism.

6.4 The Contingency of Media Effects on Political Support

Empirical research on the micro-level link between media and political support has generally not found strong effects. Multiple studies do find significant effects from media on political trust and cynicism. However, these effects are mostly modest and hardly ever seen as the main drivers of political trust. For instance, Aarts and colleagues (2012) show in their study of six Western countries that the effect of news exposure on political trust is weak and mostly disappears after controlling for education. "Education is the main driver of trust (and knowledge), not the media—and this point can hardly be overemphasized" (Aarts et al. 2012: 117). Earlier Moy et al. (1999: 149) concluded along the same lines that "factors other than the media must be examined when seeking to explain America's confidence crisis" (see also Gross, Aday, and Brewer 2004; Moy and Scheufele 2000). Another important nuance is that the effects of media exposure are most outspoken on political cynicism and much less on the more general indicators of political trust. For instance, based on experiments, Jackson (2011) finds that people became more cynical after exposure to strategic news coverage. However, the effect is only significant for the specific politicians featured in the (experimental) news story and not for the general confidence in politicians or the working of democracy (but see Shehata 2014). In short, the effects of media on political trust are often absent and when present mostly modest at best.

Although the ongoing discussion on the potential positive or negative role of the media in politics sparked a lively debate, given the empirical findings mentioned earlier, one might raise the question of how useful it is to keep the clear distinction between "media malaise" versus "media mobilization," or "spiral of cynicism" versus "virtuous circle." Also Curran and colleagues (2014: 15) complain in a recent article that scholars are forced to choose between "the view that the media radiate democratic influence in a nimbus of virtue or the opposing view that the media turn people off by distorting its true nature." To move beyond the discussion of the media as good cop or bad cop, it is more useful to investigate under what conditions media can have certain effects. Also in the empirical literature, there is a growing consensus that impact of the media on the public is *contingent* on the medium, the message, and the receiver. Thinking in terms of contingency of media effects is nothing new. In the debate on the democratic role of the media, however, the focus has perhaps been too much on stressing the positive or negative outcomes, rather than their conditional nature. Studies show that both medium, message, and receiver characteristics mediate the effects of news exposure.

It has become common sense in media effect research that media messages are not received in a similar way by a passive, homogeneous audience, but rather actively processed and dependent on different personal characteristics of the *receiver* (McQuail 1993). Also in the debate on media and trust, scholars have devoted extensive attention to the moderating role of individual features. A central dispute in the literature deals with the role of political sophistication, mostly operationalized in terms of political knowledge, political interest, and education. The question is whether the media mainly influence more highly educated people who follow politics closely or the politically less sophisticated. In general, the picture is not straightforward. For education it seems that most studies do not find any interaction effect: trust levels of more highly educated people are not more or less influenced by media coverage than those of lower-educated people (e.g. Aarts et al. 2012; Valentino et al. 2001). The results on the moderating role of political knowledge are mixed. Some studies find stronger effects on people with low political knowledge and political interest (e.g. Jackson 2011; Schuck, Boomgaarden, and De Vreese 2013), while other have found some indications that actually the more knowledgeable (De Vreese and Elenbaas 2008) and those more interested (De Vreese 2005) are affected more. This difference might be explained by the specific types of frames under investigation. While presenting politics using a general "game frame" (e.g. referring to winning and losing) might be more likely to influence the less sophisticated, De Vreese and Elenbaas (2008) argue that more knowledgeable citizens can make more sense of complex strategic news frames (e.g. stressing the role of spin doctors in influencing media coverage), and therefore are more influenced by them. Another related variable of importance, in particular in the US, is partisanship. For instance, Valentino and colleagues (2001) show that in the US only the trust of non-partisans is negatively affected by strategic news coverage, while most partisan voters are left unaffected. Finally, a Dutch study finds that, in particular, levels of cynicism about politics among young people are affected by campaign coverage. The effect is, however, not negative but positive: more substantive news coverage leads young people to trust politics more, not less (Adriaansen et al. 2010).

In terms of the *medium* the classical distinction is made between the role of television versus newspapers. In general, newspaper-reading is associated with higher levels of trust, while the relationship with television-viewing is mostly neutral (Ceron 2015; Newton 1999). Avery (2009) shows with his panel study of a US election that watching television leads to more cynicism while reading a newspaper rather boosted trust. However, these effects are only present among voters with relatively high levels of trust. No effects are found among those already mistrusting the government at the start of the campaign. This confirms the downside of the virtuous circle of Norris: those who are cynical and not engaged are unlikely to get positive attitudes from the media, which they often also mistrust (see also Earl Bennett, Rhine, Flickinger, and Bennett 1999). When we further differentiate between types of television there is a growing consensus that public broadcasting is most likely to contribute to a virtuous circle of media exposure, political knowledge, and attitudes. Most recently, an eleven-country study confirms the importance of public television (Curran et al. 2014; Soroka et al. 2013). Without claiming a causal relationship, watching public broadcasting stations (PBS) is positively connected to knowledge, interest, and confidence toward politics (see also Hooghe 2002). This positive relationship is absent for viewers of commercial television. However, when we focus on the relationship between public broadcasting and political trust, the relationship is less straightforward. Aarts et al. (2012) find a positive relationship in Sweden and Belgium, but not in Norway, the UK, and the Netherlands. Also the seminal study of Aarts and Semetko (2003) clearly shows that in the Netherlands watching public television was correlated with higher political knowledge and turnout, but again there was no correlation with political trust. In a recent study Strömbäck and colleagues (2015) confirm the positive link between watching public service television and political trust, although this relationship has become weaker in the last three decades.

A third and most recent evolution in studying the conditions of media effects on political attitudes and participation is also taking into account the *message*, or more correctly the actual media content that people consume. For instance, Elenbaas and De Vreese (2008) find that following the news about an EU referendum in the Netherlands on the public broadcasters has the strongest effect on political cynicism. This can simply be explained by the fact that in this campaign the public news broadcast had the highest amount of strategically framed campaign news. More and more, studies that test the effect of strategy news (e.g. Adriaansen et al. 2010) or soft news (e.g. Boukes and Boomgaarden 2014) on political cynicism have combined content analyses data with news exposure measures. This allows researchers to better measure the amount and type of content people actually received. In this way, for instance, Shehata (2014) shows that Swedish voters who consume a larger diet of strategy rich news become more cynical and less trusting, but that also the opposite effect is significant: the more voters receive substantive news coverage of the election the less cynical and the more trusting they turn out to be.

In sum, studying the conditionality of media exposure is necessary to nuance both positive and negative effects the media might have on feelings of trust and legitimacy toward the political system. The combination of content analysis with public opinion data seems to be the most fruitful way forward. The challenges for this line of research are, however, not small. The growing proliferation of media outlets and the increasing importance of the new media make it more difficult to "capture" the actual news content people consume. Furthermore, these studies often focus on specific events or specific periods that make it difficult to study the long-term implications of the relationship between media and political legitimacy.

6.5 Summarizing: How Media Affect Political Support

In this chapter I tested two related claims of the media malaise theory. First, that there is a decline in political support because of increased negative and cynical political news coverage of politics. Second, to support this longitudinal view, that this type of media coverage has an immediate harmful effect on citizens' political trust and support for the political system. To start with the second claim: is there a negative link between news coverage and political attitudes? As our analyses of public opinion data and an extensive discussion of the literature indicates, the answer is probably "no," but perhaps the safer answer would be "it depends." First, we showed empirically that media use is not negatively but *positively* correlated with political support in nine Western European democracies. Controlling for several relevant characteristics, people who use more media are more satisfied with the functioning of democracy than people who have low levels of media use. Furthermore, this relationship seems to have become somewhat stronger in recent decades. Although these findings go against media malaise theories, they do not prove a causal relationship. Therefore, we took a closer look at existing studies.

Overall, a majority of studies do not find a strong causal relationship between media use and measures of political trust. Research that focuses especially on political cynicism, operationalized as the opinions about what drives individual politicians, does find a media effect more often, but again seldom a very strong one. On the basis of the modest and mixed findings in his study on political cynicism in Denmark and the Netherlands, De Vreese even concludes that "cynicism is perhaps little more than an indication of interested and critical citizenry" (De Vreese 2005: 294).

In that respect there is very little reason to assume that media are the drivers behind a decline of legitimacy, if such a trend existed (see van Ham and

Thomassen, Chapter 2, this volume). This being said, scholars seem to recognize that news coverage of specific events or periods can have both negative as well as positive consequences for political trust. The effect is, however, seldom straightforward but contingent on the predispositions and characteristics of the receiver, and more importantly on the exact amount and type of news that people consume. In that sense, the research shifts from measures of mere news exposure to integrating actual content analyses into research designs are welcome. So overall this overview provides little support for the media malaise theory, but on the other hand, there is also not that much proof for the "virtuous circle" that Norris (2000) suggested. This is mainly due to the focus of this chapter on the political trust dimension of the virtuous circle and not so much on knowledge, interest, and participation. For these other dimensions news consumption might be more beneficial, even if the coverage is not that positive for politics. For instance, there is evidence that conflictual campaign coverage mobilizes people to turn out to vote (e.g. De Vreese and Boomgaarden 2006; De Vreese and Tobiasen 2007; Lengauer and Holler 2012), but simultaneously has negative effects on levels of trust. This indicates that some news content might be "good" for interest and participation, but "bad" for political support.

Even more difficult than linking media coverage and political trust in the short term, is judging the claim that the rise in critical news coverage is responsible for the gradual erosion of political legitimacy in the long term. Although a causal claim cannot be made, we must acknowledge that both trends, at least in the US, have taken place around the same time. So, at least there is ground for concern. At the same time, there is scholarly consensus that people need information about politics to act as citizens in a democracy and that the news media are an important source of information in this respect. Even Patterson, one of the most outspoken critics of the media, states that: "There is something worse than exposure to persistently negative news, and that is no news exposure at all" (Patterson 2002: 97). In this respect Patterson was worried that the decreasing amount of campaign coverage in the 1990s would lower the involvement of the American voter. Also other US scholars warn us that the real problem for democracy is the decreasing amount of hard news in combination with growing numbers of commercial channels and new media opportunities. This creates a context in which people can more easily avoid political information altogether and can go "newsless" (Bennett and Iyengar 2008; Prior 2007). Ironically, in the initial video malaise thesis of Robinson (1976) the inadvertent audience was considered the most vulnerable group for the damaging influence of the news media. Forty years later the analysis has been turned upside down: not the presence of these accidental news viewers, but rather their disappearance is seen as problematic. The question is whether this shrinking supply and demand of news is a general trend. Recent comparative studies show that the US is clearly different from most European countries, with a relatively low amount of attention for news during prime time and in comparative perspective an extremely low amount of people watching it. "The US stands out as a low-trust, low-knowledge and low news-consumption country" (Aarts et al. 2012: 117). In the future, the ongoing commercialization and fragmentation of the media landscape might bring Europe somewhat closer to the US situation. In particular, the growing importance of new and social media might be important to scrutinize.

This chapter is mainly concerned with traditional media as they still outweigh the new media in terms of political news; and at this stage the most important "new" media are still the online versions of traditional news media (Mutz and Young 2011; Shehata and Strömbäck 2014). However, the rapidly growing success of social media indicates a transition from low to high choice media environments. More than ever, people can choose when, how, and what kind of news they consume. As a consequence, people might be more influenced by the information of likeminded (virtual) friends, and no longer confronted by traditional news that sometimes challenges their preexisting views. This trend raises democratic concerns about citizens increasingly living in algorithm-shaped "filter bubbles" (Pariser, 2011) and reinforcing "echo chambers" (Sunstein, 2007). This means that people might further narrow their information diet and increasingly live in homogeneous information environments. However, at this stage, the extent to which this trend will influence levels of political support remains unclear.

Therefore, future research will need to devote more attention to social media as alternative sources of information with potential positive and negative effects on political attitudes (Kenski and Stroud 2006; Moy and Hussain 2011). Recently, some scholars have looked at the relationship between political trust and social media. Based on Eurobarometer data Ceron (2015) comes to the conclusion that people who consume more news via social media have significantly lower levels of trust in political institutions. Johnson and Kaye (2015), on the other hand, find that in the US only the use of some types of social media (blogs, YouTube) are related to lower levels of trust, while others such as Twitter and Facebook are slightly positively correlated with political support. Both the negative and positive relationships are weak, again. These studies give us a first insight on how social media and political trust correlate, but we need more advanced studies to know what people consume, share, and produce on social media, before we can actually take into account potential effects of social media on political support (e.g. Gil de Zúñiga, Jung, and Valenzuela 2012 on social media use and social capital). This future research agenda becomes more relevant in countries where trust in traditional media is declining and people are relying more, or even exclusively, on social media.

We need only think of the prevalence of fake news stories on Facebook and Twitter during the 2016 US election (falsely accusing Trump and Clinton of acts they did not perform) to understand how problematic low-quality information on social media can be for people's trust in political actors.

6.6 Conclusion: What is Bad News and Who is to Blame?

At this stage neither old nor new media seem to be the drivers behind long-term trends in political support, though they may well be associated with short-term fluctuations in political support. This general conclusion might sound reassuring, however, at the same time, studies have shown that under certain circumstances cynical or negative coverage can have potentially negative consequences for public support of political actors and institutions. This raises more fundamental questions about what political news is or what it should be. We address two related issues: When is the news about politics too negative and who is to blame for that?

The discussion on what kind of political news we consider most appropriate for citizens is not an easy one to answer. Of course, this is related to broader views on news and democracy (Strömbäck 2005), but also more concretely to the nature of politics itself. For instance, can we expect media to present an issue in a non-conflictual manner if there is open and intense disagreement between politicians? In line with the work of Schattschneider (1960) conflict, defined as the competition of ideas, can be considered as a natural part of a healthy democracy. So it would be strange to expect the media to ignore the conflictual nature of politics, or to consider the attention for conflict in the news as merely something that journalists independently add to make their coverage more attractive. Probably, the critique is not that the media report political conflicts, but rather that they create conflicts, or at least over-represent them. The same goes for the attention to strategy and electoral competition: not their presence, but their dominance is considered problematic. To determine when media "distort" political reality requires a kind of benchmark to place media coverage in perspective. These benchmarks are, however, not easy to define. Lengauer, Esser, and Berganza (2012) for instance, argue that it is hardly possible to empirically distinguish between "media-initiated" negativity added by journalists and "media-disseminated" negativity added by political actors or others. They are probably right when it comes to a stand-alone content analysis. However, some studies have tried to overcome this issue by using alternative benchmarks. For instance, Kahn and Kenney (1999) asked US campaign managers to judge the degree of negativity of campaign ads and news coverage. It turned out that they were able to distinguish between criticism and "mudslinging" in both ads and news coverage.

This distinction proved to be highly relevant as negative ads and news coverage increased turnout, while mudslinging had the opposite effect. The authors conclude that "negative information is helpful and motivates participation as long as is addresses relevant topics and is presented in an appropriate manner" (1999: 878).

This brings us to the question to what extent the media can be blamed for the sometimes negative effects their coverage has. A revealing study in this respect has been conducted by Mutz and Reeves (2005). In three experiments they test the potential negative effect of "uncivil" political debates on television viewers. It turns out that when politicians in the debate interrupt each other, raise their voices, and show non-verbal disrespect for their opponent, viewers trust in politics goes down. The effects are substantial and not only affect trust in politicians, but also in institutions such as Congress and the presidency. When viewers watched a debate with exactly the same level of conflict, but with "civil" politicians, the negative effects on trust remained absent. Can the media, or in this case television, be held responsible for the damaging influence on citizens' confidence in politics? Of course the media cannot be blamed for simply broadcasting a political debate. On the other hand, we should not be naïve as we know that media favor at least some drama and tension to make a political debate more attractive for the audience. In fact, the study of Mutz and Reeves also shows that the uncivil debates are considered as more interesting and exciting. This leaves political journalists with the dilemma that making political programs that are the most thrilling, probably also have the most negative influence on political trust.

The attention for what "bad news" is and how it is caused remains an important challenge for future studies. However, a future research agenda should perhaps also look at the potential opposite effect of "good news" on political support. Until now, the research agenda was perhaps too much occupied with the potential link between "political malaise" and "media malaise." Even Norris (2011), in her most recent opposition against media pessimists focused more on showing that a negative relationship is absent, rather than clarifying or deepening the potential positive relationship. This is perhaps not surprising as scientists may be—just like journalists—more focused on the negative and less on the positive (Lau 1985). But maybe it is time to put the opposite questions center stage. What amount and types of news content might enhance political trust and limit cynicism? Which people might benefit most from following the news? When do social media have a positive impact on confidence in politics? Some studies discussed earlier fit this research agenda. For instance, Adriaansen et al. (2010) indicating that substantial news coverage was able to reduce cynicism among younger citizens is intriguing, while Shehata (2014) shows that in Sweden even institutional trust can be enhanced when campaign news is mainly about issues and policy, instead of focusing on politics as a game. Also the study of Kahn and Kenney (1999) is worth mentioning as they suggest ways to distinguish between substantial disagreement with its positive effects and aggressive personal attacks that lead to the opposite. These findings require more investigation before we can generalize them. Of course, even a research agenda that looks for positive effects, should not be blind to the many shortcomings and distortions in how media portray politics and its potential detrimental consequences. Or to put it in the words of the famous media sociologist Michael Schudson (1995: 3): "Everyone in a democracy is a certified media critic, which is as it should be."

Notes

1. Using a slightly different approach, Zaller (1999) finds for the same time period an increase from 5 percent to 20 percent negative news. Benoit and colleagues (2005) don't find an increase of negative campaign news in the *New York Times* between 1952 and 2000, as campaign news has always been more negative than positive. They do confirm an increase of more strategic news coverage over time.
2. The trend file was updated until 2014 for all variables as media use questions not asked in the 2015 Eurobarometers.
3. While online media use has increased in recent years, questions about online news media use were not asked in earlier Eurobarometers. Hence to ensure comparability of our data over the thirty-year period analyzed here, we only consider media use of these three more traditional media sources.
4. Note that the media use index variable in the Mannheim Trend File is coded from very high to very low, but we reversed the scale to make the interpretation of results more intuitive.
5. Note that in Table 6.1. we report results for media use taking media use as a quasi-continuous variable, in order to ease interpretation of results for the interaction term with year. The predicted probability graphs that are shown in Figure 6.2 are based on analyses with media use index as a categorical variable, combining low and very low media use to prevent empty cells in some country-years. The results of these models are substantively the same as the ones presented in Table 6.1 and are available on request from the author.
6. Note that these categories include a substantial proportion of respondents. In the pooled data set across the nine European democracies, forty-eight percent of respondents fell into the very high media use category, thirty-three percent fell into the high media use category, and nineteen percent into the low and very low media use categories.

Part III
Diverging Trends?

Explaining Within and Between Country Differences in Political Support

7

Institutions and Political Support

How Much do Institutions Matter?

Shaun Bowler

7.1 Introduction

This chapter focuses on the question to what extent variation in political institutions affects political support. The absence of a uniform decline of political support (see Chapter 2) suggests that we need to shift our research focus to explanations that can account for differences between countries in levels and trends of political support. In a cross-national context institutional differences broadly understood are likely suspects for factors that would help us explain cross-national variation in public support. For example, political institutions that are inclusive might improve the quality of representation (or at least generate perceptions among citizens that they are being represented well), which in turn might increase citizens' political support for these institutions and/or the political system at large. Moreover, should we find that institutional variation helps to explain cross-national variation in political support then, as a consequence, some form of institutional reform could help address citizen discontent. After all, while it may be difficult to bring about a given institutional change it is often easier to reform institutions than accomplish other kinds of reform, such as changing the political culture of a nation.

Before engaging in the question of what kinds of reform may be helpful, however, we need to show that institutions do have some effect on citizens' political support. Even if institutional change does offer some prospects for helping to address citizen discontent, if the impact of institutions on political support is relatively modest, institutional reform might not provide the optimal solution to address citizen discontent. The core focus (and substantive contribution) of this chapter is therefore to better understand what proportion of the variation in citizen political support can be explained by variation in political institutions. In addition, this chapter argues that the role of institutions in shaping political support is under-theorized. We think that "institutions matter," yet we are less clear about which institutions matter and why. It is not entirely clear, for example, what kinds of institutions should produce what kind of effects. As a result, it is also not entirely clear how sizable any such effects would be, and hence, how effective a solution institutional reform would be.

This chapter, therefore addresses three questions:

- Do institutions matter, and if so, which institutions matter and why?
- If institutions matter, how much do they matter?
- What are the prospects for institutional reform in strengthening political support?

The chapter is divided into three main sections. Section 7.2 examines variation in citizen opinions across Europe toward democratic governance and outlines theoretical expectations about which institutions should matter and why. Section 7.3, analyzes data from the European Social Survey from 2012 on sixteen established democracies in Western Europe (ESS 6) to examine the link between institutions and political support.[1] More specifically it considers the relationship between institutions and three indicators of political support: trust in politicians, trust in the national parliament, and satisfaction with democracy. Section 7.4 of the chapter discusses the broader implications of the results noting that institutions do matter for political support, but effects found are generally weak and inconsistent. The chapter concludes with suggestions for further research.

7.2 Framing the Problem: *Can* Institutions Make a Difference to Political Support?

In Chapter 2 of this volume, Van Ham and Thomassen cast doubt about whether there has been a secular decline in political support but do point out that there is variation both across countries and across time. In this chapter it is cross-country variation that is of interest and that we seek to explain, in particular whether institutions are an important source of that variation.

One preliminary point to make is that it is not citizen support for the idea of democratic governance that is at stake but support for the national political institutions as they work in practice—a quite different entity. Most of our evidence for this claim comes from the responses to the European Social

Survey from 2012 (ESS 6). This is an especially interesting round of the ESS because of the serious and sustained attention the survey pays to questions of democratic governance. Respondents, for example, were asked a battery of questions first about democracy and democratic principles in general, and then specifically about how those principles are put into practice in their country.

The specific questions were of the form:

> Now some questions about democracy. Later on I will ask you about how democracy is working in [country]. First, however, I want you to think instead about how important you think different things are for democracy in general. There are no right or wrong answers so please just tell me what you think.

Respondents were asked their views of fourteen elements of democracy and asked to rate how important they were for democracy in general on an eleven-point scale (0–10). For example respondents were asked how important it is for democracy in general that the government explains its decisions to voters, that the media be free to criticize the government, and so on. Respondents were then asked about their responses to the same fourteen dimensions and asked:

> Now some questions about the same topics, but this time about how you think democracy is working in [country] today. Again, there are no right or wrong answers, so please just tell me what you think.

One of the striking patterns we see is that citizens across the sixteen countries have remarkably consistent views of what matters to democracy in principle. One way of getting a feel for the data is Figure 7.1, which shows national level averages in response to the question how important free and fair elections are and compares them to national averages for how well elections are working in practice in the respondent's country. It becomes clear from Figure 7.1 that there is very little variation across countries in how important citizens find free and fair elections for democracy: the vast majority of respondents find elections very important. Yet, when asked about how well elections are working in practice, respondents are much more critical, and responses vary more strongly from one country to the next. In broad terms these patterns occur as well with the other measures on the survey.

Table 7.1 gives a more precise overview of the fourteen elements of democracy covered in the survey, and shows the means and standard deviations for both how important elements are as well as how well they are working in practice.

The pattern shown in Figure 7.1 is largely confirmed for all of the fourteen elements. With only one exception out of the twenty-eight comparisons we see that the mean evaluations of national political institutions are lower than

119

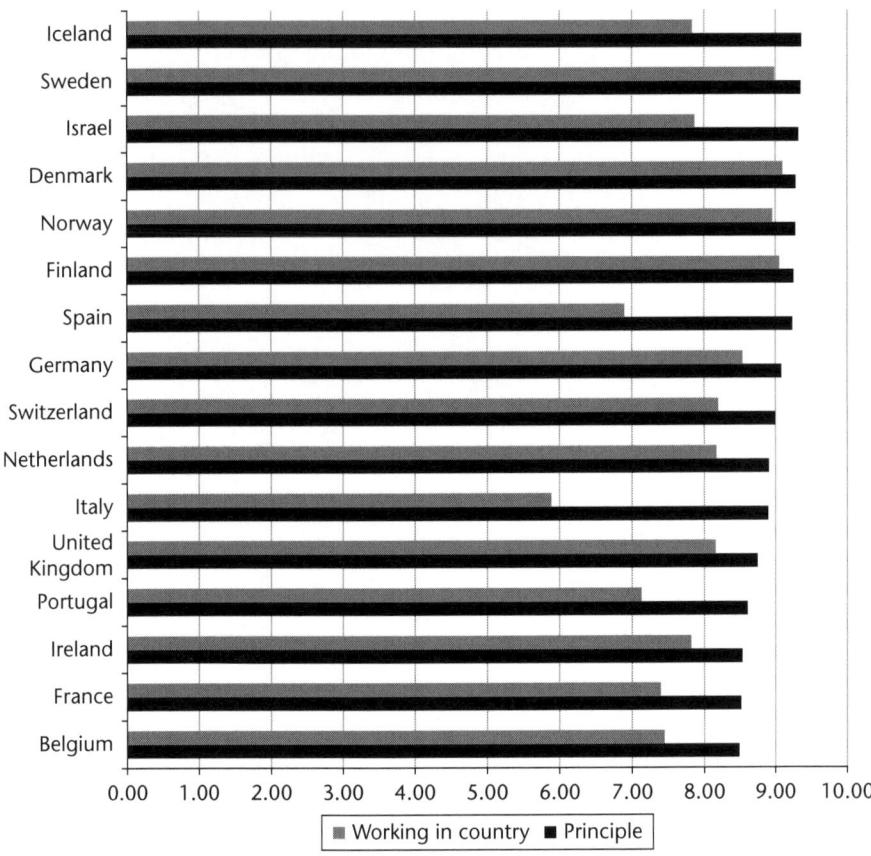

Figure 7.1 How important are elections to the principle of democracy and how well are elections working in your country?
Source: European Social Survey, round six (2012).

the assessments of how important the various properties are in principle. We also see that standard deviations for the assessments of how well the principle is being applied in practice are higher than for the measures of importance.[2]

What we take these data to be saying is that there is an impressive degree of consensus among citizens across Europe of how democracy *should* be. When it comes to how democracy is *actually* operating within one's own country, however, the numbers become much more spread out, and national political systems are generally seen to fall short in varying degree. While there may be a great deal of consensus on what should happen in principle there is a lot less consensus about what is happening in practice.

Table 7.1 Assessments of principles of democracy and how well they are working in the country

	Importance for democracy in general		Degree to which applies in country	
	Mean	SD	Mean	SD
The courts treat everyone the same	9.25	0.37	4.86	1.87
National elections are free and fair	8.98	0.36	6.91	1.77
The government explains its decisions to voters	8.87	0.36	4.57	1.23
The media provide citizens with reliable information to judge the government	8.76	0.41	5.86	0.80
The government protects all citizens against poverty	8.73	0.46	3.88	1.49
Governing parties are punished in elections when they have done a bad job	8.40	0.39	5.38	1.38
The rights of minority groups are protected	8.36	0.51	6.17	1.15
Opposition parties are free to criticize the government	8.30	0.42	7.36	0.91
Citizens should have the final say on the most important political issues by voting on them directly in referendums	8.30	0.46	4.9	1.30
The government takes measures to reduce differences in income levels	8.27	0.66	8.27	0.66
The media are free to criticize the government	8.25	0.49	7.21	1.04
Different political parties offer clear alternatives to one another	8.00	0.45	5.40	0.84
Voters discuss politics with people they know before deciding how to vote	7.42	0.38	6.48	0.56
Politicians take into account the views of other European governments before making decisions	6.62	0.73	5.53	0.62

Source: European Social Survey, round six (2012)

These patterns give some grounds for optimism when discussing legitimacy because we see that a fairly cohesive set of attitudes towards the principles of democracy exists across a range of European nations. What varies is not a sense of what democratic government should be but assessments of how well those principles are practiced at the national level.

In seeking to explain this cross-national variation in how citizens evaluate democratic governance in practice, political institutions offer an intuitively appealing avenue of inquiry. Institutions could affect political support in two ways: first, by connecting citizens to public decision-making, shaping the degree of "input" or influence citizens have on public decisions and policies; and second, by shaping the "output" or benefits citizens receive from government policies (Dahlberg and Holmberg 2014). On the output side, both substantive performance (such as economic growth, high employment rates, low inflation, and generous welfare state provisions) as well as procedural performance (such as high quality of government, low levels of corruption, and impartiality and fairness of government institutions) have been shown to be important for political support (see Peffley and Rohrschneider 2014, and chapters by Van der Meer and Magalhães in this volume). Institutional differences may very well explain differences in substantive and procedural performance across political systems (Acemoglu and Robinson 2012; Lijphart 1999, 2012), and thereby affect political support indirectly. However, as these topics are covered in the subsequent chapters by Van der Meer and Magalhães, this chapter focuses on the "input" side, i.e. how well institutions connect citizens to public decision-making.

Here, it is important to note that the literature still lacks an overarching understanding of which kinds of rules and institutions should have what kind of effects. One difficulty with the argument that institutions should help shape popular attitudes is not so much its plausibility as its lack of specificity. The literature is not always clear on which institutions should produce what kind of effect although in general we expect that institutional arrangements have the capacity to improve political support because citizens will respond when they are given an increased sense of connection to, and regard for, the political process. In general then, we should expect that institutions that strengthen the quality of representation will strengthen political support (Peffley and Rohrschneider 2014; Dahlberg and Holmberg 2014; Thomassen 2014).

An important debate in the literature on political institutions refers to the difference between majoritarian and consensual democracies (Lijphart 1999, 2012). One strand of this research focuses on electoral and party systems, and their consequences for the composition of the legislature and executive, investigating how these institutional differences affect the quality of representation, and subsequently citizens' political support. The other strand of this research focuses on federalism, decentralization, and division of power between political institutions, investigating how these institutional differences affect the quality of representation, and subsequently citizens' political support.

Broadly, the argument is that consensual democracies (i.e. democracies with proportional electoral systems, multiparty governments, and institutional division of power) are more inclusive and therefore generate higher responsiveness (Lijphart 1999; Norris 1999b; Powell 2000; Peffley and Rohrschneider 2014). The counterargument is, however, that majoritarian democracies (i.e. democracies with majoritarian electoral systems, single-party governments, and concentrated power) have higher clarity of responsibility and therefore are more accountable (Powell and Whitten 1993; Sanders et al. 2014). An additional counterargument is that majoritarian systems have fewer veto players and are therefore more efficient in terms of policy implementation (Tsebelis 1995), which can in turn make those systems more responsive. Yet, empirical evidence is still decidedly mixed.

With regard to *electoral systems*, it has been argued that proportional electoral systems lead to higher political support because they generate more inclusive outcomes and enhance broad representation of citizen's interests. Indeed, Van der Meer and Dekker (2011) and Rose and Mishler (2011) find that political trust is higher in countries with proportional electoral systems. However, Banducci, Donovan, and Karp (1999) find only a weak effect of proportional electoral systems on satisfaction with democracy, Dahlberg and Holmberg (2014), Holmberg (2014), and Norris (2011) find no effect, and Karp and Bowler (2001) and Aarts and Thomassen (2008) appear to find slightly higher levels of satisfaction with democracy in majoritarian electoral systems.[3] As electoral systems are the main institutional locus of where citizens choose their representatives, we test the effect of the disproportionality of the electoral system here, hypothesizing that political support will be higher in countries with more proportional electoral systems. In addition, we also test the effect of the choice available to voters in elections, and some proportional systems allow greater choice than others. The single transferable vote system (STV) or systems with *panachage*, for example, allow voters to express a choice over candidates, while others are more closed. As a straightforward hypothesis then, we might expect closed-list elections to produce unhappier voters as compared to other kinds of systems (see also Farrell and McAllister 2006). Summarizing, our expectations for the effect of electoral systems on political support are:

H1: Political support is higher in more proportional electoral systems
H2: Political support is lower in closed-list electoral systems

Another institutional factor that might shape opinions is whether the current government is a single party government or *multiparty government* and in particular a multiparty government of three or more parties. Multipartyism in the executive is clearly related to the level of proportionality of the electoral system but here we are interested in the responsiveness of governments. In line with the arguments about the pros and cons of majoritarian versus consensual systems, here we have competing expectations. Under a veto-player argument (Tsebelis 1995) we would see it harder to move policy under multiparty governments and, therefore, multiparty governments to be less responsive in the sense that they would not change in response to voter opinions. On the other hand, the work of Powell, in particular, would note that multiparty governments are likely to be closer to the policy/ideological preferences of the median voter and so be responsive in that sense (Powell 2000). So while one-party governments may be responsive in the sense that they can move quickly (fewer veto points) to respond to citizens, multiparty coalitions will be closer to the median voter and might receive more support from citizens for that reason. While empirical research on the consequences of multiparty government for political support is scarce, empirical research on policy representation has demonstrated that ideological congruence between citizens and their representatives—in either the legislature or government— significantly strengthens political support (Erber and Lau 1990; Miller and Listhaug 1998; Flavin 2013; Holmberg 2014; Dahlberg and Holmberg 2014). We therefore have competing expectations over what effect the number of parties in power should produce, but given the importance of policy representation for political support, as a working hypothesis we would expect that multiparty governments will raise levels of political support.

H3: Political support is higher in political systems with multiparty governments

Apart from the electoral system providing choice and generating subsequent multiparty governments that may be more responsive, the quality of representation can also be strengthened by giving citizens frequent opportunities to participate in politics. Everything else being equal, shorter legislative terms for the national parliament means more frequent elections and so more frequent opportunities for voters to instruct politicians and hold incumbents to account. Similarly, we might expect that with fewer veto players (Tsebelis 1995), governments will, *ceteris paribus*, be more responsive to citizens. One institutional form of veto player is a strong upper chamber. Everything else being equal, then, we would expect unicameral legislatures with frequent elections to be more responsive than other kinds of arrangements.

H4: Political support is higher in political systems with unicameral legislatures with frequent elections

The other strand of research on the consequences of political institutions on political support focuses on federalism, decentralization, and division of power between political institutions, investigating how these institutional differences affect the quality of representation, and subsequently citizens' political support. Broadly speaking we expect governments that are closer to citizens to be seen to be more responsive and there are a series of ways in which we may see that. For example, legislatures that are more closely in contact with voters are likely to be seen to be more responsive (Parker and Parker 1993). In nations with comparatively larger legislatures in relation to their population, MPs each represent a comparatively smaller proportion of the population and therefore might be better able to represent voters. In addition, federalism and decentralization may also contribute to bringing politics closer to citizens. Fitzgerald and Wolak (2016: 1) find that "when opportunities for voice in local government are high, as in decentralized systems, people report greater trust in local government."

Likewise, Heijstek-Ziemann (2014) found that decentralization tends to increase satisfaction with the working of democracy.[4] Peffley and Rohrschneider (2014) find no significant effect of federalism on political support, however. We therefore also test the following hypotheses:

H5: Political support is higher in political systems with more members of parliament per head of the population

H6: Political support is higher in more decentralized political systems

So, do institutions matter, and if so, which institutions matter and why? In this section we have proposed that while an overarching theory of institutional effects on political support is lacking, institutions that increase the quality of representation and bring citizens in closer connection with government are likely to increase political support. In Section 7.3 we test our hypotheses on the connection between institutions and political support and seek to gain some sense of the size of the relationships, to get a sense of whether institutions indeed matter, and if so, how much they matter.

7.3 Do Institutions Make a Difference for Citizen Political Support? Some Empirical Evidence

ESS round six provides us with appropriate data against which to test the extent to which we can see institutional effects, for a number of reasons. It provides us with a range of established democracies that provide us with institutional variation across electoral systems, party systems, legislatures, and degree of decentralization.[5] It also contains a large and varied set of measures of attitudes toward politics that lend themselves to analyzing political support. It therefore allows us to test the hypotheses presented in Section 7.2.

We do still need to outline our dependent measures. In this project we are interested in the likely effect of our independent measures—characteristics of political institutions—on citizens' political support for those institutions as well as the political system as a whole. For that reason we take as our main dependent variables trust in parliament and satisfaction with democracy in one's country. In addition, we also test to what extent institutions affect public support for political actors, measured as trust in politicians. These measures are also in keeping with the operationalization of political support outlined in Chapter 1 and applied throughout this volume.

After having established our measures of political support, how should we expect institutional factors to drive these assessments? The discussion earlier emphasized the quality of representation and is a plausible starting point for looking at the effects of institutions: citizens will be more supportive of institutions that provide higher-quality representation, be it because they are more inclusive, provide greater choice, generate better responsiveness and accountability, or are closer to citizens.

To briefly reiterate our empirical expectations: first, we expect citizens to demonstrate lower levels of political support when the electoral system is less inclusive (H1) and does not allow candidate choice (H2). In terms of the arrangement of executive power we expect multiparty governments to be seen as more responsive by citizens and therefore raise political support (H3). Also, we expect unicameral legislatures with short terms to be seen as more responsive and therefore more highly regarded by voters (H4). Institutions closer to voters, either because there are more representatives per head of population (H5) or because power is decentralized (H6), will also generate higher political support.

We measure our institutional variables as follows. Disproportionality of the electoral system is measured using the Gallagher Index of proportionality of the most recent election.[6] Whether the most recent elections were run under a closed-list electoral system was coded by the author as a dummy variable (country scores are displayed in Appendices: Table 7.1B). Whether countries had a multiparty government or single-party government in 2012 was coded by the author as well. Legislative responsiveness was coded by the author, scoring countries as 1 when they had unicameral legislatures with a term of four years, as -1 when countries had a bicameral legislature with a term of five years, and a score of 0 for other scores. The number of seats in the legislature per head of the population was calculated by the author. Finally, decentralization was measured using the regionalization index developed by Marks et al. (2008). Appendices: Table 7.1A gives an overview of the coding and sources of all variables used in the analyses, and Appendices: Table 7.1B gives an overview of country scores for all the variables coded by the author.

In addition to the institutional variables, the analyses include a battery of control variables at the individual level that have been shown to affect political support: age, education, gender, religious attendance and affiliation, being discriminated against, interest in politics, level of political engagement, whether one feels close to the party in government, one's left–right self placement, and one's self-reported place in society. Coding of all measures is reported in Appendices: Table 7.1A.

Finally, the analyses also include several control variables that measure substantive and procedural performance (see Chapters 8 and 9 in this volume, which address these issues in greater detail). Economic performance and unemployment in 2012 (the year of the ESS survey) are taken from the World Bank Development Indicators.[7] Corruption is measured using Transparency International's Corruption Perceptions Index.[8]

In discussing the results of our models we will tend to downplay discussion of whether specific parameters are statistically significant or not. Recall that

Table 7.2 Variance explained of the models in Appendices: Tables 7.2A, 7.2B, and 7.2C

	Random intercept	Individual level	Individual level + institutions	Individual level + performance	Individual level + institutions + performance
Trust parliament					
ICC	0.22	0.17	0.02	0.02	0.009
R-squared:					
Snijders/Bosker Level 1		0.12	0.27	0.27	0.27
Snijders/Bosker Level 2		0.28	0.93	0.93	0.96
Bryk/Raudenbush Level 1		0.08	0.08	0.08	0.08
Bryk/Raudenbush Level 2		0.28	0.93	0.93	0.96
Trust politicians					
ICC	0.23	0.20	0.01	0.01	0.001
R-squared:					
Snijders/Bosker Level 1		0.13	0.30	0.30	0.31
Snijders/Bosker Level 2		0.25	0.95	0.95	0.99
Bryk/Raudenbush Level 1		0.10	0.10	0.10	0.10
Bryk/Raudenbush Level 2		0.25	0.95	0.95	0.99
Satisfaction with democracy					
ICC	0.20	0.17	0.02	0.02	0.009
R-squared:					
Snijders/Bosker Level 1		0.12	0.27	0.27	0.27
Snijders/Bosker Level 2		0.28	0.93	0.93	0.96
Bryk/Raudenbush Level 1		0.08	0.08	0.08	0.08
Bryk/Raudenbush Level 2		0.28	0.93	0.93	0.96

the research goal here is not so much to establish specific institutional effects on specific measures of political support, but rather to try and gain some broader sense of the size of effects we may see that are due to institutions, i.e. to try and gain a sense of *how much* institutions matter. In order to help accomplish that goal it was necessary to develop some arguments and hypotheses about ways in which institutions could affect political support but over and above the question of whether specific parameters are statistically significant we are interested in two related questions: first, how much of the variance in political support is explained once we add in institutional factors to models predicting political support with individual level covariates? And how much variance explained by institutions remains once we control for performance covariates as well? Second, and relatedly, what is the substantive size of the effects of the institutional variables compared to the effects of individual level attributes or performance attributes?

The full models estimating these effects are reported below in the Appendices: Tables 7.2A–7.2C. In each of these we report an estimation of a baseline model in which country level intercepts are allowed to vary (column one of Appendices: Tables 7.2A–7.2C). We then estimate a model in which individual level measures (of SES, partisanship, and so on) are included (column two of Appendices: Tables 7.2A–7.2C). The third model adds institutional variables to the model (column three of Appendices: Tables 7.2A–7.2C). The fourth model examines performance indicators (corruption, economic growth, and so on). And finally, the fifth model (column five of Appendices: Tables 7.2A–7.2C) adds in both performance and institutional factors at the same time.

As can be seen from a quick glance at the tables the number of independent variables and the number of models makes the results themselves quite cluttered, which makes overall patterns difficult to assess. In order to try and simplify the clutter we report summary information on our analyses in order to get some handle on the size of institutional effects in two ways. First, we will briefly discuss the results of the statistical models presented in Appendices: Tables 7.2A–7.2C, focusing our discussion of results on the institutional variables, and shortly discuss to what extent our hypotheses hold. Second, to get a feel for the substantive size of effects, we will present some simple graphs showing the substantive effects of the various measures. Third, we will examine the change in R^2 in each model and Table 7.2 presents the R^2 for each of the models predicting satisfaction with democracy, trust in parliament and trust in politicians.

Looking across the models predicting satisfaction with democracy, trust in parliament and trust in politicians (Appendices: Tables 7.2A–7.2C), we find that in models only including individual level covariates and the institutional variables (model three in each table), closed electoral systems are indeed associated with lower levels of support, as are more disproportional electoral systems (though not significant in all models). Multiparty governments are also consistently related to higher levels of political support, as are responsive legislatures (though the latter is not a significant predictor of trust in politicians). Decentralized power also appears to be positively related to political support in models predicting satisfaction with democracy and trust in parliament, but is never significant; and—contrary to our expectations—the number of representatives per head of the population appears to be negatively related to political support, though again not reaching statistical significance in any of the models.[9]

Broadly then, when we only consider institutional effects (controlling for individual-level variables), we can confirm the positive effects of multiparty governments and responsive legislatures, and the negative effect of closed electoral systems on political support, but find no significant effect for the other institutional variables. Moreover, when adding controls for substantive and procedural performance (model five in each table), most of the institutional control variables are no longer significant. Also, some of the institutional effects are quite unstable (compare columns three and five in any of the tables). That instability should perhaps be unsurprising given both the relatively small number of countries (N = 16) and the likely relationships between these institutional measures and other aggregate measures. However, even with high levels of multicollinearity we can use the results to say something about the scope of institutional effects by focusing not so much on the statistical significance (or otherwise) of individual parameters but focusing on both the substantive size of parameters and variance explained, to which we turn now.

Figures 7.2 to 7.4 show the substantive effects of the institutional measures in relation to each other and also in relation to the non-institutional effects. The bars for each variable show the change in the predicted level of satisfaction with democracy (Figure 7.2), trust in parliament (Figure 7.3), and trust in politicians (Figure 7.4). We calculate the change by looking at the change in the prediction of the dependent variable as the independent variable moves from its minimum to maximum value. Parameters are taken from the "full" models (i.e. column five in each of the models).

The measures are grouped according to whether they are institutional level variables (the first group) or individual level measures (the second group). While collinearity affects the statistical significance of parameters it should

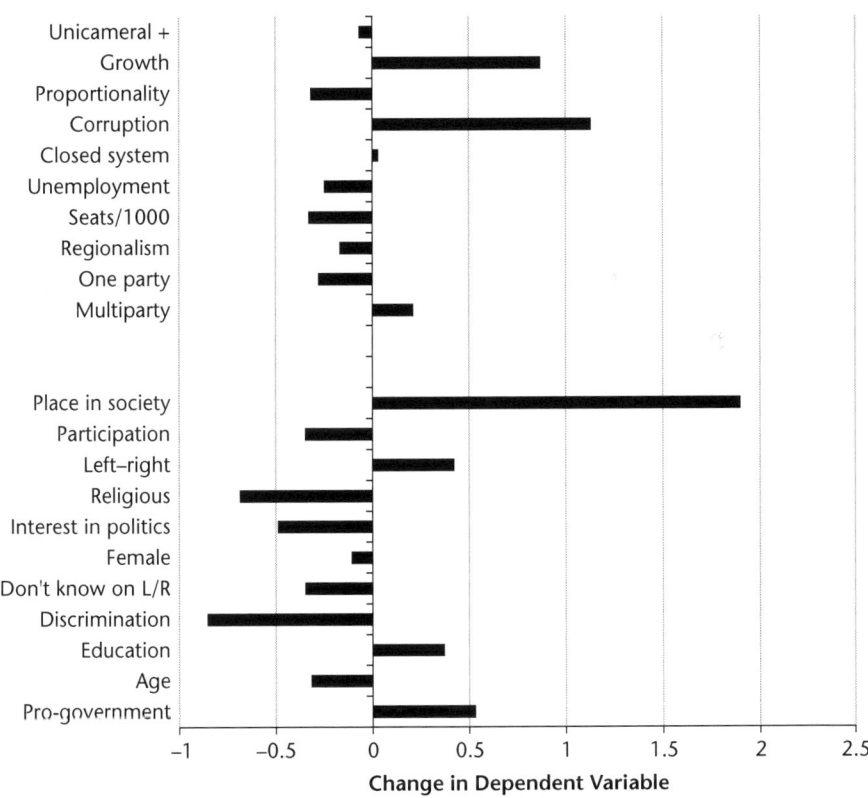

Figure 7.2 Effect of independent variables across their range of satisfaction with democracy

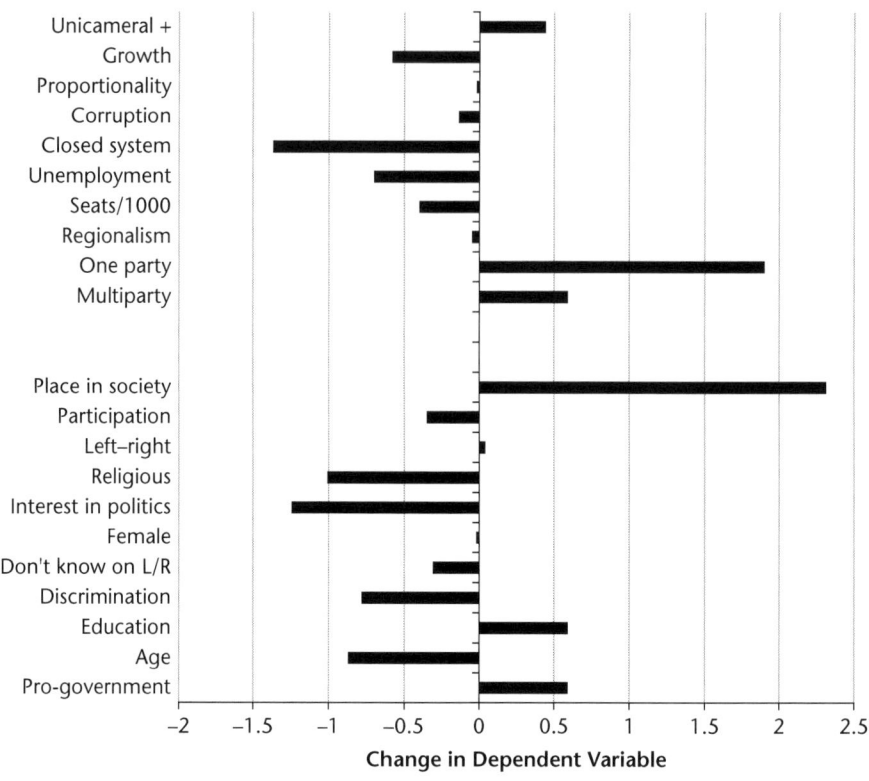

Figure 7.3 Effect of independent variables across their range on trust in parliament

not affect their substantive effect. As can be seen from the Figures the substantive effect of institutional variables is often quite modest. Some of the macro-level variables do have notable effects as we move across their range. In particular the level of corruption in a country shifts the dependent variable by just over one point (on the eleven-point 0 to 10 scale). However, the institutional variables do not seem to have such a large effect, at least not as large as we might be led to believe given the literature on institutions. As an (admittedly limited) summary indication, the average impact of all institutional effects on satisfaction with democracy is 0.36. That is if we simply average the effect across the measures listed in the first group, then a given institutional measure will shift satisfaction with democracy around one third of a point. For trust in politicians the average effect is around 0.48, while for trust in parliament the institutional effect is 0.61. While there are institutional effects it is hard to claim that they are major ones, especially compared to the effects of the individual level measures, many of which have more sizable effects when moving from their minimum to maximum value.

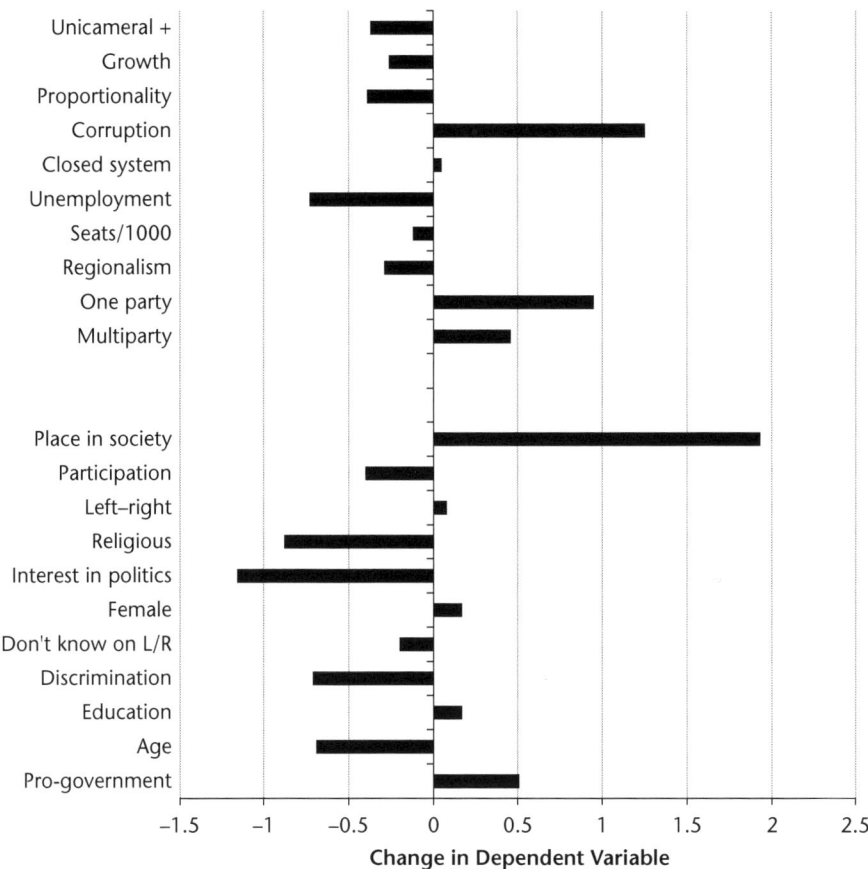

Figure 7.4 Effect of independent variables across their range of trust in politicians

Another way of trying to assess just how much institutions matter is to look at the variance explained (R^2) of these models. The simple random intercept model (column one) suggests that roughly twenty percent of the overall variance is at the national level. At the very least this suggests something of an upper limit to how much cross-national variation can be explained by our independent variables.

So how much do institutional variables contribute? A model only including individual level variables (demographics and similar factors) shows these to be strong and consistent predictors of political support. Adding in institutional factors does boost the total variance explained for all three dependent variables, and adding the institutional variables roughly doubles the variance explained at the individual level, and almost fully explains variance at the country level. This gain in variance explained is roughly equal to variance explained by performance measures. In models that have both attributes of individual survey respondents plus country-level performance measures plus the institutional measures, total variance explained increases only marginally, suggesting that institutional and performance measures tap into the same variance in political support.

Taken together these results allow us to make several points that essentially speak to the limits of institutional effects. First, yes, there are some effects of institutions. The substantive effects shown in Figures 7.2–7.4 demonstrate that institutional variables can shift political support between 0 and 1 point on an eleven-point scale as they move from their minimum to maximum values. Also, when adding institutional variables to models explaining political support with individual-level covariates variance explained roughly doubles. There are, then, substantive effects of institutions.

That said, the point of this exercise has been to gain some sense of where the limits are of those kinds of relationships. As the model results in Appendices: Tables 7.2A–7.2C show, the statistical significance of parameters for institutional effects may be fragile, the signs of effects can change when performance indicators are taken into account, and sometimes the signs of effects are "wrong." For example, the sign on the parameter for "legislative seats per capita"—a proxy measure of how in touch the national legislature may be— is consistently negative, i.e. legislatures with more seats are seen as related to lower levels of trust and confidence (see columns three and five of Appendices: Table 7.1A). Model specification issues typically throw conceptual issues into sharp relief. One of the points here is that, since institutional effects do seem subject to specification issues, then there are plainly some theoretical issues to be worked out.

7.4 Discussion: How Much do "Institutions Matter" to Political Support?

On the basis of these results we can draw several conclusions. First, there is considerable agreement across established democracies about the components of democracy in principle. The idea of what democracy should be is remarkably similar across Europe. It is hard to understate the importance of this takeaway. There is little scope for value conflict over some of the fundamental ideas of democracy. Second, there is quite a bit of disagreement about how well democracy is being implemented in the respondent's own country. The principle of democracy may not be ailing, but there is some discontent among European publics about how democracy is working in practice. The distinction between democracy in principle and democracy in practice would seem to be an important difference when compared to European attitudes in the 1930s when it seemed that the idea of democracy was contested. Third, while institutional factors do give us some purchase on explaining cross-national variation it is unclear just how much purchase they give us. Institutions may well matter, but they do not seem to matter very much to citizens. On the face of it, emphasizing the limitations of institutional explanations may seem both somewhat negative and also somewhat at odds with the thrust of the literature that argues that "institutions matter." In this instance we have explored the question of just how much institutions matter when it comes to the issue of political support in democratic societies. While there are strong theoretical presumptions that institutions should make a difference to political support, the evidence to support such a claim is less than compelling.

There is evidence that institutions do make some difference. Roughly speaking, and referring back the patterns of Figures 7.2 to 7.4, it seems that there is some potential for institutional change to provide an effect of around one point in the average measures of satisfaction with democracy and of trust in parliament and politicians. Giving voters more of a choice about candidates, having responsive legislatures, and multiparty governments seem to be the most consistent effects that we see when modeling individual-level and institutional effects. But while we have seen some effects of institutions we have also seen non-effects, inconsistent effects, and small effects. Institutional reform in general, then, is not likely to have major consequences for political support.

There are a number of caveats to this conclusion, however. First, in this chapter we have only considered direct effects of institutions, while institutions might very well have differential effects on different groups of citizens. The winner–loser literature demonstrates that electoral systems can exacerbate or diminish the differences in political support between winners and losers of elections (Anderson and Guillory 1997; Anderson et al. 2005), and hence when the effects on different groups of citizens are taken into account, institutions may make more of a difference to political support. Secondly, we have not considered possible interactions between institutions. For example, some research suggests that substantive performance affects political support more strongly in majoritarian democracies (Criado and Herreros 2007) or in political systems with lower quality of government (Magalhães in this volume). Hence, it could very well be that certain combinations of institutions in particular lower political support, while the individual effects of these institutions are each relatively small. Third, institutions might, in part, shape political support indirectly, through their effect on procedural and substantive performance, further underscoring the need to better understand interactions between institutions.

What these caveats do illustrate, however, is that our understanding of institutions in relation to public attitudes remains under-theorized. While the analyses presented here show that institutions do matter for political support, and show that the direct effects of institutions on political support are relatively modest, it is much less clear which institutions matter (most) and why. Consequently our ability to predict changes in political support that may be brought about by institutional change is also uncertain. In addition, evaluating the prospects for institutional reform to strengthen political support would also require longitudinal research designs that build on instances of actual institutional change to evaluate changes in political support before and after institutional reform took place, and such instances are relatively rare.

In terms of broader takeaway points what this study suggests is that we should rethink a little whether we expect too much of institutions. To be sure, part of the issue is that perhaps we need to think more carefully about the consequences of institutions at the level of mass political support: what institutions do we expect to affect political support and why? What benchmarks should we use? And, in particular, given the kinds of discussion earlier, what size of institutional effect can we reasonably expect to see? Here we have focused on the quality of representation as a dimension of importance, and tested the effects of a large variety of institutions, but it is true that there may well be others. We should also note that even if we have established clear theoretical expectations, a benchmark, and have some idea of the size of the effect it is not always clear that the effect of any institutional change is to produce a permanent improvement. While electoral systems have been given a great deal of attention this may not be the only or biggest lever we can use to bring about change. Political systems comprise bundles of institutions and changes in one institution may be offset or dampened by the remaining ones (Sanders et al. 2014). Moreover, even if we expect that citizens do have concerns relating to political institutions they are likely to have other concerns, too. Even if we grant that there are, indeed, effects of institutions on political support, citizens may still have other priorities in mind: unemployment or economic growth are two obvious "performance" issues that may color opinion even as citizens acknowledge that institutions matter. Institutional reform may well be important to (some) citizens but perhaps just not as important as other issues to many more. At present, therefore, the conclusion is that institutional change may have some possibility to offer some help—but it is clearly no panacea.

Notes

1. Specifically: Belgium, Switzerland, Denmark, Germany, Spain, Finland, France, the UK, Iceland Ireland, Israel, Italy, Netherlands, Norway, Portugal, and Sweden.
2. The one exception is that the standard deviation of assessments of whether politicians should consult with other European leaders is smaller for the assessment of country-level practice than for how important it should be in principle.

3. Marien (2011b) argues that these contradictory findings are due to majoritarian electoral systems increasing citizens' possibilities to hold their governments to account, while proportional electoral systems increase inclusiveness, both leading to higher levels of political trust, and demonstrate that indeed the relationship between electoral system proportionality and political support is curvilinear. For a similar argument, see Sanders et al. 2014.

4. Note that I do not investigate the effects of direct democracy on political support here, but instead focus on institutional differences that shape the quality of representation. On the one hand there are those who argue that introducing forms of direct democracy will strengthen political support (compare Cain, Dalton, and Scarrow 2003; Zittel and Fuchs 2007), others suggest that citizens prefer "stealth democracy" over more opportunities for direct influence (Hibbing and Theiss-Morse 2002). But this analysis seeks to link variation in political support to real existing institutions, and these tend to be institutions of representative democracy.

5. The non-democracies in the ESS sample—Albania, Russia, and Ukraine were excluded from all analyses. As were the "new democracies" to leave a sample of sixteen countries: Belgium, Switzerland, Denmark, Germany, Spain, Finland, France, the UK, Iceland, Ireland, Israel, Italy, Netherlands, Norway, Portugal, and Sweden. Portugal and Spain have now been democracies since the 1970s. A forty-year tradition would presume that they are no longer "new" democracies. Israel may strike some as problematic and is dropped from some models due to missing values on the regional devolution variable. The main conclusions hold even when we consider an N of twenty-five, only excluding the three obvious non-democracies noted at the beginning of this footnote.

6. Source: <http://www.tcd.ie/Political_Science/staff/michael_gallagher/ElSystems/Docts/ElectionIndices.pdf>.

7. Source: <http://data.worldbank.org/data-catalog/world-development-indicators>.

8. Source: <http://www.transparency.org/research/cpi>.

9. As for the effects of the control variables, the effects of the individual-level variables are all in line with expectations: citizens who feel closer to the government, who have a more right-wing ideological position, who are more politically interested (note reverse scale), who feel they belong to a higher social class, and who are higher educated have higher levels of political support. Conversely, citizens who don't know where they stand on the ideological left–right position, who participate more in politics, who personally experienced discrimination, are older and female have lower levels of political support. The only two surprising findings here are the negative effect of political participation on political support—indicating that the causal relationship might be the other way around, less supportive citizens might feel the need to engage more in politics—and the finding that more religious citizens are less supportive. The effects of the performance variables are generally also in line with expectations: unemployment lowers political support, and corruption lowers political support in all but one of the models (note reverse coding). The effect of economic growth is only significant and positive when predicting satisfaction with democracy, and not in the other models.

8

Dissecting the Causal Chain from Quality of Government to Political Support

Tom van der Meer

8.1 Introduction

Lacking empirical evidence for secular decline of political support in advanced industrial democracies, the question is what explains differences between countries in levels and trends of political support? This chapter proposes that the quality of government is a key factor explaining such divergence. "The 'Western model' [of liberal democracy] is best symbolized not by the mass plebiscite but the impartial judge," wrote Fareed Zakaria (1997: 27) in the late 1990s. A decade later, Rothstein and Teorell (2008: 180) laid down their framework of quality of government: "Democratic legitimacy requires that political rights, such as freedoms of association and expression, must be secured within a legal framework, and this framework must, in turn, be impartially applied to all its subjects." All three authors put impartiality, procedural fairness, and quality of government at the heart of democratic legitimacy.

It is by now well-established that citizens are more likely to support the regime and its institutions when they evaluate governmental procedures to be neutral (Ulbig 2002) and fair (Carman 2010). Panel studies show that "these effects prevail even once prior attitudes and the substantive outcomes of the contact are taken into account" (Grimes 2016: pp. 262; Tyler 1990; Kumlin 2004; Grimes 2006). But although these studies provide a strong argument that impartial and fair institutions raise political support, they ultimately rely on citizens' subjective perceptions rather than actual rules and practices. Evidence for the effect of actual practices of good government commonly rely on within-country variation in the interactions with street-level bureaucrats in organizations such as airports or employment agencies (e.g. Esaiasson 2010; Hasisi and Weisburd 2011).

By and large, cross-national research on the determinants of political support overlooked quality of governance indicators, at least until recently (see Dahlberg and Holmberg 2014; Rohrschneider 2005; Peffley and Rohrschneider 2014; Sanders et al. 2014). Rather, cross-national studies traditionally focused on three other explanations. First, a wide range of cross-national studies emphasizes the relevance of governmental output, most notably macroeconomic performance, as a crucial explanation of cross-national differences in political support, with varying empirical support (Miller and Listhaug 1999; Taylor 2000; Van der Meer and Hakhverdian 2017; Van Erkel and Van der Meer 2016; and Magalhães in this volume). Second, scholars have studied the impact of representative democracy: whereas some scholars found evidence that majoritarian systems stimulate political support, supposedly by emphasizing concentration of power and governmental accountability (Castles 1994; Norris 1999b; Aarts and Thomassen 2008; Bowler in this volume), others conclude that proportionality boosts political support, supposedly because of its inclusive character (Lijphart 1999; Anderson and Guillory 1997; Banducci et al. 1999; Van der Meer 2010), or find mixed results (Marien 2011b). Third, and most importantly, corruption has been found to erode legitimacy quite consistently (Dellaporta 2000; Hakhverdian and Mayne 2012; Van der Meer and Hakhverdian 2017).

In this set of empirical analyses on contextual explanations of political support in democratic regimes, quality of government has remained somewhat of a missing link. Democratic legitimacy goes beyond input (government by the people) and output (government for the people). Scharpf's (1997; 1999) conceptualization of input legitimacy and output legitimacy does not advocate "simple" majority rule and policy outputs in line with citizens' preferences, but rather emphasizes the importance of impartiality and rule of law (Scharpf 1999: 7–10): institutions should "hinder the abuse of public power" (Scharpf 1999: 13). Inhabitants of established democracies do not only relate to their state by functioning as clients in relation to (governmental) output and as an electorate in relation to the representative element of democratic rule, but also as citizens who hold inalienable rights in the face of governmental power. The quality of government perspective implies that the executive ought to be bound by its own rules: impartiality and rule of law. Government legitimacy, by extension, depends on the quality of these binds.

Theoretically, it is surprising that the quality of government hardly found its way into cross-national studies of political support. While quality of government is rather difficult to classify in existing models of democratic legitimacy—such as the distinction between Madisonian and populistic democracy (Dahl 1956), and constitutional and popular democracy (Mair 2013: 10)—its emphasis on impartiality and rule of law puts it closer to the former categories than the latter. Empirically, this lacuna can be explained by the lack of cross-national data on this topic. Moreover, perceived corruption functioned as a general epitome of the quality of government (Rothstein and Teorell 2008), and had such a strong effect in models of political support, that it tended to crowd out alternative explanations (Van der Meer 2010; Oskarsson 2010; Van der Meer and Hakhverdian 2017). In recent years, research groups such as the Quality of Government (QoG) and Varieties of Democracy (V-Dem) institutes have made great progress in gathering and sharing expert judgments on a range of quality-of-government indicators. Therefore, cross-national analyses of the relationship between quality of government and political support have been made possible.

This chapter sets out to explain cross-national variation in political support for the regime (democracy) and its main representative institution (parliament) by variation in the quality of government. More precisely, it formulates hypotheses on the effects of governmental impartiality, rule of law, and bureaucratic professionalism to rival with the more common explanations of economic performance, electoral representation, and particularly corruption, which is closely—but inversely—related to quality of government and drives most of the cross-national differences in earlier studies. As such, the chapter provides a stringent test of the quality of government thesis.[1]

Moreover, to the extent that political support is an evaluation of the regime and its institutions by citizens (Hardin 2000; Anderson and Singer 2008; Van der Meer and Dekker 2011), any statistical effect of country level characteristics on political support ought to be both mediated and moderated by citizens' evaluations and perceptions of these characteristics. This study will therefore test the whole causal chain that would relate quality of government to political support.

8.2 Theory and Hypotheses

8.2.1 *Political Support as an Evaluation*

Conceptually, citizens' satisfaction with democracy and trust in political institutions are relational characteristics: they entail an evaluation of the object (the regime and its institutions) by the subject (the citizen) (compare Hardin 2000). To the extent that this evaluation is rational, it is based on four characteristics of the object: competence, care (inherent commitment to the subject), accountability (commitment that can be enforced by the subject), and reliability (Kasperson et al. 1992; Van der Meer 2010). The quality of government perspective relates to all four of these aspects, but most notably to care (fairness) and reliability. Impartiality and rule of law imply an executive that is bound by its own laws and treats similar cases similarly. The perspective that satisfaction with democracy and trust in political institutions are evaluation-based has strong empirical implications. First, there should be an empirical relationship between objective characteristics of the regime and its institutions and citizens' satisfaction with and trust in them. Second, this relationship should be mediated by citizens' perceptions and evaluations of these objective characteristics. Third, this relationship should be conditional on the importance citizens attach to the objective characteristics that are evaluated.

Each of these three implications from the quality of government perspective is discussed in the next subsection.

8.2.2 *Quality of Government*

In their seminal article, Rothstein and Teorell (2008) conceptualized quality of government, that encompasses various interrelated elements such as rule of law, impartial government, professionalism, and lack of corruption.

Most fundamentally, Rothstein and Teorell see quality of government reflected in the *impartiality of the executive*. The impartiality of the executive should be distinguished from the (im)partiality of the substance of the laws that are executed. The former specifically concerns the extent to which civil servants *implement* laws without regard to specific individuals, social groups, or firms: similar cases are treated similarly. The procedural norm of impartiality of the executive may be considered the benchmark that determines other aspects of what is widely considered to be quality of government (Rothstein and Teorell 2008: 171, 181).

A second factor, closely related to impartiality of the executive, is *rule of law*. Rule of law is a "key feature of contemporary liberal democracy" (Sanders et al. 2014). It includes the consistent application of the law to all subjects by courts and the police, including those who formulate and execute it (Rothstein and Teorell 2008). More broadly, it also encompasses the guarantees that are set in place for that purpose, such as civic oversight of the police, independent courts, and defendant rights in criminal cases. Whereas impartiality of the executive thus refers to the neutral implementation of policies by civil servants, rule of law refers to (the set of guarantees for) the neutrality of the judiciary and police, as well as government in general respecting civil liberties. Citizens who perceive government to respect civic liberties and human rights are more likely to be satisfied with the way democracy works in their country (Sanders et al. 2014). Yet, earlier studies report an effect of actual civil rights enforcement on political support that was at best inconsistent (Van der Meer 2010; Van der Meer and Hakhverdian 2017).

Third, *professionalism of the bureaucracy*—in which recruitment is based on meritocracy rather than on clientelism—is conceptually related to impartiality as well (Rothstein 2009) and empirically related to the quality of public services (Rauch and Evans 2000). However, professionalism of the bureau-cracy does not directly concern the services provided to citizens but rather the internal organization of the state bureaucracy: the selection of personnel and extent of discretionary powers. Direct experiences with discretionary powers that are not used in an impartial way are likely to undermine political support (Kumlin 2004: 274, 289). Professional bureaucracies may limit partiality in the face of unavoidable discretionary powers.

Finally, *absence of corruption* has been found to be such a strong determinant of political support (e.g. Dellaporta 2000; Hakhverdian and Mayne 2012) that it has crowded out many rivaling explanations (Van der Meer and Hakhverdian 2017). Corruption is strongly related to partiality, clientelism, and discretionary powers (Rothstein and Teorell 2008) and as such, is corrosive to political support in any aspect of the trust relationship between the regime and its citizens: corruption reveals lack of competence, care, commitment, and reliability (Van der Meer 2010).

Hence, I formulate the following hypotheses:

H1: Impartiality of the executive is positively related to political support.
H2: Enforcement of rule of law is positively related to political support.
H3: Professionalism of the state bureaucracy is positively related to political support.
H4: Absence of corruption is positively related to political support.

8.2.3 *Mediating the Quality of Government Effect*

In her overview of the field Grimes (2016: pp. 260) juxtaposes two groups of studies on procedural fairness and political trust. Some "tend to see a strong link between *perceived* procedural fairness and political trust as sufficient corroboration of the procedural justice theory," others see that link mainly as a "theoretically compelling argument" that still requires "evidence linking variations in political trust to variations in actual procedures." This chapter argues that neither the effect of perceived procedural fairness (e.g. Grimes 2006; Tyler 2006) nor the effect of actual quality of government (e.g. Dahlberg and Holmberg 2014) are—by themselves—sufficient evidence. Rather, the effects of actual quality of government ought to be mediated by citizens' perceptions in order to establish a true causal chain linking quality of government to citizens' political support.

In recent years various cross-national studies have investigated mechanisms that relate country-level effects at the macro level to individuals' political support at the micro level, but generally without great success. Although macroeconomic performance has no significant effect on political trust in cross-national analyses once corruption is taken into account (e.g. Van der

Meer 2010; Oskarsson 2010; Van der Meer and Hakhverdian 2017), citizens' subjective evaluations of the economy have a very strong effect (Van der Meer and Dekker 2011) and there are strong macroeconomic effects in longitudinal studies (e.g. Van Erkel and Van der Meer 2016). The design of the study (cross-national versus longitudinal) had a strong effect on the conclusion. Rather than a methodological artefact, it is likely that these differential findings are caused by implicit assumptions in the model choice about the respectively cross-national and longitudinal comparisons behind these effects (Van der Meer 2016).

The mechanisms behind the effect of the electoral system on political support are equally puzzling. Aarts and Thomassen (2008) found that satisfaction with democracy is lower in proportional systems than in majoritarian systems. However, this effect cannot be due to the conventional mechanisms (perceived accountability, perceived representation): proportional systems score (surprisingly) better on perceived accountability, not worse on perceived representation, and the effect of proportionality is not at all explained by these mechanisms (Aarts and Thomassen 2008: 16).

To date, studies on the causal mechanisms that explain how macro-level factors affect political support have therefore not been encouraging. Nevertheless, tests for mediating mechanisms remain relevant. To the extent that the cross-national effect of quality of government reflects an evaluation, the effect should be mediated by citizens' perceptions and judgments. While cross-national studies on the direct effects of quality of government on political support are already scarce (Dahlberg and Holmberg 2014), there seem to have been no cross-national studies that attempted to unravel this causal chain. To test for mediating mechanisms connecting macro-level quality of government to citizens' perceptions and subsequently to political support, I therefore propose the following hypothesis:

H5: The relationship between quality of government and political support (in H1–H4) is mediated by citizens' perceptions of impartiality.

8.2.4 Conditional Effects of Quality of Government

Finally, the quality of government is unlikely to be equally important to all citizens' evaluations. Mishler and Rose (2001b: pp 36) argue that "evaluations of performance reflect not only the aggregate performance of government but also individual circumstances and values." Citizens may have different criteria in mind or attach different priorities, and only be affected by behavior on matters that they prioritize (Van der Meer and Hakhverdian 2017). But which values might induce these differential criteria and priorities? Anderson and Singer (2008) propose that ideology functions as a screen that citizens use when they evaluate the performance of the regime and its institutions. Their study focuses on the effect of income inequality, which ought to be conditional on citizens' left–right position. Similarly, I argue that citizens' evaluations of the quality of government are likely to depend on citizens' democratic norms: the extent to which they think quality of government is important for democracy. Citizens who think quality of government is important will be more likely to relate it to their support for the regime and its institutions. Hence, the final hypothesis is:

H6: The more citizens prioritize impartiality, the stronger the positive relationship between impartiality and political support.

8.3 Data and Methods

8.3.1 Cross-sectional, Multilevel Analysis

The hypotheses call for a multi-evel research design. As argued earlier, to the extent that political support is a more or less cognitive evaluation of a relationship, it is compared to an absolute or relative benchmark. Citizens' evaluation of the legitimacy of the regime and its institutions may be directly or indirectly (e.g. by copying dominant frames used in media reports or by politicians) based on an absolute standard (that holds irrespective of culture and time), on a cross-national comparison (to other countries), or on a historical comparison (to past performance of their own country). A cross-national comparison implies a cross-sectional analysis, while a historical comparison implies a longitudinal analysis. The choice of model in scholarly analyses thus implies assumptions on the nature of the relationships that are tested. Ideally, both analyses are run simultaneously. Unfortunately, to date only a cross-sectional analysis is possible due to data limitations: crucial contextual level determinants and individual level mediators and moderators are only available at one point in time. Moreover, unlike, for instance, economic performance, the quality of government is unlikely to change much in the short term.

This chapter therefore performs a cross-sectional, multilevel analysis with individuals (level one) who are nested in their country of residence (level two). Multilevel models are estimated in MLwiN 2.29 (Rabash et al. 2012). These models are built up in a stepwise fashion from empty (variance) models, and random intercept models to random slope models.

8.3.2 Contextual Level Data

This chapter models contextual determinants that were collected one or two years before the individual level data (ESS 2012, see subsection 8.3.4) were collected.

The measure of the *impartiality of government* is derived from the Expert Survey of the Quality of Government Institute (Dahlberg et al. 2012). The QoG Expert Survey was held in three waves between 2008 and 2012, includes a multitude of experts per country, and has been tested for reliability. It combines expert judgments on five aspects of the impartiality of the executive (most notably impartiality of policy implementation by the state bureaucracy) into a single index.[2] The use of a single, encompassing measure instead of separate measures did not affect the findings reported.

Rule of law is based on the index offered by Freedom House in 2010. The index, ranging from 0 (worst) to 16 (best) is based on a range of characteristics, including (but not limited to) civil control over the police, protection from political terror, unjustified imprisonment, and equal treatment. Covering 194 countries and fourteen territories, the assessment was done by fifty analysts and eighteen advisers.[3]

The level of *professionalism* of the state bureaucracy is an index from the Quality of Government Expert Survey. It is based on four questions, measuring meritocracy in and politicization of the state bureaucracy via recruitment procedures: the extent to which skills and merits of applicants matter; the extent to which political connections matter; the extent to which senior public officials are recruited from within the ranks of the public sector; and the extent to which the top political leadership hires and fires senior public officials.

By its nature *corruption* cannot be measured directly. Hence, we rely on expert perceptions of corruption as measured in the Corruption Perception Index (CPI), issued by Transparency International in 2010. The CPI is based on multiple expert surveys per country. The variable was coded in such a way that it ranges from 0 (highly corrupt) to 10 (highly clean).[4]

We test these effects against more conventional, rivaling explanations discussed in the previous sections (see also Chapters 7 and 9 in this volume): economic development (e.g. Van Erkel and Van der Meer 2016) and proportionality (e.g. Marien 2011b). Both control variables are derived from the Quality of Government standard data set (Teorell et al. 2013), based on the indicators of 2010. *Economic development* is measured as GDP/capita PPP, as provided by the World Development Indicators. To measure the *proportionality of the electoral system*, we use data from the Database of Political Institutions, which distinguishes between majoritarian and proportional systems, scoring electoral systems as proportional if any part of the legislature is elected using proportional representation.

8.3.3 *Contextual Determinants and the Risk of Harmful Collinearity*

Various contextual measures overlap, both conceptually and empirically. Conceptually, corruption (as a general societal phenomenon), impartiality (confined to the executive), and rule of law (as formal and practical independence of the judiciary) are intrinsically related, whereas the professionalism of the bureaucracy may be a precondition for especially the latter two. Indeed, the operationalizations partially overlap. Theoretically, though, this chapter will assess which of these concepts is most closely related to political support. For the tests of mediating and moderating effects the conceptual and operational overlap does not matter at all, as findings are robust regardless of the simultaneous inclusion of all measures.

Empirically, various measures correlate quite strongly, especially when less well-established democracies (i.e. Ukraine, Albania) are included in the model (but see Section 8.5 for the robustness check). Most notably, corruption (according to the expert survey by Transparency International) and impartiality (according to the expert survey by Quality of Government) are strongly related: impartiality statistically "explains" eighty-three percent to eighty-seven percent of the variance in corruption. This signals a serious risk of harmful collinearity. There are basically two ways to deal with that problem. The first is to exclude one or more determinants or combine them into an index. However, that prevents us from opening the causal blackbox. The second is to proactively deal with and test the effect this multicollinearity has on the estimates. For that purpose, we perform several checks including perturbation analyses in Section 8.5, showing that the main conclusions are not affected by any harmful collinearity.

8.3.4 *Individual Level Data: ESS 2012*

Our individual level data need to cover a broad set of countries that diverge in terms of institutional quality and output, but are rather similar in other (cultural) aspects. Moreover, they need to include evaluations of support for the regime and its institutions, as well as a set of mediators (subjective evaluations of the quality of government) and moderators (subjective salience of the quality of government).

These demands are best met by the European Social Survey of 2012. The ESS 2012 wave includes a special module on citizens' evaluations of democracy. It covers a broad range of thirty European countries across the continent, as well as Israel. Cyprus was excluded because of missing data. Kosovo was excluded because it was not yet a fully functioning state. Russia was excluded for two reasons: it is a highly influential case on the effect of "Rule of Law," and it is the sole non-free country in the list according to Freedom House. As the focus of this volume is exclusively on established democracies, Russia is excluded. To ensure sufficient variance, Ukraine and Albania remain included in the analyses for now. However, Section 8.5 in this chapter will test whether any effect found in the models is driven by their inclusion, i.e. whether any cross-national effect is primarily due to the difference between more and less established democracies rather than due to differences within the set of established democracies.

8.3.5 Dependent Variables

Political support in this chapter is measured as satisfaction with the functioning of democracy and trust in parliament, in line with the now common focus in the literature (Dalton 2004; Norris 2011; see also Chapter 1 in this volume). These are "middlerange indicator[s] of support between the specific political actors in charge of every institution and the overarching principles of democracy in which specific institutions are embedded in a given polity" (Zmerli et al. 2006: pp. 41).[5] The 2012 wave of the ESS covers two aspects of political support defined in the introduction: satisfaction with democracy and trust in parliament. All measures range from 0 (extremely dissatisfied/no trust at all) to 10 (extremely satisfied/complete trust). The use of rating scores sets the measures in the ESS apart from more conventional answer categories that use dichotomies (e.g. Eurobarometer for trust in government) or Likert scales (e.g. EVS/WVS, EB for satisfaction with democracy, national election surveys).

8.3.6 Mediators, Moderators, and Controls

MEDIATORS
To measure subjective evaluations of the quality of the government, I employ the question battery that poses respondents the question: to what extent fifteen aspects of democracy actually apply in their country (range from 0—does not apply at all, 10—applies completely). Five of these items deal with the subjective perception of impartiality and rule of law (of the executive and the judiciary), impartiality toward input processes (elections, opposition parties, media), and impartiality of output agencies (minority rights, neutral courts).[6] These are not ideal measures of subjective perceptions of impartiality and rule of law: they do not line up well with the expert survey measures of impartiality of the executive (that is explicitly confined to executive agencies). Nevertheless, they are the best measures available and tap into general perceptions of impartiality.

MODERATORS
The moderators reflect the importance respondents attach to the quality of government. The ESS 2012 offers an additional question battery on sixteen aspects that respondents may consider important for democracy in general, including the same five aspects mentioned under Mediators (see note 6). I will use "free and fair elections" and "courts treat everyone the same" to tap into impartiality, with the explicit caveat that this impartiality does not refer to the

executive but to input institutions and the judiciary. The other three measures deal with aspects of civil rights and rule of law. I will model these individual considerations as moderators of the contextual effects.

CONTROL VARIABLES
Finally, all models control for respondents' gender, age, level of education, religiosity, citizenship, country of birth, and television watching.

8.4 Results

8.4.1 Main Effects

Model 1 in Table 8.1 displays the random intercept models that simultaneously include individual and state-level characteristics as determinants of political support. To a large extent the models paint the same picture. The impartiality of the executive has a consistent, strong, significant, and positive effect on political support: the more impartial the executive, the higher the level of satisfaction with democracy (b = 1.28) and trust in parliament (b = 1.27).

Table 8.1 Multilevel random intercept models: determinants of satisfaction with democracy, trust in parliament

	Satisfaction with democracy		Trust in parliament	
	Model 1	Model 2	Model 1	Model 2
Level 2 (countries)				
Impartiality executive	1.28 (0.53)**	1.00 (0.44)**	1.27 (0.56)**	0.96 (0.50)**
Rule of law (FH)	−0.11 (0.10)	−0.07 (0.08)	−0.14 (0.11)	−0.12 (0.09)
Professionalism bureaucracy	0.07 (0.23)	0.18 (0.18)	−0.20 (0.24)	−0.12 (0.21)
Lack of corruption	0.16 (0.18)	−0.09 (0.14)	0.25 (0.18)	0.06 (0.16)
GDP/Capita (eff: *1000)	0.02 (0.02)	0.00 (0.02)	0.04 (0.02)	0.02 (0.02)
Electoral system (ref: majoritarian)				
• Proportional	0.66 (0.38)*	0.63 (0.31)**	0.50 (0.40)	0.47 (0.36)
Level 1 (individuals)				
Evaluation: Free and fair elections		0.25 (0.00)**		0.19 (0.01)**
Evaluation: opposition free to criticize		0.01 (0.01)		−0.02 (0.01)**
Evaluation: media free to criticize		0.05 (0.01)**		0.02 (0.01)**
Evaluation: protection of minority rights		0.06 (0.00)**		0.05 (0.01)**
Evaluation: courts treat everyone same		0.18 (0.00)**		0.18 (0.00)**
N(L1)	46,285	41,746	46,719	41,796
N(L2)	26	26	26	26

Source: ESS 2012
Random intercept model
Controls (L1): gender, age, level of education, religiosity, citizenship, country of birth, television watching.
Standard errors between brackets; one-sided tests; * p<0.05,** p<0.01

These significant effects oppose the null-findings by Dahlberg and Holmberg (2014) but support Hypothesis 1. Once impartiality is taken into account, rule of law has no significant effect on satisfaction with democracy and trust in parliament. Hypothesis 2 thus finds no support. The third aspect of the quality of government focuses on the level of professionalism of the state bureaucracy. The level of professionalism has no significant effect on satisfaction or trust. Hence, Hypothesis 3 is also rejected. This is in line with the findings of Dahlberg and Holmberg (2014).

Surprisingly, the level of corruption has no significant effect on satisfaction with democracy and trust in parliament, once I control for the other variables. Inclusion of corruption in the same model does reduce the effect of impartiality of the executive somewhat, but not to the extent that the latter effect turns non-significant. Therefore, Hypothesis 4 is rejected. The consistent effect of impartiality instead of corruption is irrespective of the model specification (both those shown here and additional models). This suggests that the commonly found effect of corruption is explained by impartiality.[7] Of all aspects of quality of government that corruption points to (including inefficient public services, the undermining of collective action), it seems to be (the lack of) impartiality of the executive that particularly affects political support (compare Warren 2004). This would imply that impartiality mediates the corruption effect.

When we move the focus to the country-level control variables, economic development has no significant effect on satisfaction with democracy or on trust in parliament. This confirms the pattern found in earlier cross-sectional studies: once procedural characteristics are included, effects of economic performance are no longer significant (compare Van der Meer 2010; Oskarsson 2010; Hakhverdian and Mayne 2012). The electoral system does have a significant effect, but only on satisfaction with democracy: satisfaction with democracy is higher in countries with a proportional system than in countries with a majoritarian system. This effect is robust, but suppressed when no controls for other procedural characteristics are included (compare Van der Meer and Hakhverdian 2017, who find the same on the data of the European Values Survey 2008).

8.4.2 Intermediary Effects

If the country-level effects of impartiality indeed reflect a conscious evaluation, these effects should be mediated by individual-level judgments by citizens within these countries. Model 2 in Table 8.1 shows that a positive evaluation of the quality of government generally stimulates satisfaction with democracy and trust in parliament. The evaluation that elections are free and fair and the evaluation that courts treat everyone the same have the strongest effects. By contrast, the evaluation of opposition parties' freedom to criticize the government has no significant effect on satisfaction with democracy and a negative (albeit substantively weak) effect on trust in parliament.

The five individual evaluations only explain a small part of the contextual effect of impartiality, however. The effect of impartiality is reduced by approximately a quarter, but remains positive and significant in all models. The subjective evaluations thus only partially intermediate the contextual effect. It is important to note, though, that the measures of these subjective evaluations do not line up ideally with the impartiality measure. Regardless, although the evidence for intermediary effects supports Hypothesis 5, most of the impartiality effect remains unexplained.

8.4.3 Conditional Effects

If the positive effect of an impartial government reflects citizens' evaluation of the quality of the government, this effect should be stronger among respondents who consider free and fair elections and an impartial judiciary important. Table 8.2 models these conditional effects of subjective values and evaluations.

Table 8.2. Multilevel random intercept models: conditional intermediary effects

	Satisfaction with democracy	Trust in parliament
	Model 3	Model 3
Level 1 (individuals): Main effects		
Evaluation: free and fair elections	0.10 (0.02)**	0.07 (0.02)**
Evaluation: opposition free to criticize	0.02 (0.02)	0.04 (0.02)*
Evaluation: media free to criticize	0.02 (0.02)	0.01 (0.02)
Evaluation: protection of minority rights	−0.03 (0.02)*	−0.00 (0.02)
Evaluation: courts treat everyone same	0.15 (0.02)**	0.15 (0.03)**
Importance: free and fair elections	0.00 (0.02)	−0.02 (0.02)
Importance: opposition free to criticize	0.01 (0.02)	0.05 (0.02)**
Importance: media free to criticize	−0.08 (0.01)**	−0.08 (0.02)**
Importance: protection of minority rights	−0.05 (0.01)**	−0.02 (0.01)
Importance: courts treat everyone same	−0.07 (0.01)**	−0.09 (0.02)**
Level 1 (individuals): Interaction effects		
Evaluation*Importance: free and fair elections	0.02 (0.00)**	0.01 (0.00)**
Evaluation*Importance: opposition free to criticize	−0.00 (0.00)	−0.01 (0.00)**
Evaluation*Importance: media free to criticize	0.01 (0.00)**	0.00 (0.00)
Evaluation*Importance: Protection of minority rights	0.01 (0.00)**	0.01 (0.00)**
Evaluation*Importance: courts treat everyone same	0.00 (0.00)	0.00 (0.00)
N(L1)	*40,873*	*40,880*
N(L2)	*26*	*26*

Source: ESS 2012
Random intercept model
Controls (L1): gender, age, level of education, religiosity, citizenship, country of birth, television watching.
Controls (L2): impartiality executive, rule of law, professionalism bureaucracy, corruption, GDP/capita, electoral system.
Standard errors between brackets; one-sided tests; * p<0.05,** p<0.01

Table 8.3 Multilevel random slope models: the conditional effect of impartiality

	Satisfaction with democracy	Trust in parliament
	Model 4	Model 4
Level 2 (countries)		
Impartiality executive	−0.24 (0.39)	−0.72 (0.50)
Level 1 (individuals)		
Importance: free and fair elections	0.13 (0.02)**	0.09 (0.02)**
Importance: courts treat everyone same	−0.05 (0.01)**	−0.08 (0.01)**
Cross-level interactions		
Impartiality * Importance Elections	0.16 (0.03)**	0.14 (0.03)**
Impartiality * Importance Courts	0.10 (0.02)**	0.09 (0.02)**
N(L1)	*41,746*	*41,796*
N(L2)	*26*	*26*

Source: ESS 2012
Random intercept model
Controls (L1): gender, age, level of education, religiosity, citizenship, country of birth, television watching.
Controls (L2): rule of law, corruption, GDP/capita, electoral system.
Standard errors between brackets; one-sided tests; * $p<0.05$, ** $p<0.00$

Again, the effects are quite consistent across the two dependent variables and mostly in line with expectations.

Next, Table 8.3 displays the cross-level interaction effects, showing to what extent the subjective importance attached to democratic norms affects the impact of the (macro-level) impartiality of the executive. Based on the estimates in Table 8.3, we can calculate the marginal effects. The significant and positive cross-level interaction effects signal that the positive impact of impartiality on satisfaction and trust increases with the value respondents attach to impartiality. Among respondents who consider impartiality to be extremely important for a democracy (and score 10 on both measures), the marginal effect of impartiality increases to +2.4 on satisfaction with democracy and +1.6 on trust in parliament. By contrast, citizens who do not consider impartiality to be important (and score 0 on the interaction effect) are not or hardly affected by it.

These conditional effects are substantially impressive (see Figure 8.1, which visually displays the marginal effects). They would suggest that citizens who consider impartiality extremely important would on average score approximately five points higher on the 11-point scale of satisfaction with democracy when they live in the most impartial country in the data set (Norway) instead of in the least (Ukraine). All in all, while I find little evidence for the theoretically expected mediation effects, the moderating effects are quite substantive.

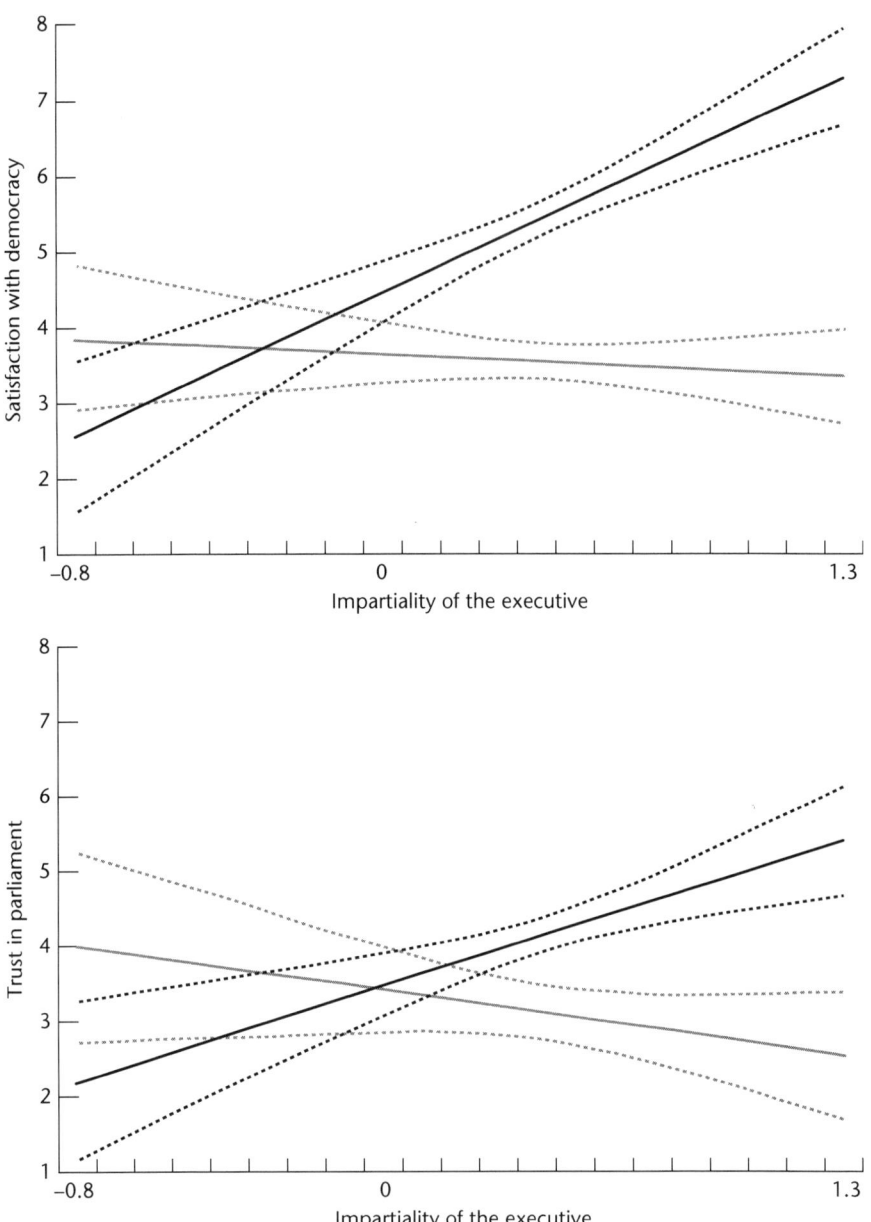

Figure 8.1 Marginal effects plots of Table 8.3

Straight lines represent point estimates, dashed lines the 95% confidence intervals.

Black lines represent citizens who consider free and fair elections and impartiality of courts extremely important to democracy.

Grey lines represent citizens who consider free and fair elections and impartiality of courts extremely unimportant to democracy.

8.5 Robustness Checks

8.5.1 *Sample: Excluding Less-established Democracies*

The inclusion of less-established European democracies in the data set gave the models more statistical power to test rivaling hypotheses simultaneously. However, as a result the findings may be driven by the difference between established and less-established democracies, and not necessarily hold in either of the subsets. To test this, I re-estimated models 1, first by excluding Albania and Ukraine and subsequently by also excluding all countries that transitioned into democracy after 1980. The sample is now much smaller: containing respectively twenty-four and sixteen countries. This smaller sample has various costs: it lowers the statistical power, imposing a larger risk of misestimation and collinearity. Especially with only sixteen countries I therefore excluded the non-significant effects from the earlier models. The effects, shown in Table 8.4, are essentially robust compared to those in Model 1 (Table 8.1).

In additional analyses I also estimated interaction effects similar to Model 4 (Table 8.3), though without any contextual control variables. These interactions are substantially similar as well: no effect of impartiality among those who hardly value it, and strong positive effects among those who value it the most. This suggests that the effects in the main analysis are not primarily due to a sharp distinction between established and less well-established democracies, but also relate to differences within the subset of the former. In other words, quality of government does not only explain differences between democracies and semi-democracies, but also differences between and within established democracies.

Table 8.4 Multilevel random intercept models (subsample of established democracies)

	Satisfaction with democracy		Trust in parliament	
	excl Alb, Ukr	est < 1980	excl Alb, Ukr	est < 1980
Level 2 (countries)				
Impartiality executive	1.39 (0.60)**	1.72 (0.59)**	1.19 (0.63)**	1.67 (0.75)**
Rule of law (FH)	−0.11 (0.12)	–	−0.13 (0.12)	–
Professionalism bureaucracy	0.03 (0.25)	–	−0.17 (0.26)	–
Lack of corruption	0.14 (0.18)	0.16 (0.18)	0.25 (0.19)	0.14 (0.23)
GDP/capita (eff: *1000)	0.02 (0.02)	–	0.04 (0.02)	–
Electoral system (ref: Majoritarian)				
• Proportional	0.67 (0.40)*	0.67 (0.36) *	0.49 (0.41)	0.62 (0.47)
N(L1)	*28,890*	*28,890*	*28,977*	*28,977*
N(L2)	*24*	*24*	*16*	*16*

Source: ESS 2012
Random intercept model
Controls (L1): gender, age, level of education, religiosity, citizenship, country of birth, television watching.
Standard errors between brackets; one-sided tests; * p<0.05, ** p<0.01

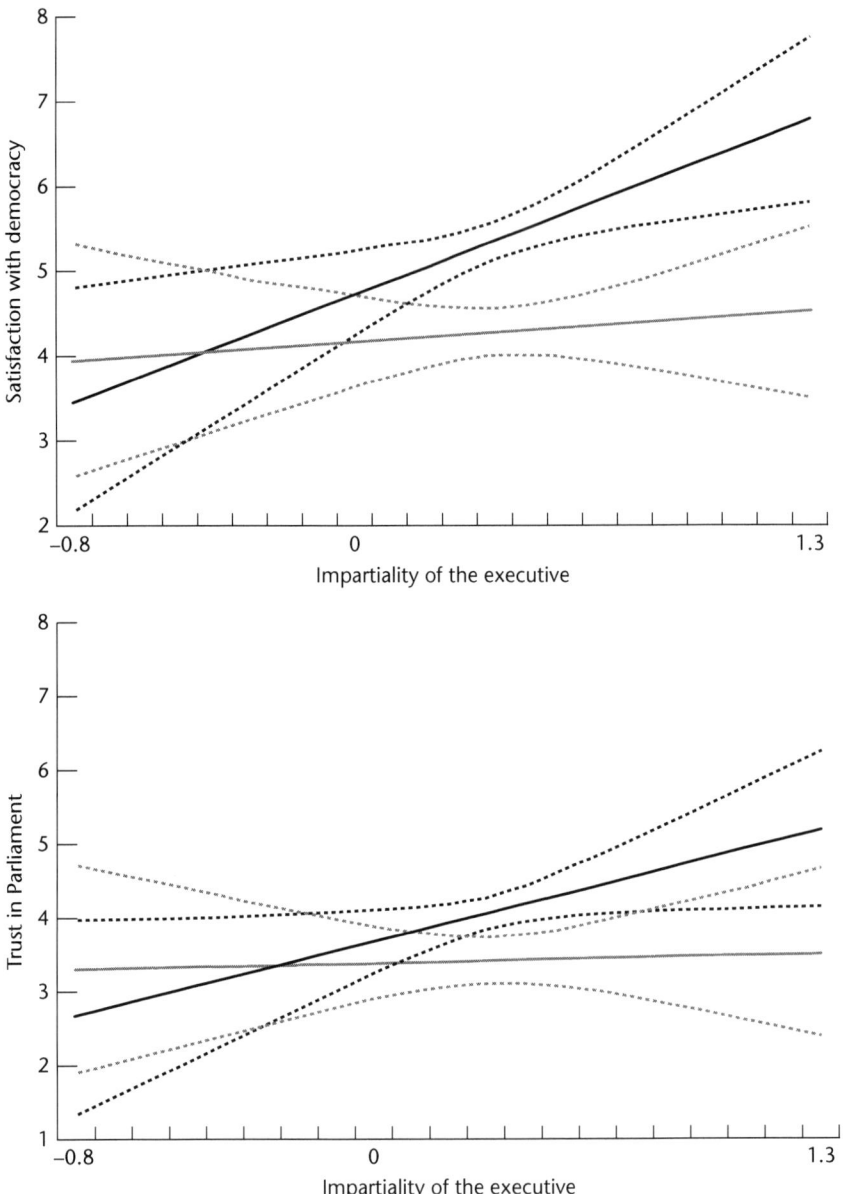

Figure 8.2 Marginal effects plots, two categories (importance 0–6; importance 10)

8.5.2 *Distribution of the Moderating Effect*

The moderators in Table 8.3 are highly skewed: the majority of respondents consider each of the five criteria extremely important (score of 10 on the scale). Consequently, although the interaction effects were estimated linearly, the conclusions may be based on outliers at the bottom who rate the importance of, for instance, free and fair elections extremely low. As a check I re-estimated Models 4 in Table 8.3 after recoding all moderators into three groups: scores between 0 and 6, scores between 7 and 9, and the score of 10. This did not affect the substantive interpretation of the interaction effects whatsoever: impartiality continues not to affect political support among the group that attaches the lowest importance (now encompassing 0–6), and continues to have a strong positive effect among the group that attaches the highest importance (score 10). This is reflected in Figure 8.2.

8.5.3 *Harmful Collinearity*

To deal with potentially harmful collinearity, I ran various robustness checks of the results presented here.

The results are quite robust already, for four reasons. First, all models were carefully built up in a stepwise fashion. The effect of impartiality was consistently significant regardless of the inclusion of corruption. Second, the effect of impartiality was found in all models regardless of the dependent variable. Third, the mediation and moderation analyses led to the same conclusion even when I modeled the effect of impartiality but not corruption, or vice versa. Fourth, the effect of impartiality is robust to the inclusion or exclusion of less well-established democracies (Ukraine, Albania).

However, to test harmful collinearity directly, I rely on perturbation analyses (Belsley 1991). Harmful collinearity implies that the estimated parameters (direction and/or significance of the estimators) are sensitive to the addition of small random noise to the potentially collinear measures. To test whether this is the case, I re-estimated each of the three models 1 in Table 8.1 one hundred times, after first adding unique random error terms to the contextual determinants in each re-estimation (see Appendices: Tables 8.5A–8.5B). The outcomes in Appendices: Tables 8.5A–8.5B show that the effects of impartiality (as described in Table 8.1) are all highly robust. This underscores our finding that cross-national differences are primarily driven by impartiality.

8.6 Conclusion

Rather than the quality of the economy (output) or the quality of democracy (representation), the findings in this chapter suggest that the quality of governmental procedures have the strongest effect on political support at the macro level, at least in the set of European democracies on which this chapter focuses. Most notably, the impartiality of the executive (measured via expert surveys) has a strong positive and consistent effect on satisfaction with democracy and trust in parliament. The strength of this effect is underpinned by the vast reduction of the effect of corruption that had consistently been the strongest determinant of political trust and satisfaction with democracy in earlier cross-national studies. While impartiality and corruption have a considerable (but not perfect) conceptual and empirical overlap, it is consistently the former that affects satisfaction with democracy and trust in parliament whereas the latter does not. This has two potential implications. On the one hand, the original effect of corruption may have been largely *due to* the partial treatment of citizens (rather than, for instance, due to the personal gains for civil servants or politicians). On the other hand, the effect of corruption may have had little to do with it altogether, so that it is not the misuse of public power for personal benefit but rather the structurally unequal chances for different groups is society that affects political trust. I would argue that the former (specification/mediation effect) is a more likely explanation of the findings than the latter (a spurious effect of corruption), though it is impossible to pull them apart statistically.

Yet, the strong relationship between impartiality of the executive and political support is not as straightforward as it appears. If political support is the outcome of a conscious evaluation of the impartiality of government by citizens, one would expect that the impartiality–support relationship is mediated by these evaluations. However, empirical evidence that such evaluations function as the mechanism linking impartiality to political support is limited at best: the relationship is hardly explained by the inclusion of such evaluations. This may simply reflect limitations of the data that cover evaluations of the impartiality of elections and the judiciary but not the impartiality of the executive or the street-level bureaucrats who implement policies. Nevertheless, this raises new questions on the missing explanatory link between impartiality of the executive and political support.

By contrast, the strong evidence for conditional effects works in favor of the conclusion that political support is based on citizens' conscious evaluations. As can be expected, impartiality has no effect whatsoever on citizens who consider impartiality to be unimportant to democracy. By contrast, impartiality has a major effect on citizens who consider it to be extremely important. This suggests that citizens evaluate their regime and its institutions by their own core values.

Ultimately, this chapter shows that the quality of government, measured as impartiality of the executive and state bureaucracy, is *the* crucial factor that explains cross-national differences in political support. It does not only explain differences between full democracies and semi-democracies, or differences between established and young democracies, but also variation between and within the established democracies of Western Europe. These findings suggest that we should move beyond the more conventional explanations of democratic legitimacy in the literature that emphasize government by the people (i.e. the quality of representative institutions) and government for the people (i.e. the quality of governmental output). Rather, to a large extent public support for democracy and its institutions seems to hinge on the liberal aspect of governments that are bound to impartiality by their own laws.

Notes

1. This chapter differs methodologically from Dahlberg and Holmberg (2014) in three ways. First, this chapter tests the effects of impartiality, rule of law, and bureaucratic professionalism against both corruption and economic development as rivaling explanations. Second, this chapter studies a sample of Western and Central European countries that allow a more focused comparison than the globe-spanning data of the CSES used by Dahlberg and Holmberg (2014). Finally, this chapter explicitly breaks down the causal chain that would relate quality of government to political support, by focusing on mediating mechanisms and moderating conditions.
2. It covers (1) how often public procurement contracts are awarded to firms that provide favorable kickbacks to senior officials; (2) how often public-sector employees treat some societal groups unfairly; (3) how often public-sector employees favor applicants for licenses for private firms with whom they have strong personal contacts; (4) how often public-sector employees act impartially in individual cases; (5) percentage of poor relief that actually reaches the needy poor.
3. Source: <https://freedomhouse.org/report/freedom-world/freedom-world-2010>.
4. Source: <http://www.transparency.org/research/cpi>.
5. While the judiciary is not part of the analyses in this volume, we find highly similar effects on trust in the judiciary as on the other dependent variables.
6. (1) National elections are free and fair. (2) Opposition parties are free to criticize the government. (3) The media are free to criticize the government. (4) The rights of minority groups are protected. (5) The courts treat everyone the same.
7. Statistically, though, it might also signal spuriousness.

9

Economic Outcomes, Quality of Governance, and Satisfaction with Democracy

Pedro C. Magalhães

9.1 Introduction

Citizens' satisfaction with the way democracy works in practice varies considerably across countries, people, and time. As Linde and Ekman (2003: 396–7) put it, such satisfaction is an "instrumental" and "output-oriented" dimension of political support, and it is thus likely to be driven by political systems' outputs and outcomes, such as economic performance. In recent years, for example, there has been a precipitous decline in people's satisfaction with democracy in Southern European countries (Alonso 2013), a decline that can hardly be understood without considering the economic and financial crisis in which these countries were engulfed. Many studies focusing on the individual-level determinants of political support have indeed confirmed that the subjective evaluation of economic performance has "a strong and highly significant effect (...) on support for national democracy," emerging in fact, according to some, as its strongest individual-level predictor (Armingeon and Guthmann 2014: 439). And economic growth, unemployment, or inflation seem to perform well and in the predicted directions in explaining trends over time in levels of popular satisfaction with democracy (Wagner, Schneider, and Halla 2009). Hence, we should expect economic outcomes to be an important factor in explaining variation in political support across countries and over time.

However, there are two caveats that should be considered when studying the effect of economic outcomes on political support. First, there is no such thing as unanimity about the effect of economic performance, with some studies failing to find systematic effects (McAllister 1999; Nye et al. 1997; Wells and Krieckhaus 2006; Dalton 2004). Second, people's views about political authorities cannot be described purely in the instrumental terms presumed by the relationship between economic outcomes and satisfaction. Political support also responds to other factors, particularly to a constellation of aspects that might be designated as "quality of governance" (Rothstein and Teorell 2008). Social psychologists have long told us that authorities, above and beyond their ability to deliver favorable outcomes, are also evaluated on the basis of the perceived fairness of decision-making procedures (Thibaut and Walker 1975), and have shown that this also applies to political authorities (Tyler 2006). In political science, many studies have repeatedly shown how individual-level perceptions (Rose, Mishler, and Haerpfer 1998; Seligson 2002; Linde and Erlingsson 2013) and aggregate measures based on expert and stakeholder surveys (Anderson and Tverdova 2003; Norris 2011; Wagner, Schneider and Halla 2009; Curini et al. 2012; Dahlberg and Holmberg 2014) of (absence of) corruption, fair and honest treatment by political officials, or impartiality affect popular satisfaction with the way democracy works.

This chapter takes the view that both economic outcomes and quality of governance should go a long way indeed in explaining political support. However, it takes an additional step: it suggests that the effect of economic performance is contingent on the quality of governance. A fundamental insight of procedural fairness theories in organizational psychology is the existence of a fundamental *process-outcome interaction*, through which procedural fairness moderates the effects of outcome favorability in the explanation of support for decision-makers and authorities in organizations (Brockner and Wiesenfeld 1996, 2005; Brockner 2002). This chapter shows that the same occurs when we move from the meso level of organizations to the macro level of entire political systems. In particular, it argues that citizens' satisfaction with the performance of democracy is most affected by economic outcomes in those countries where the quality of governance is lowest. In contrast, in contexts where institutions and policy-making adhere to high standards of quality and impartiality, political support is less sensitive to short-term fluctuations in the economy.

This hypothesis is tested with the help of the high-quality survey data provided by the European Social Survey, conducted in more than thirty countries throughout six rounds from 2002 to 2013. This study also resorts to data on economic outcomes, which are aggregated into a single Economic Performance Index (EPI)—combining data on economic growth, unemployment, inflation, and budget deficits (Khramov and Lee 2013)—as well as data on the *Quality of Governance* (QoG) drawn from the World Bank Worldwide Governance Indicators (Kaufmann, Kraay, and Mastruzzi 2010)[1] and on the *Impartiality* in the exercise of public power, obtained from an expert survey conducted in ninety-seven countries (Dahlberg et al. 2013).[2] The next section—Section 9.2—presents the main argument: that the effects of economic outcomes on satisfaction are moderated by procedural fairness and the quality of governance in general. Section 9.3 presents the results of our analysis, while Section 9.4 concludes.

9.2 Outcome Favorability, Procedural Fairness, and Political Support

The contingent effects of economic performance on satisfaction with democracy can be described with an illustrative example. Figure 9.1 shows two dual y-axis graphs. The black lines in each graph, scaled along the left y-axis, represent the EPI—*Economic Performance Index* (Khramov and Lee (2013), a composite measure of yearly economic performance, including growth, unemployment, inflation, and budget deficit (to be fully explained in the data and methods section). The grey lines, scaled along the right y-axis, represent the sample mean level of *Satisfaction with democracy*, for each year when the European Social Survey was conducted in each of the countries.[3]

There are at least two interesting aspects about these graphs. The first is that it seems that people in Greece have already been, on average, as satisfied with the way democracy works in their country as people in Sweden. By the beginning of the twentieth century, aggregate levels of satisfaction with democracy in both countries were very similar. The second interesting aspect in these graphs is the relationship between aggregate trends in satisfaction with

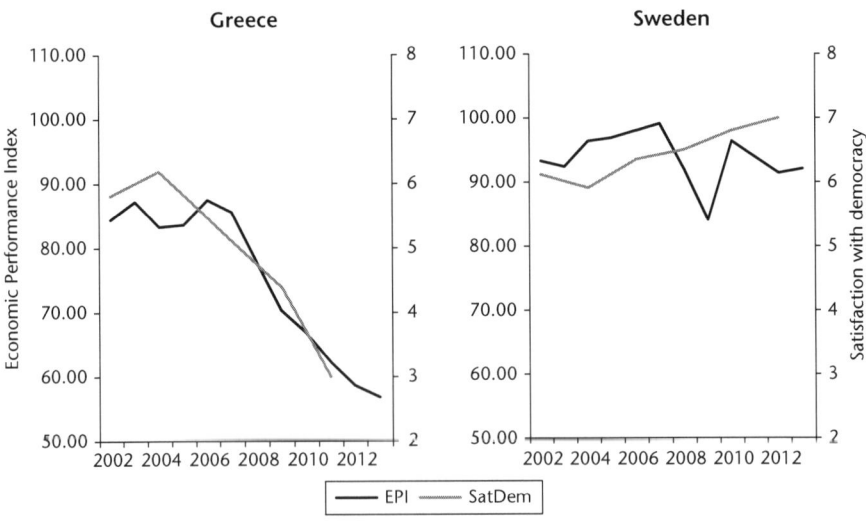

Figure 9.1 Economic performance and satisfaction with democracy in Greece and Sweden

democracy and economic performance in both countries that emerges from visual inspection. In Greece, the accelerated decline in the performance of the economy that has taken place since 2006 seems to be accompanied by a steep decline in satisfaction. In Sweden, in contrast, the steady rise in aggregate satisfaction since 2004 seems completely insensitive to economic performance, namely to the effects of the global financial crisis that shook the world economies, including the Swedish one. To be sure, these graphs can be deceptive, as these are just two countries and a relatively short time series. However, they also suggest a question: should we really expect the relationship between economic performance and levels of satisfaction with the way democracy works to be the same in all contexts and for all people? Indeed, the cases of Greece and Sweden illustrate that the ability of regimes to elicit support from people is not equally driven by the delivery of favorable economic outcomes. This chapter suggests that this is part of a broader phenomenon, which characterizes not only the relationship of citizens with political authorities but also other kinds of social exchanges. This phenomenon is the interaction between outcome favorability and procedural fairness in determining positive attitudes and behaviors vis-à-vis authorities and organizations.

9.2.1 *Outcome Favorability and Procedural Fairness*

In the social psychology of organizations, many laboratory experiments and observational studies of workplaces, courts, universities, and other settings have supported the notion that positive attitudes and behaviors—measured in expressed satisfaction, organizational trust and support, organizational commitment, acceptance of decisions, and affect towards authorities—are explained by two main factors. The first is "outcome favorability," the extent to which an individual receives a beneficial or valued outcome such as, for example, a favorable ruling in a court, a pay raise, or even the acceptance of an article in a journal. The second is "procedural fairness," the adoption of rules and procedures that allow for a real or perceived treatment of individuals by organizational authorities that is characterized by transparency, impartiality, and the right to be heard (Thibaut and Walker 1975; Folger and Greenberg 1985; Lind and Tyler 1988).

What happens when we move to the larger and more impersonal level of a national political system? First, economic performance, particularly in terms of economic growth and prosperity, is an aspect likely to be seen as favorable in any polity and by any citizen. Thus, many studies find economic performance to be related in predictable ways with citizens' satisfaction with the way the regime works in their country (Clarke, Dutt, and Kornberg 1993; Anderson 1998; Rose, Mishler, and Haerpfer 1998; Wagner, Schneider, and Halla 2009; Kotzian 2011; Fails and Pierce 2010; Ezrow and Xezonakis 2011; Norris 2011;

Kumlin and Esaiasson 2012; Voicu and Bartolome Peral 2014; Armingeon and Guthmann 2014).[4] It should be noted, however, that others fail to confirm that relationship. For example, although they focus on institutional confidence rather than satisfaction with democracy, McAllister (1999) and Nye et al. (1997), find it unrelated with objective economic performance. Wells and Krieckhaus (2006), replicating previous studies with different methodologies, do not confirm a relationship between GDP growth and democratic satisfaction. And more generally, Dalton (2004: 111) argues that there is "little evidence that economic performance is a major reason for the decline in political support."

Second, the study of the determinants of political support has also begun to focus not only on the "what" citizens get from government, but also on the "how." Social psychologists who have applied the concept of "procedural fairness" beyond the realm of organizations to the level of political institutions and regimes have confirmed its relevance there, too (Tyler 1984; Lind and Tyler 1988; Tyler 2001; Grimes 2006). And in a closely related literature, political scientists have focused on the concept of "quality of governance," conceived as having at its very core the notion of "impartiality in the exercise of public authority," a procedural norm presiding over how power is exercised by political bodies, the courts, and the state as a whole (Rothstein and Teorell 2008; Rothstein 2011). Several studies have shown the importance of different measures of such "quality of governance," including the functioning of courts, transparency/control of corruption, checks and balances, or the quality of public policy-making, treated either as system attributes or as individual-level perceptions of such attributes. Invariably, when such variables are employed, they emerge as powerful predictors of popular satisfaction with the way democracy works (Rose, Mishler, and Haerpfer 1998; Anderson and Tverdova 2003; Wagner, Schneider, and Halla 2009; Norris 2011; Curini et al. 2012; Linde and Erlingsson 2013; Dahlberg and Holmberg 2014).

9.2.2 Why Procedural Fairness Moderates the Effect of Outcome Favorability

There is, however, an implication of the studies of procedural fairness in organizations that remains unexplored in the study of political support: the notion that outcomes *interact* with procedural fairness in explaining satisfaction. Why should this be the case? There are several arguments in social psychology pointing in this direction (Brockner and Wiesenfeld 1996; Brockner 2002; Brockner and Wiesenfeld 2005). The first, a so-called "instrumental" argument, is that when individuals perceive procedures as being fair, allowing them voice and influence, for example, they become more likely to discount present bad outcomes in favor of expected positive outcomes in the future (Thibaut and Walker, 1975; Brockner and Wiesenfeld 1996: 199). A second argument focuses on accountability attributions: when people perceive that there is an adherence to fairness norms, they are less likely to believe outcomes could have been more favorable and, thus, also less likely to hold authorities directly responsible for negative outcomes (Folger and Cropanzano 1998; Brockner et al. 2007). A third and related argument, resulting from referent cognitions theory, suggests that people's reactions to outcomes are referential, deriving from a mental comparison between the outcomes they got with what they could get in other circumstances (Kahneman and Tversky 1982). The more fairness rules are broken or perceived to be broken, the more referential people's thinking is likely to become, creating a gap between actual and referent outcomes that is a source of resentment and negativity (Folger 1986). Finally, relational theories suggest that fairness impinges on the social relationship between people and the authorities employing the procedures: if procedures are fair, outcomes can lose importance in favor of other intangible benefits, such as the perception that one is respected and held in high regard. In contrast, lack of fairness may lead individuals to see their relationship with authorities as purely instrumental, heightening the impact of tangible benefits and self-interested considerations on satisfaction (Tyler and Lind 1992; Lind 2001).

Reviewing forty-five different studies addressing the determinants of positive evaluations and behaviors within organizational settings, Brockner and Wiesenfeld (1996) find that the modal result is indeed one of an interaction between outcome favorability and procedural fairness. In particular, "when procedural justice is relatively low, outcome favorability is more apt to be positively correlated with individuals' reactions" (Brockner and Wiesenfeld 1996: 191). Later reviews of extant research confirm that "across a wide variety of studies, high procedural fairness has been found to reduce the effect of outcome favorability on people's support for decisions, decision-makers, and organizations, relative to when procedural fairness is low" (Brockner and Wiesenfeld 2005: 548).[5]

What are the implications of these findings when we move to the macro-political level of political systems and regimes? If they do travel to such contexts, a fundamental hypothesis should hold: the relationship between economic outcomes and satisfaction with democracy should be strongest in situations where the quality of governance is lowest. In a recent study, I show that, across Europe, although satisfaction with democracy is indeed strongly related to both evaluations of economic performance and the perceived prevalence of procedural fairness in the political system (conceived as a combination of impartiality, standing, and trust), the latter exerts a relevant moderation over the effect of the former (Magalhães 2016). In other words, the process-outcome interaction found in organizational studies seems to be present as well when we move to the macro-political level. However, important questions can be raised about the use of subjective perceptions of the economy in explaining political support, particularly the possibility of endogeneity and the possibility that varying perceptions over the same object-ive economic data may reflect little else than random or systematic measure-ment biases (Van der Brug et al. 2007). Does the finding of a process-outcome interaction survive when we move from the use of subjective perceptions of the economy to the use of objective economic conditions? This is the question addressed in this chapter.

9.3 Data and Analysis

Data on people's satisfaction with the way democracy works in practice in their countries comes from six rounds of the European Social Survey, con-ducted between 2002 and 2013. The ESS1-6 Cumulative Data File, updated November 26, 2014, is used here.[6] It includes 152 surveys conducted in thirty-two countries. Our major dependent variable of interest is *Satisfaction with Democracy* (*stfdem* in the ESS dataset, "How satisfied are you with the way democracy works in [country]?," ranging from 0 to 10). Given that our focus is on satisfaction with *democracy*, we exclude from the analysis countries whose status as "democracies" is unclear throughout the period under analysis. In other words, we only include countries that have consistently scored seven or more in the Polity IV data set between 2002 and 2013.[7] This leads to the exclusion of Ukraine, Croatia, and Russia.[8]

Our crucial independent variables are *economic performance* and *quality of governance*. To measure economic performance, instead of relying on individual-level perceptions of the state of the economy, I resort to a macro-level variable based on objective economic data: the Economic Performance Index (EPI) proposed by Khramov and Lee (2013). EPI aims at measuring the general macroeconomic performance of a nation, comprising information on four variables about three primary segments of the economy, households, firms, and government: "the inflation rate, as a measure of the economy's monetary stance; the unemployment rate as a measure of the economy's pro-duction stance; the budget deficit as a percentage of total GDP as a measure of the economy's fiscal stance; and the change in real GDP as a measure of the aggregate performance of the entire economy" (Khramov and Lee 2013: 3).[9] Starting from a set of benchmarks about the desirable economic performance of a country—inflation at 0 percent, unemployment at 4.75 percent, govern-ment deficit at 0 percent as a share of GDP, and GDP growth at 4.75 percent—the optimal EPI score is normalized to 100 percent. Current performance is compared with these benchmarks, allowing for a simplified formula:

$$EPI = 100\% - \lceil Inflation\ (\%)\rceil - Unemployment(\%) - \frac{Deficit}{GDP}(\%) + \Delta GDP(\%)$$

Using Eurostat and World Bank Development Indicators data, a value for EPI is calculated for each country-year. In this, we take into consideration fieldwork date. For example, several surveys contained in each of the six ESS rounds considered (2002, 2004, 2006, 2008, 2010, and 2012) took place in particular countries, not in the "official" round year but rather in the following one. For example, for round one, when fieldwork is actually conducted in the second semester of 2003, economic data for 2003 was used rather than 2002. Values for EPI in our sample range from 60.6 (Spain in 2012) to 114.9 (Norway in 2006). Although the primary analysis in the chapter will employ EPI, I will also assess the robustness of the results with a more conventional—although narrower—measure of economic performance, real GDP growth.

To measure quality of governance, I rely on two alternative sources, which are employed alternatively in the analyses. First, the World Bank Governance Indicators: each country-year is matched with an average of the indicators of government effectiveness, control of corruption, rule of law, and voice.[10] Effectiveness captures "perceptions of the quality of public services, the quality of the civil service and the degree of its independence from political pressures, the quality of policy formulation and implementation, and the credibility of the government's commitment to such policies." Control of corruption "captures perceptions of the extent to which public power is exercised for private gain, including both petty and grand forms of corruption, as well as 'capture' of the state by elites and private interests." Rule of law "captures perceptions of the extent to which agents have confidence in and abide by the rules of society, and in particular the quality of contract enforcement, property rights, the police, and the courts, as well as the likelihood of crime and violence." Finally, voice captures "perceptions of the extent to which a country's citizens are able to participate in selecting their government, as well as freedom of expression, freedom of association, and a free media" (Kaufmann, Kraay, and Mastruzzi 2010). Across the world, values for each of these variables range from −2.5 to 2.5, although in our sample the index ranges from −0.01 (Bulgaria in 2008) to 2.16 (Denmark in 2004). At the time of this writing, WGI data is available only until 2012, which resulted in surveys conducted in 2013 (in Lithuania and Italy) being dropped from the analysis in this case.

Alternatively, a different variable is used to code "quality of governance": *impartiality* measures the extent to which, "when implementing laws and policies, government officials shall not take into consideration anything about the citizen/case that is not beforehand stipulated in the policy or the law" (Rothstein and Teorell 2008: 170). One disadvantage of employing this variable is that, unlike the World Bank WGI Indicators, we don't have measures per year of impartiality, as it results from a single expert survey conducted between 2008 and 2012.

Impartiality is thus taken to characterize each country throughout the entire period of data collection. The advantage, however, is that, unlike what occurs with the more general measure derived from World Bank's WGI, the notion of "impartiality" taps what is arguably the core of both the "quality of government" (Rothstein and Teorell 2008; Holmberg et al. 2009) and "procedural fairness" (Leventhal 1980; Lind and Tyler 1988) concepts. The impartiality index is built on five items from the QoG expert survey, with higher values meaning greater impartiality. In our sample of cases, it ranges from -0.46 (Bulgaria) to 1.33 (Norway). On this variable, no data is available for Cyprus, Iceland, and Luxembourg. These cases are thus dropped in the models where impartiality is employed.

Besides these crucial dependent and independent variables, several macro- and micro-level controls are employed in the analysis. First, country-level measures of how consensual democratic regimes are in terms of their basic institutions, a variable that has been found to increase political support in some studies (Rose and Mishler 2011; Bernauer and Vatter 2012). Readily available measures of consensual democracy—in the executive-parties dimension—exist only for nineteen of the thirty-two European countries available in our initial sample (see the web appendix in Vatter, Flinders, and Bernauer 2014). However, the average Effective Number of Parliamentary Parties (ENPP) for those countries in the 1997–2010 period is correlated at 0.87 with the measure of consensual executive-parties democracy. Thus, ENPP is considered to be a good proxy of consensual democracy for all the ESS countries. It is coded, for the 1997–2010 period, using the Vatter, Flinders, and Bernauer (2014) data for nineteen countries and using Gallagher (2014) for the remaining ones.[11] It ranges from 2.25 (Turkey) to 7.02 (Israel).

Income inequality has also been found to be a correlate of satisfaction with democracy and even some aspects of diffuse support (Fails and Pierce 2010; Andersen 2012; Schäfer 2012), at least for some individuals (Anderson and Singer 2008), and in some polities (Boda and Medve-Bálint 2014). Here, the net Gini index of income inequality, post-taxes, and post-transfers, described in Solt (2009), is used.[12] Data for Ireland, Israel, Italy, Lithuania, and Turkey were not yet available for the year 2012 at the time of this writing, and thus these cases for that year are also dropped. Values range from 22.1 (Slovenia in 2002) to 40.9 (Turkey in 2004).

Finally, at the macro level, we control for level of economic development (GDP per capita at constant thousands of 2005$, from the World Bank) and for the age of democracy (number of continuous years with a Polity score greater than or equal to seven, from the Polity IV data set). Thus, we rely on a maximum of 130 surveys in twenty-nine countries, with a total of respondents above 200,000 for the entire six rounds of the ESS. At the individual level, we control for age, years of education, gender (female), social trust,[13] religiosity, political interest, unemployed, and left–right self-placement (as well as LRSP squared, to allow for the possibility of non-linear effects).

Some variables vary only across countries, such as 1997–2010 ENPP, our measure of consensual democracy, or impartiality. Others vary across countries and time, such as economic development, income inequality, and age of democracy, as well as economic performance and quality of governance. Finally, satisfaction with democracy, the main dependent variable, as well as the individual-level controls, varies across individuals. We take into account this three-level structure of the data—countries, country-years, and individuals—by estimating multilevel linear regression models. Satisfaction with democracy is treated as a continuous variable, and the model includes predictors at the three levels of analysis, as well as varying intercepts and error terms for country (and year). Crucially, to test our hypothesis, the model includes an interaction term between economic performance and, alternatively, quality of governance or impartiality. We allow the effect of economic performance to vary by country-year, in the models with quality of governance, and by country, in the models with impartiality. Table 9.1 shows the results.[14]

Table 9.1 Economic performance, quality of governance, and satisfaction with democracy

	Model 1	Model 2
EPI	.08 (.02)***	.05 (.008)***
QoG	3.54 (.99)***	–
Impartiality	–	2.29 (.77)***
QoG*EPI	−.04 (.01)***	–
Impartiality*EPI	–	−.03 (.01)***
Contextual controls		
ENPP	−.01 (.09)	−.003 (.09)
GDP per capita	.02 (.01)*	.02 (.02)
Age of democracy	.0002 (.009)	.004 (.01)
Income inequality	−.006 (.02)	−.01 (.02)
Individual controls		
Female	−.20 (.01)***	−.20 (.01)***
Age of respondent	−.005 (.0003)***	−.005 (.0003)***
Years of education	.01 (.001)***	.01 (.001)***
Religiosity	.05 (.002)***	.05 (.002)***
Social trust	.30 (.003)***	.31 (.003)***
Political interest	.18 (.006)***	.19 (.006)***
LRSP	.22 (.007)***	.23 (.007)***
LRSP squared	−.01 (.0007)***	−.01 (.0007)***
Constant	−5.32 (1.57)**	−2.36 (1.10)**
Variance components		
Country-year intercept	.11	.13
Economic performance	.00	.00
Country intercept	.14	.00
Countries	29	26
Country-years	130	122
Respondents	207,919	201,097

*p<.10; **p<.05; ***p<.01 (two-tailed tests).

Both economic performance and quality of governance, the latter measured either through the index derived from the World Bank data or through the *Impartiality* index, have a positive effect on specific support. However, more importantly for our purposes, the interaction term between economic performance and our measures of quality of governance is negative, as expected, and statistically significant. Results for the contextual control variables suggest that Europeans who live in more economically developed democracies tend to be more satisfied with the way they work, but only in one specification and only at $p<0.10$. All remaining contextual controls are very far from conventional statistical significance. At the individual level, males, as well as younger, more educated, and more religious individuals display higher levels of satisfaction with democracy. Social trust and political interest are also positively related with support, while ideology displays a non-linear pattern, through which both satisfaction and political trust increase as individuals move from the extreme left to the center and then stabilize.

Table 9.2 in the appendices shows results of other analyses that suggest the robustness of the findings presented in Table 9.1. First, an additional interaction is included in relation to Model 1: between EPI and *Age of Democracy* (Model 3), taking into account the possibility that the results obtained in Table 9.1 might be a function not so much of the process-outcome interaction, but rather of a dampening of the effects of economic performance on satisfaction that might increase as democracies become older. Second, Model 1 is estimated replacing EPI by a more conventional measure of economic performance, real GDP growth (Model 4). Third, Model 1 is re-estimated replacing EPI with the difference between the yearly EPI and the "normal" performance within each country, i.e. a benchmarked EPI, centered around the country mean for the entire 2002–13 period (Model 5). Finally, Model 1 is re-estimated including only the more established democracies, i.e. dropping the Eastern European/post-Communist countries (Bulgaria, Czech Republic, Hungary, Latvia, Lithuania, Poland, Slovakia, and Slovenia). In all these cases, the main result—the interaction between economic performance and quality of governance—stands.[15]

Figures 9.2 and 9.3 show the estimated marginal effects of *Economic performance* on *Satisfaction with democracy* across levels of *Quality of governance* (Figure 9.2) and *Impartiality* (Figure 9.3) on the basis of, respectively, Models 1 and 2. The solid black line shows the marginal effects, dotted lines the ninety-five percent confidence intervals, and the grey bars represent the distribution of values of both our WGI-based measure of quality of governance and our impartiality measure across the sample.

Clearly, the effect of economic performance on satisfaction with democracy decreases as quality of governance increases, becoming indistinguishable from zero at the highest levels of quality of governance. To put this in a different

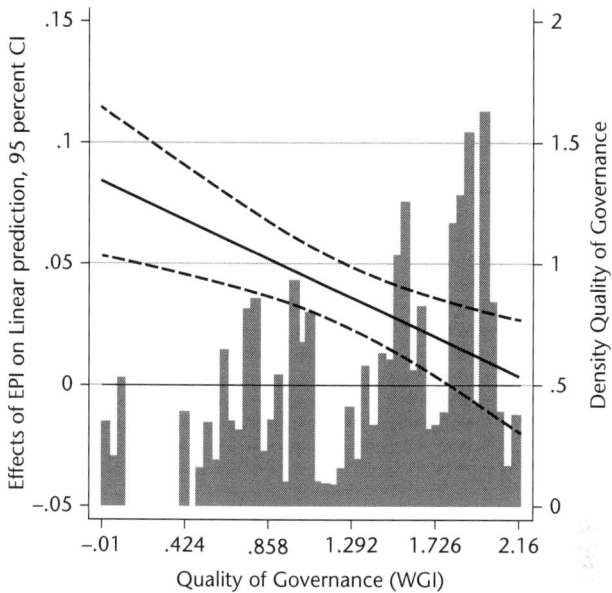

Figure 9.2 Marginal effect of economic performance (EPI) on satisfaction with democracy, across the range of levels of quality of governance

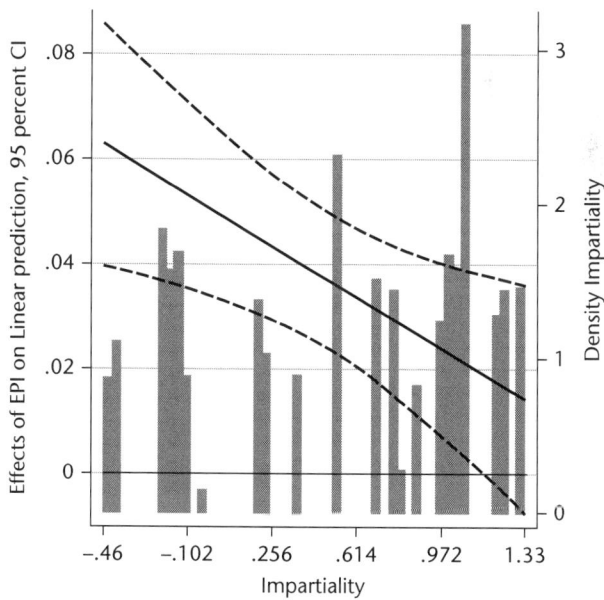

Figure 9.3 Marginal effect of economic performance (EPI) on satisfaction with democracy, across the range of levels of impartiality

way, in a country such as Italy in 2004 (with *Quality of governance* at about 0.7, the average value minus one standard deviation), a one standard deviation increase in EPI is predicted to increase satisfaction with democracy by 0.45 in a 0 to 10 scale, about one-third of a standard deviation in the dependent variable. Conversely, in a country such as Switzerland in 2006 (with *Quality*

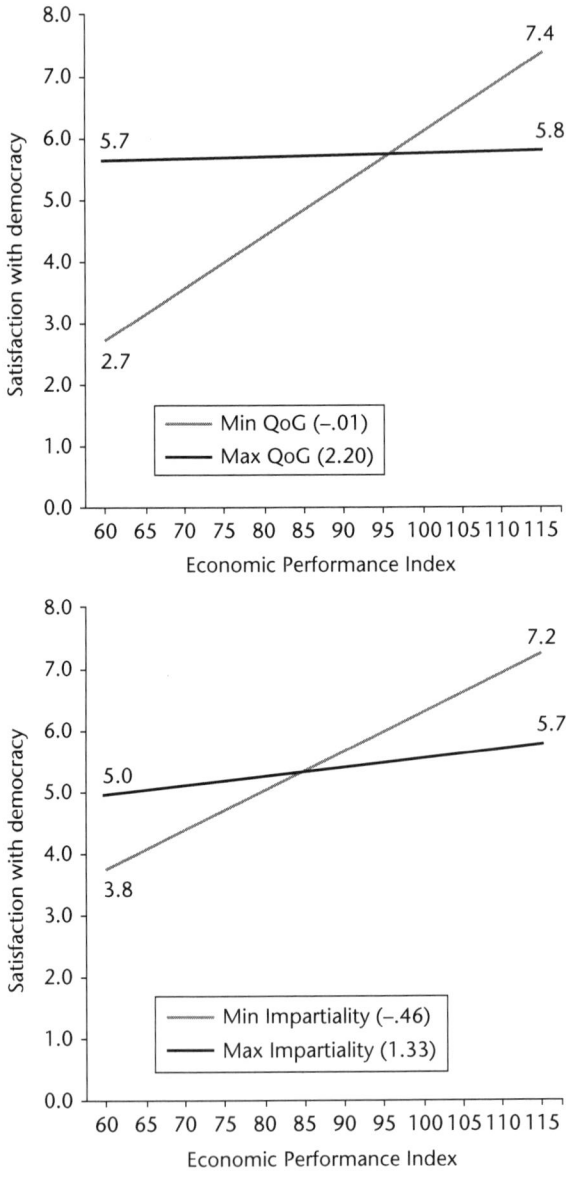

Figure 9.4 Predicted values of satisfaction with democracy for combinations of values in EPI and QoG, with all remaining variables at their mean values

of Governance at 1.9, the average value plus one standard deviation), the estimated effect is less than half as large (0.18) and is not significantly different from zero. A very similar pattern and the same magnitude of effects is obtained when we look at the role of *Impartiality* as a moderator.

Another way of looking at the results is to estimate how the predicted levels of satisfaction with democracy change as the values of economic performance increase, under different quality of governance contexts. Figure 9.4, compares the effect of EPI under the lowest (−0.5) and highest (2.2) levels of the *Quality of governance* variable. On the right, the same approach is used, in this case under the lowest and highest levels of *Impartiality*. Clearly, countries with very high quality of governance exhibit a gentle slope, showing how people's satisfaction with democracy there is nearly insensitive to economic performance. This raises the possibility that some of the discrepancies in extant findings concerning the relationship between the economy and democratic satisfaction may be a function of the sample of countries employed: when that sample is limited to countries with a relatively high quality of governance, little to no effects of the economy are to be expected. In contrast, people living in countries with lower quality of governance in Europe show a much stronger sensitivity to economic outcomes when evaluating the performance of the democratic regime.

9.4 Conclusion

When examining correlates of political support in democratic regimes, many studies have observed how citizens react both to economic outcomes and to prevalent procedural rules and norms. When the economy is doing well, or at least for people who perceive it as such, satisfaction with the way democracy works tends to increase. However, citizens do not care only about "what" regimes deliver: they also care about "how" regimes work. When the state apparatus, political institutions, and public officials are perceived to be transparent, impartial, and fair, satisfaction with democracy also rises. Nobody wants a bad economy and "everybody wants good government" (Dahlberg and Holmberg 2014: 125).

However, these two aspects are related in ways that organizational psychologists have emphasized for long, but political scientists have, so far, mostly neglected. Procedural fairness and favorable economic outcomes interact in the explanation of people's evaluation of democratic performance. There are different arguments about why such interaction should occur, provided by "instrumental," "relational," "fairness," and "referent cognitions" theories in social psychology. However, they all point to a clear generic hypothesis that has found systematic empirical support: procedural fairness moderates the effects of outcome favorability. In other words, there are contexts where the extent to which individuals form positive evaluations and sentiments about authorities and institutions is very contingent upon the delivery of favorable economic outcomes, while there are other contexts where political support is more immune to outcome delivery. The latter are those where procedural fairness prevails.

Elsewhere, I tested this hypothesis at the macro-political level, confirming it from the point of view of people's perceptions of both the state of the economy and of the extent to which procedural fairness prevailed in the regime (Magalhães 2016). In this chapter, I extend those findings and assess their robustness by employing objective measures of economic performance, irrespective of how the economy might be perceived. Furthermore, the chapter employs measures of quality of governance that, although still relying on perceptions, are at least partially exogenous to the views of survey respondents, by being based on views of experts and stakeholders. The basic finding about a process-outcome interaction is confirmed. In contexts where the "quality of governance" is low or where government officials display low levels of impartiality in their decisions and dealings with citizens, satisfaction with democratic performance is both lower in general, and also more sensitive to the delivery of negative or positive national economic outcomes. The contrast exposed in the beginning of the chapter, the one between the cases of Greece and Sweden, can now be better understood. In a country such as Greece, with comparatively low quality of governance, political support can rise high under a good economy, but it also drops to very low levels when that falters. In a country such as Sweden, political support is less sensitive to economic conditions. This result is obtained even when we control for how long countries have been democratic, how economically developed they are, the extent to which their institutions are consensual, or their level of economic inequality.

Having said that, we still know little about the specific causal mechanisms that drive the process-outcome interaction in determinants of political support we observed in this chapter. Does it result from the way in which impartial and high-quality governance affects the attribution of responsibility for outcomes, deflecting blame from authorities for short-term economic failures? Or because it changes the time horizon of individuals when making judgments about authorities, leading them to discount present or recent outcomes and heightening the importance of expected future benefits? Or is it because, when living under conditions of high-quality governance, individuals attribute greater value to intangible benefits, to being heard and respected and treated with equity and impartiality, than to short-term tangible benefits? All these mechanisms have been advanced in the study of procedural fairness and outcome favorability in organizations, and all of them are promising lines of further inquiry in the study of support for political authorities, institutions, and regimes.

Notes

1. Available at: <http://data.worldbank.org/data-catalog/worldwide-governance-indicators>.
2. Available at: <http://qog.pol.gu.se/data/datadownloads/qogexpertsurveydata>.
3. The question posed on the survey is "How satisfied are you with the way democracy works in [country]?" and respondents use an eleven-point scale, from "Not at all satisfied" (0) to "Very satisfied"(10).
4. Not to mention the equally large literature showing that positive subjective *perceptions* of economic outcomes are correlates of satisfaction with democratic performance (Anderson and Guillory 1997; Rose, Mishler, and Haerpfer 1998; Mishler and Rose 2001a; Chu et al. 2008; Thomassen and van der Kolk 2009).
5. To be sure, one can imagine a relationship of reverse causality, where satisfaction with authorities increases perceptions of fairness. However, the hypothesis posed in this chapter is that low levels of procedural fairness increase the effects of economic outcomes on satisfaction in comparison with situations of high procedural fairness. This means that high satisfaction can perfectly coexist with low procedural fairness, provided economic outcomes are positive. If confirmed, these results cannot be driven by the reverse causality mechanism described.
6. Downloaded December 5, 2015, from <http://www.europeansocialsurvey.org/downloadwizard/#>.
7. Available at: <http://www.systemicpeace.org/polityproject.html>. Although Luxembourg and Iceland are not included in the Polity IV data set, we considered these countries to be democratic since the Second World War.
8. See Appendices for more information.
9. Sources for primary data: Eurostat and World Bank Development Indicators. Available at: <http://ec.europa.eu/eurostat/data/database> and <http://data.worldbank.org/data-catalog/world-development-indicators>.
10. Available at: <http://data.worldbank.org/data-catalog/worldwide-governance-indicators>.
11. Available at: <http://www.tcd.ie/Political_Science/staff/michael_gallagher/ElSystems/Docts/ElectionIndices.pdf->.
12. Available at: <http://myweb.uiowa.edu/fsolt/swiid/swiid.html>.
13. This is the average of three items in the ESS questionnaire, measuring trust in others, their expected fairness, and their helpfulness.
14. Collinearity tests show that the highest values of the variance factor are below 6, suggesting that no harmful collinearity exists (Kennedy 2008: 199).
15. Although the coefficient of the interaction between GDP growth and QoG is not significant, examination of the marginal effects show that GDP growth effects decrease as QoG increases, and are only significant at conventional levels at GoG levels below 1.8, which is substantively close to the results presented here.

10

Political Support in the Wake of Policy Controversies

Peter Esaiasson, Mikael Gilljam, and Mikael Persson

10.1 Introduction

Given the weak empirical evidence for a secular decline in political support across advanced industrialized democracies (Van Ham and Thomassen in this volume), this chapter studies how support attitudes are affected by idiosyncratic factors unique to each country.[1] Specifically, we direct attention to the critical event literature. The basic assumption in this literature is that events of certain qualities trigger re-evaluations of political leaders (Mueller 1973) and of the system in which they act (Parker 1995; Hetherington and Nelson 2003). As critical events occur irregularly across countries, they are potentially a source of diverging trends and varying levels of political support.

Following John Mueller's landmark *War, Presidents, and Public Opinion*, events are critical when they are "specific, dramatic and sharply focused" (Mueller 1973: 208). The literature in the field has focused on two types of events thus defined: external threats, and norm violations by political decision-makers. Events associated with external threats regarding national security (Mueller 1973; Brody 1991) and acts of terrorism (Putnam 2002b; Hetherington and Nelson 2003; Wollebæk et al. 2012; Dinesen and Jæger 2013) typically generate rally effects that increase political support. Conversely, critical events that are triggered by norm violations such as political scandals (Chanley, Rudolph, and Rahn 2000; Bowler and Karp 2004; Maier 2011; Dancey 2012; Kumlin and Esaiasson 2012) and man-made disasters (Arcenaux and Stein 2006; Atkeson and Maestas 2012) frequently undermine political support attitudes.

The support generating effect of external threats commonly fades after a period of time (Brody 1991; Sander and Putnam 2010; Dinesen and Jæger

2013). However, the support undermining effects of scandalous behavior from decision-makers can be more lasting, in particular if scandals expose dysfunctional governmental structures with corruption as the primary example (Van der Meer 2010 and in this volume; Dancey 2012; Wroe, Allen, and Birch 2013; Kumlin and Esaiasson 2012; Allen and Birch 2013). For example, studies of political support attitudes during economic crisis find that the perception that government is corrupt is more detrimental than austerity measures and deteriorating material conditions (Torcal 2014; Erlingson, Linde, and Öhrvall 2016).

Acknowledging the potential importance of support undermining critical events, this chapter goes beyond previous event research in two ways. First, we expand the universe of critical events by moving the concept to a setting of normal politics. By critical events in a setting of normal politics we mean policy controversies in which politicians propose a policy that evokes strong protests from affected citizens. Second, we examine not only the support undermining effects of policy controversies but also various mechanisms through which support may be regained. By considering support maintaining mechanisms we highlight the need to learn about processes that preserve a working relationship between citizens and their representatives during conflictual periods.

Empirical studies of critical events require temporal data that are difficult to obtain. To help overcome methodological obstacles, we suggest a "fire house" approach to data collection. This approach relies on monitoring citizens' reactions to a controversial policy decision over time using web surveys of targeted groups of citizens, and estimates of an "artificial T0 measure" to estimate citizens' support before the policy was proposed (see Zaller 1992). Demonstrating the usefulness of this approach, we examine how political support develops in association with a local policy controversy over school closures in Sweden.

We begin by outlining the reasons why policy controversies are critical events that may undermine political support, and by developing four mechanisms that may sustain support in the face of such critical events. Having presented our analytical framework, we then turn to empirical matters and our illustrative local case study. Following discussions on case selection, data collection, and measurements, we present empirical findings. Results confirm that a controversial policy proposal may undermine political support among protesting citizens, and that support undermining forces are mitigated by policy concessions from politicians and multilevel institutional arrangements. A final section concludes and draws out implications of the study.

10.2 Policy Controversies as Critical Events

Politicians sometimes find it necessary to introduce controversial policy proposals that go against strongly held preferences among citizens. Examples include: increased taxes on income and housing; cutbacks on central welfare state responsibilities such as pensions for the elderly and schooling for the young; regulation of internet use; and the right to wear religious symbols in public places. Propositions of this nature will affect the everyday lives of significant groups of citizens. Under the influence of psychological mechanisms such as loss aversion and dissonance avoidance, protesting citizens might re-evaluate their support of the regime and of regime institutions (e.g. Anderson et al. 2005). Indeed, for affected individuals these events will appear as "specific, dramatic and sharply focused" (Mueller 1973: 208).

Critical events involving external threats and norm violations are spectacular incidents that go beyond the expected. In contrast, as elected politicians have the formal right to decide common matters between elections (Pitkin 1967), events involving controversial policy decisions are normal procedure in a representative democracy. Nevertheless, in these cases protesting citizens find reasons to object to politicians' exercise of power. In terms suggested by Jane Mansbridge (1997), it is a case of "contestedly legitimate coercion." Because policy controversies unfold regularly at all levels in a political system, and because they make it clear to affected citizens that they have surrendered power to their representatives, we argue that the handling of these policy controversies is important for democratic legitimacy.

Policy controversies follow a certain dynamic. To capture this dynamic, and to identify triggers of support undermining processes, we use a standard typology from policy-making research: politicians propose policies that trigger negative reactions from groups of citizens (policy initiation). After a period of contention, which frequently involves demonstrations and other expressions of citizen dissatisfaction, politicians decide whether to follow through with the proposal (policy decision). If they do, the decision is eventually implemented and citizens will have to adjust to the new conditions (policy implementation). In a policy controversy, thus, initiation, formal decision, and implementation are focal points that may motivate citizens to re-evaluate their political support attitudes.

10.3 Support Maintaining Mechanisms

We know from experience that advanced industrialized democracies have regained citizen support following periods of contention. How is this achieved in the wake of policy controversies? Many theories about democratic legitimacy center on electoral accountability (e.g. Przeworski, Stokes, and Manin 1999). When applied to policy controversies this means that the prime mechanism for support maintenance is the possibility for protesting citizens to sanction politicians at the following election. However, for citizens with acute concerns over unwelcome policy proposals the next election is in the distant future.

To learn about support maintenance in the wake of policy controversies, we identify four mechanisms that jointly or independently might mitigate the support undermining forces in play. Three of the support-maintaining mechanisms are directly tied to the policy-making process: high quality decision-making procedures (SMM 1); concessions to the policy preferences of protesters (SMM 2); and fading memories among protesters (SMM 3). The fourth mechanism (SMM 4) considers an institutional arrangement—vertical division of power—that might contain the support undermining forces to a singular branch of government.

10.3.1 *SMM 1: Fair Decision-making Procedures Win Back Support Once the Decision is Made*

SMM 1 derives from the importance people ascribe to fair decision-making processes. A large literature demonstrates that perceptions of procedural fairness are consequential for willingness to accept unfavorable decisions and for legitimacy beliefs (e.g. Tyler 2006; MacCoun 2005; see also Magalhães in this volume).

Considering that protesting citizens have exercised their constitutional right to voice concerns about the proposal, a straightforward application of procedural fairness theory maintains that political support will return to its original level shortly after the formal decision is taken. In other words, protesters will be reassured by the fact that the decision was made by their authorized representatives and, while they might not like the decision in itself, they take comfort in the procedural qualities of representative decision-making.

An alternative, and more realistic, application of procedural fairness theory adds that representatives are required to be responsive toward the wishes and views of the represented (Pitkin 1967: 209–10). Hence, political support will be restored to the extent politicians have been acting responsively during the process leading up to the decision.

It is not clear precisely what it means to be responsive in the context of policy controversies. According to a common understanding, responsiveness requires representatives to adapt to the policies preferred by protesters, but with the important qualification that protesters must be supported by a majority of citizens (Dahl 1989; Powell 2004). However, since no serious representation theory maintains that representatives are obligated to blindly follow instructions from voters (Pitkin 1967), responsiveness is perhaps best seen as a promise of sincere communication. With a communicative under-standing, politicians act responsively not only when they adapt to majority preferences but also when they provide good reasons for their actions (Esaiasson, Gilljam, and Persson 2013).

10.3.2 SMM 2: Concessions to Protesters Substantial Preferences Win Back Political Support

SMM 2 emphasizes the effectiveness of conceding to some of protesters substantial preferences. In the negotiation literature, offering a compromise solution is a generic strategy to move out of conflict-ridden situations (Fischer et al. 1997). By allowing both negotiating parts to gain at least something from the process, the strategy avoids the psychologically detrimental situation in which one part comes out as a loser. Moreover, by showing goodwill the part offering the compromise invites the other to reciprocate (Falk and Fischbacher 2006).

The compromise strategy and its mechanisms readily translate to policy controversies: by conceding to some of protesters' policy preferences politicians show goodwill. As a consequence, protesting citizens will be relatively better off than they originally feared, and there is less reason for them to feel psychologically as losers.

Although similar to SMM 1 (adaptive responsiveness), SMM 2 differs by ascribing weight to material considerations; protesters become more supportive because their substantial preferences have been met, and not because they reward politicians for acting procedurally fair. Obviously, this subtle difference is difficult to study empirically. However, the two mechanisms differ in observable ways in case policy concessions satisfy the preference of only a subgroup of protesters. In this situation, the mechanisms associated with compromise solutions will only play out among the camp of protesters whose preferences have been satisfied. Precisely, differential reactions from protesters that are tied to the favorability of the outcome signal that support maintaining processes are driven by material concerns (SMM 2) rather than by procedural concerns (SMM 1).

10.3.3 SMM 3: With Time, Unwelcome Decisions Fade in Protesters' Memory

SMM 3 is tied to the implementation phase—support will grow as a consequence of forgetfulness and interest in other topics as time moves on. The precise mechanisms at play involve individual-level information processing and saliency reduction. Research on trust in government observes that trust levels are contingent upon the criteria people employ when they evaluate government, and that these criteria are primed by the flow of information (Hetherington and Husser 2012). When applied to the present setting, the theory suggests a cyclical pattern in protesters' political support. During the height of the conflict dissatisfied citizens think about politicians in terms of the proposal and hence evaluate them negatively, but with time other aspects of the representative relationship become more salient.

A complementary mechanism is dissonance reduction after the cutback proposal has been implemented. When forced to adjust to new circumstances, protesting citizens who have at least some positive experiences of their polity might re-evaluate their support attitudes to reduce dissonance. In other words, protesters might find it mentally taxing to remain politically unsupportive as they continue with their lives. Psychological research has found evidence for this kind of mechanism in car drivers' attitudes toward road pricing. Although initial resistance might be strong, the new charge is more easily accepted when car drivers believe that it has come to stay (Schade and Baum 2007).

10.3.4 *SMM 4: A Vertical Division of Power Contains Dissatisfaction to Singular Branches of Government*

Under multilevel institutional arrangements, welfare state commitments and other political issues are handled by a specific branch of government (e.g. Downs 1999). Provided that protesters attribute blame to politicians who have primary responsibility for the specific proposal, this vertical division of power can contain support undermining mechanisms to one particular branch of government and not to the overall political regime. Precisely, if blame is to be found at one particular level of government, there is no reason for protesters to re-evaluate their overall level of political support. Moreover, if protesters keep track of specific levels of governments, chances increase that negative experiences with regard to welfare state arrangements at one level of government are countered by positive experiences at other levels of government, thus making the overall tally positive.

An objection against containment of this sort is that dissatisfied citizens might be unwilling to undertake the required cognitive effort. For instance, the literature on critical events related to external threats reports cross-border effects on political support attitudes (e.g. Mueller 1973; Parker 1995; Hetherington and Nelson 2003; Dinesen and Jæger 2013). However, studies that directly focus on citizens' blame attributions find that citizens do make distinctions among levels of government in terms of the issues they handle (Arcenaux 2006; Arcenaux and Stein 2006; Atkeson and Maestas 2012).

10.4 Case Selection

Policy controversies are by definition tied to specific cases. To begin exploring the processes in play, we will target citizen reactions toward a proposal to restructure the local school system in a Swedish municipality. Cutbacks in central welfare state functions are generally unpopular among citizens (Kumlin 2009), and for parents few issues are more important than their children's schooling.

By most accounts Sweden is a well-functioning democracy, but it is not conflict-free. In a 2012 survey of a nationally representative sample of elected politicians at all branches of government, sixteen percent reported that they had been maltreated at least one time during the past year, and that a significant share of assaults (up to twenty percent) originated from cutbacks on welfare state arrangements at the local and regional level (Brå 2012). With regard to school closures specifically, one estimate reports that there are forty to fifty significant protests per year in Sweden (Uba 2010).

The study is situated in Suburbia, an affluent municipality in a metropolitan area. The precise study location was selected for practical reasons. We monitored several municipalities in planning this research, and Suburbia provided the first example of a relevant policy controversy.

10.4.1 *Case Description*

In the fall of 2010, shortly after joint local and national elections in which the ruling center-right coalition in Suburbia secured a new term in office, politicians and administrators intensified plans to restructure the local school system. The plans involved ten school and pre-school units, five of which would be closed down completely, which would affect nearly 600 children and their parents (of a total population of 34,000). The restructuring was deemed necessary for budgetary reasons—as a consequence of a national voucher system, public schools are losing students in many municipalities—but was not discussed during the election campaign.

Following an article in the local press, news about the plan spread quickly in mid-December 2010. Within days, critical parents had started a Facebook group, 500 individuals had signed an online petition against the proposal, local and regional news media had published follow-up stories, and politicians and administrators had called a public meeting. In these and other forums, an intense debate raged for more than a month. Having postponed the decision once, the local government decided in March 2011 for a compromise outcome which involved only six school units and affected fewer children than the original plan. The decision began to be implemented after the summer break in August 2011, and after further adjustments the process was completed a year later.

When matched against our criteria for a critical event, the Suburbia case fits the requirements: initially, the introduction of a policy proposal generated a heated debate with many critical voices. Protesting citizens engaged actively on Facebook, in public meetings, and by signing the online petition drive. The formal decision was a compromise that met the demands of some but not all protesters. (Hence, there is analytical leverage with regard to SMM 1 and SMM 2.) Moreover, the decision was implemented after a reasonably extended period of time. Overall, while no single case study is representative in a statistical sense, we argue that the restructuring of Suburbia's school system shares essential characteristics with other cases in the universe of controversial policy propositions to which we ultimately want to generalize.

10.5 A Fire-House Approach to Data Collection

Illustrating a way to obtain data of the required temporal quality, we have conducted a multiwave web survey of protesting Suburbians and a control group of non-active Suburbians. When combined with an auxiliary survey with a nationally representative sample of adults, the web survey allows us to map political support and other relevant beliefs before, during, and after the introduction of the controversial policy proposal. We describe the key features of our fire-house approach to data collection in this section.

To recruit a sufficiently large number of protesters, we took as our point of departure the petition drive that was initiated shortly after the proposal became public knowledge. Of the 588 who signed the online petition, we were able to find contact information for 369 relevant individuals (remaining petition signers were children, persons for whom we could not find a telephone number, or individuals living in other municipalities). The 369 relevant petition signers were contacted by telephone and when reached they were asked to join a web panel on the school controversy. Overall, 237 individuals (sixty-four percent of the relevant petition signers) agreed to participate, provided a valid email address, and responded to the initial web survey.

Signing a petition is one of the least demanding forms of political partici- pation and our sample of protesters should not be seen as activists in an advanced meaning. Almost all (ninety-five percent) had children in the house- hold, ninety-five percent were fifty years or younger, sixty percent were females, sixty-five percent held a university degree, forty percent reported Facebook activities related to the protest, and fifty percent had been in per- sonal contact with a politician in relation to the protest. With regard to political predispositions, seven percent rated themselves as very interested in politics, and the median position on a self-reported left–right scale was some- what right of the middle (6.0 on a 0–10 scale) (as would be expected in a municipality which had recently re-elected a center-right coalition govern- ment). All in all, our sample of protesters shows the characteristics of con- cerned parents (and a few grandparents) who became politically engaged for the only reason that their local government was about to change the conditions for their children's schooling.

Protesters were web surveyed three times: post-proposal in January 2011 (T1); post-decision in March 2011 (T2); and post-implementation in October 2011 (T3). Three out of four protesters in our sample (n = 178) participated in all three panel waves making for an overall response rate of forty-eight percent of the relevant petition signers.[2]

A fundamental problem for event studies is to obtain a measure at T0, before the event occurred. To overcome this problem, we have estimated what is known as an "artificial T0" (Zaller 1992). The estimation followed the practice outlined by Todosijevic (2012). The core idea is to use a representative survey to simulate predicted levels of the dependent variables at T0. The procedure is based on multiple imputations and treats the dependent variables at T0 as missing values. The imputation process produces the most likely estimates of the respondents' attitudes at T0.

The estimation rests on the assumptions that the people under study in Suburbia resemble the people in a national representative sample with the same characteristics and that the factors we measure accurately predict the main variable under study. These are, of course, strong and largely untestable assumptions, and hence our estimates of protesters' attitudes at T0 should be seen as a best guess. However, while in the words of Todosijevic this practice is "still far from the mainstream statistical toolbox," simulation studies show that the procedure can generate predicted values close to observed true levels. Furthermore, belief in our artificial T0 estimates are strengthened by side information presented in the result section (as predicted, we observe a post-conflict return to the T0 position among protesters who were satisfied with politicians' decision).

Our auxiliary data are from a high-quality mail survey, which has been conducted each year since 1986 by the Society, Opinion and Media (SOM) Institute at the University of Gothenburg. It draws on a random sample of the Swedish adult population. We use variables for gender, education, age, age squared, left–right ideological placement, political interest, party choice in the elections 2010, and whether one has underage children living in the household, to construct 250 simulated records with predicted values for T0. We then calculate a mean value for each variable and for each person and use this as an artificial T0 measure.

We also use imputation to handle missing data on T1–T3 (for both the dependent and independent variables). If a respondent lacks a response at one time point we impute that observation using the variables measuring the same variable at the other time points, as well as gender, education, age, left–right ideological placement, political interest, and attitude to the proposal. Individuals with missing values on more than one time point (T1–T3) are excluded from the analyses. Hence, after imputation we have a balanced data set with information on all time points (n = 199).

The web survey was administered by the Laboratory of Opinion Research (LORE) at the University of Gothenburg. Importantly, by recruiting from its standing opt-in web panel (n = 10,000 at the time of the study), LORE also provided a small control group of individuals living in Suburbia who did not sign the online petition (n = 50). The control group, which had been surveyed a first time two months prior to the event, was surveyed parallel to the sample of protesters.[3] Table 10.1 summarizes our data collections.

10.5.1 *Measurements*

Our primary indicator of political support attitudes is satisfaction with local democracy (SWD_{local}). This is measured using the standard question about satisfaction "with the way democracy works in your local municipality." In order to test support for SMM 4 about vertical division of power, we also asked about satisfaction with national level democracy ($SWD_{national}$). (See Appendices for precise wordings of this and other survey items.)

For a robustness test we estimate changes in process preference during the conflict (Hibbing and Theiss-Morse 2002; Bengtsson and Christensen 2016). Our measure of process preference asks respondents to choose between two alternatives for citizen engagement, the one emphasizing the importance of voting in elections, the other emphasizing the importance of citizen participation between elections (Gilljam and Jodal 2002).

To capture attitudes toward the policy controversy, we described the policy proposal in neutral terms and asked respondents whether their view was positive or negative. With regard to perceived responsiveness—a key mediating variable for SMM 1—respondents were asked to evaluate the extent to which local politicians had found out about citizen wishes; explained their politics to citizens; and tried to accommodate citizen wishes (for a psychometric evaluation of this measure of perceived responsiveness, see Esaiasson,

Table 10.1 Data structure for the Suburbia study

	Pre-conflict (T0)	Post-proposal (T1)	Post-decision (T2)	Post-implementation (T3)
Citizens (self-selected sample; n = 50)	Observed*	Observed	Observed	Observed
Protesters (petition signers; n = 237)	Imputed	Observed	Observed	Observed

*Except for "process preference," which was imputed following the same procedure as for protesters

et al. Köln and Turper 2015). The measurements associated with SMM 2 (compromise decisions), and SMM 3 (fading memories) are based on comparisons between T1 and T2, and T2 and T3, respectively.

10.6 Results

As with all critical events, we expect strong initial reactions from protesting Suburbians. For an estimation of the effect, Figure 10.1 shows the mean SWD_{local} and accompanying ninety-five percent confidence interval for protesters and the control group at four time points: before initiation (T0); after initiation (T1); after decision (T2); and after implementation (T3). Our estimation method is straightforward. We calculate mean values of the dependent variable for each group at each time point and two-tailed p-values for t-tests to measure whether change over time is statistically significant (detailed statistics are presented in Appendices: Table 10.1).

Clearly, results meet expectations. Among protesters, the level of political support is twenty percent lower for our T1 observation than for the T0 observation. During the same time period the control group remained essentially unchanged (as it more or less did throughout the period we study).

Easing doubts that our T0 measure has generated an artificial effect, other indicators in the T1 survey strongly suggest that the policy proposal triggered

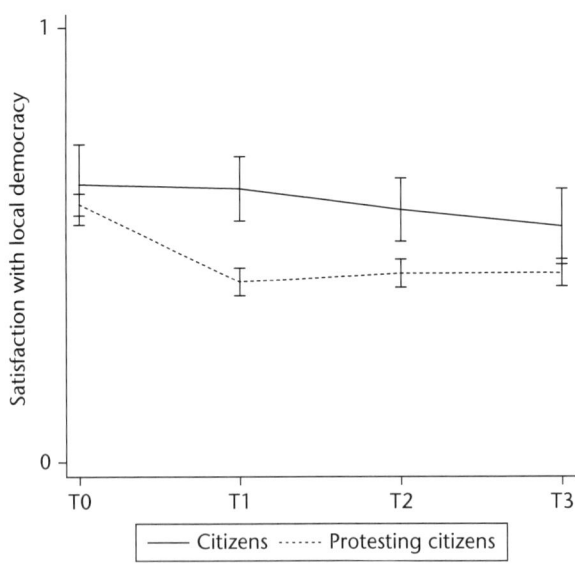

Figure 10.1 Satisfaction with local democracy among protesters and a control group of non-affected Suburbians

dissatisfaction among protesters. For instance, the vast majority of protesters (seventy-five percent) had a "very negative" view on the proposal (twenty percent "somewhat negative"). And the twenty percent of respondents who gave open-ended comments about politicians' way of handling the process used words such as "arrogance," "provocation," "ruthless," "inhumane," and "thoughtless."

A further indicator that the proposal triggered protesters is their change in process preferences. The idea that people have preferences for how politics should function originates in Hibbing and Theiss-Morse's *Stealth Democracy* (2002). The core claim is that stable, albeit individually different, process preferences guide individuals' relationship to politics (Neblo et al. 2010; Bengtsson and Christensen 2016). To measure Suburbians' process preferences we asked respondents to choose between two alternative visions of democracy, the one modeled on a Schumpeterian ideal giving priority to voting in elections, the other modeled on a participatory ideal as defended by, for example, Pateman (1970) and Barber (1984).

The question has been put twice to representative samples of Swedes, and on both occasions a majority have preferred the Schumpeterian ideal (Esaiasson, Gilljam, and Persson 2010). This is also what our artificial T0 estimate shows (Figure 10.2).[4] However, as protesting Suburbians were mobilized into politics they moved quickly toward the participatory ideal. Moreover, when the conflict over their children's school became less intense they started to move back

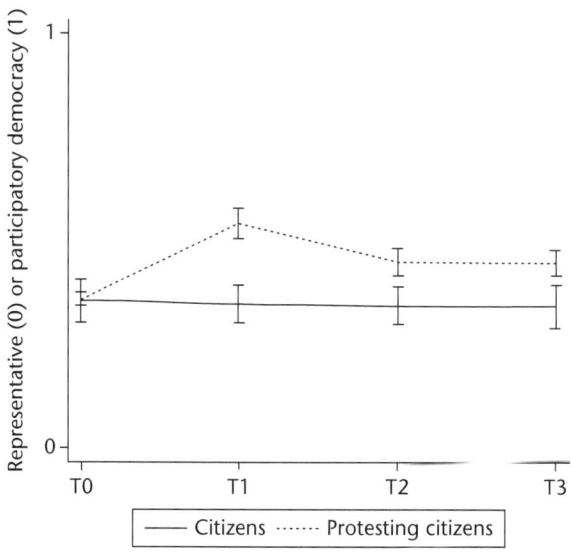

Figure 10.2 Process preferences among protesters and a control group of non-affected Suburbians

toward their original position in favor of a narrow electoral democracy in which authoritative decisions are made by politicians.[5] Corresponding movement could not be observed in the control group. Contrary to the claims made in the literature, it appears as if behavior drives process preferences rather than the reverse. For our purpose here, the cyclical movement among protesters is evidence of true change in response to a critical event.

Looking at results from the later stages in the conflict (Figure 10.1), the level of political support among protesting Suburbians began to increase post-decision, but had not returned to its pre-crisis level at T3. Thus, overall, the proposal to restructure the local school system undermined political support among protesters long-term. To learn about the processes in play, we turn to support maintaining mechanisms.

10.6.1 *SMM 1 and SMM 2: Fair Decision-making Procedures and Concessions to Protesters' Substantial Preferences Win Back Political Support*

The formal decision is a focal moment in a policy controversy. When the outcome is known, protesting citizens have a reason to reconsider their support attitudes. Was the procedure leading up to the decision a fair one (SMM 1), and did politicians offer concessions to protesters' substantial preferences (SMM 2)?

Among protesting Suburbians, the decision had a positive but small effect on aggregate support levels (Figure 10.1 and Appendices: Table 10.1A). Looking into the detailed process, we start from the fact that politicians offered a compromise solution that conceded to the interests of some but not all protesters. If SMM 2 was in play, thus, we expect differential reactions post-decision. And this is precisely what we find. Prior to the decision only five percent had a (somewhat) positive view on the proposition, after the decision forty-five percent had. As can be seen in Figure 10.3, this split among protesters translated into differential levels of support. Those with a positive view on the decision became more supportive (but still less so than before the school proposal), those who remained negative did not change.

In line with SMM 2, this result suggests that conceding to some of the protesters' substantial preferences helped to restore political support in Suburbia, but only among a subgroup of protesters and only to a degree.

Can these movements be accounted for by procedural factors as well (SMM 1)? The differential effect of outcome satisfaction makes it unlikely that objective procedural arrangements contributed to rebuilding support in Suburbia: all protesters had experienced the same decision-making procedure, yet only those who were most satisfied with the outcome became more supportive. This is far from a textbook understanding of the representative relationship,

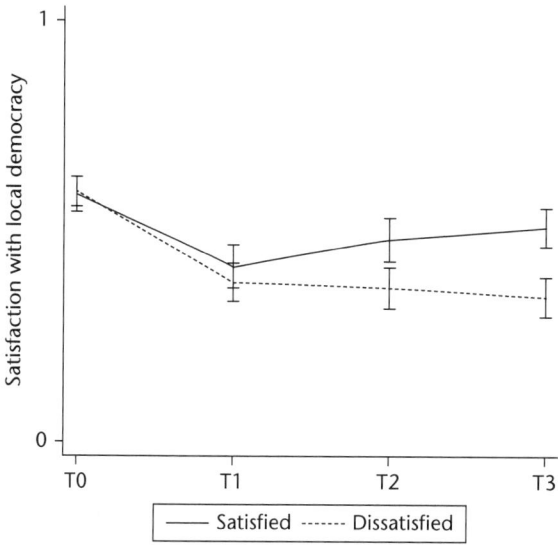

Figure 10.3 Satisfaction with local democracy among protesters who were satisfied and dissatisfied with the formal decision

according to which citizens may voice concern before the decision but after the decision let bygones be bygones.

Nevertheless, subjective procedural beliefs can play a role in support maintenance. To see how, consider that, perhaps, some protesters became more supportive, not only because policy concessions met the needs of their children, but also because they observed a group of politicians who worked hard to make the best of a difficult situation, and because they appreciated that protesting parents had been listened to during the process.

To see whether this reasoning applies to protesters, we estimated a lagged dependent variable model in which SWD_{Local} at T2 (our measure of political support post-decision) is regressed on attitudes towards the decision (T2) and perceived responsiveness (T2), controlling for SWD_{Local} at T1. To capture protesters responsiveness beliefs we asked about three responsiveness actions from politicians in the ruling majority: the extent to which they had been trying (i) to find out about citizens' wishes and views ("listening"); (ii) to explain their position to citizens (explain); and (iii) to accommodate citizen wishes and views ("adapt").[6]

Results in Table 10.2 (OLS estimates) come out in favor of subjective beliefs about procedural quality. All three responsiveness beliefs contribute independently to political support. Indeed, when "adapt" is included in Model 3, the coefficient for views on the decision becomes statistically insignificant, which suggests, that indeed "adapt" is related to concessions to the substantial

Table 10.2 Determinant of political support post decision (OLS-estimates)

	Model 1 (SE)	Model 2 (SE)	Model 3 (SE)
SWD$_{local}$T1	0.55***	0.53***	0.52***
	(0.056)	(0.054)	(0.055)
View of the decision (T2)	0.09**	0.10**	0.05
	(0.040)	(0.040)	(0.045)
Responsiveness belief—listen (T2)	0.04**		
	(0.012)		
Responsiveness belief—explain (T2)		0.07***	
		(0.023)	
Responsiveness belief—adapt (T2)			0.07***
			(0.023)
Constant	1.20***	1.16***	1.45***
	(0.229)	(0.233)	(0.275)
Adjusted R^2	0.46	0.41	0.43
Number of respondents	177	192	190

Note: * $p \leq 0.05$; ** $p \leq 0.01$; *** $p \leq 0.001$

preferences of (some) protesters. Overall, it is clear that subjective procedural fairness beliefs play a role for reactions towards the decision.[7]

To more fully understand how responsiveness beliefs contribute to attitudes toward the decision, we need to identify their sources. In particular, we should learn whether they originate from the concessions made to some of protesters' substantial preferences. However, for integrity reasons we could not probe respondents for all information needed to learn whether they benefited personally from the compromise decision.

Therefore, at this stage we must content ourselves with three substantial conclusions about the role of procedural fairness for support maintenance (SMM 1): First, subjective responsiveness beliefs are part of the motivations for why some protesters became more supportive after the decision. Second, political support would likely have increased more post-decision if more protesters had perceived that politicians were acting responsively. Third, it is not clear what actions from politicians (besides making further concessions) would have generated such perceptions.

10.6.2 SMM 3: With Time, Unwelcome Decisions Fade in Protesters' Memory

The third panel wave (T3) was conducted in October 2011, more than six months after the formal decision was taken. By then, changes in the school system had been in effect since the beginning of the new school year in August. Thus, protesting Suburbians and their children had time to adapt to the new conditions. However, as can be seen from Figure 10.3, and contrary to SMM 3, neither of the two camps of protesters who had formed immediately after the decision moved further toward regained political support. In fact, there was no systematic change at all between T2 and T3 (Figure 10.1 and Appendices: Table 10.1). Moreover, attitudes toward the compromise decision in March remained stable in October: among those who were negative at T2 only twenty percent had developed a positive attitude toward the decision in T3.

Given recurrent findings in the critical events literature about decaying effects (Brody 1991; Hetherington and Nelson 2003; Dinesen and Jæger 2013), and strong theories to back them up (Hetherington and Husser 2012; Schade and Baum 2007), the lack of support for SMM 3 is surprising. To some extent the surprising outcome can be attributed to idiosyncrasies in the case of Suburbia: some parts of the decision were to be implemented the following year, and the local administration had made changes during the process. This means that protesters were continuously reminded about the decision. However, this uncertainty cannot account for the lack of movement among protesters who accepted the compromise decision. Rather, the lack of change between T2 and T3 is a further indication that the cutback proposal generated long-lasting effect among protesters.

10.6.3 SMM 4: A Vertical Division of Power Contains Dissatisfaction to Singular Branches of Government

Arguably, policy controversies are less malign for political support if citizen dissatisfaction targets the governmental branch that is directly responsible for the unwelcome proposal. To see whether this is the case, Figure 10.4 shows the

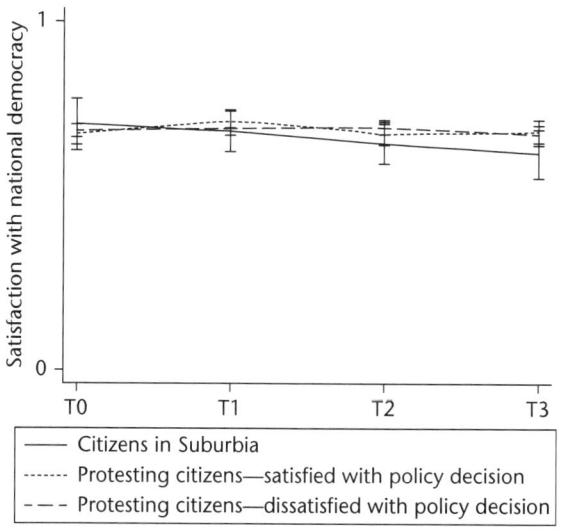

Figure 10.4 Satisfaction with national democracy (SWD$_{national}$)

development of satisfaction with national democracy for all citizen groups at T1–T4 (we refer to Appendices: Table 10.2 for detailed statistics).

Interestingly, as evidenced by three essentially flat time-series, the events in Suburbia did not spill over to satisfaction with national level democracy. This is in line with SMM 4, but surprising to the many literatures that find that citizens' attitudes seldom reflect finer distinctions in politics. If the finding is robust, and if it generalizes to national level politics as well, it has important implications. It would mean that institutional arrangements for vertical division of power help to maintain the overall level of support in a polity. Precisely, the support undermining effects of controversial policy proposals can be contained to the governmental body that is directly responsible.

10.7 Conclusion

This chapter directs attention to controversial policy proposals that trigger opposition among citizens. These situations are strenuous for the relationship between citizens and politicians. Citizens are reminded that, no matter how strongly they feel about the issue in question, they have no formal say over the decision. Politicians, in turn, must endure the ordeal of defending their proposal in a context of demonstrations and other expressions of citizen discontent. We argue that the dynamics of these situations deserve attention when researching the legitimacy of representative democracies.

Results from our case study of protesters in the Swedish municipality Suburbia confirm that policy controversies are critical events for those involved. According to our estimates, political support among protesters (as measured by satisfaction with local democracy) decreased by twenty percent as a result of the controversial proposal. After politicians decided on a compromise solution, those who had a positive view of the decision became more supportive but they did not fully regain their pre-conflict level of support. Those who remained negative to the compromise decision had not become more supportive after the decision was implemented six months later. The control group changed only little throughout the process.

In the chapter, we identify support maintaining mechanisms that may work toward regained levels of support in the wake of policy controversies. We find that policy concessions help to rebuild support among some protesters (presumably among those whose personal preferences were fulfilled), and that the effect of policy concessions are mediated by beliefs that politicians have been responsive during the decision-making process. We also find that multilevel constitutional arrangements are helpful for support maintenance in that protesters' support for the national level polity remained intact throughout the process. Surprisingly, we cannot confirm that support is maintained by saliency reduction as time goes by.

Overall, we observe substantial movement in political support in the wake of a local policy controversy. In support of the research that ties political legitimacy to regime performance, our findings indicate that politicians are not easily forgiven for interfering negatively in citizens' daily lives. Drawing out even wider implications, the handling of policy controversies (as well as other critical events) may help to explain country differences in levels and trends of political support.

However, before drawing strong conclusions we need replication studies. Although we argue that Suburbia shares basic characteristics with other relevant instances, outcomes in particular cases are produced by both systematic and non-systematic factors. For example, our case study could not fully consider the lengthy character of the implementation process that continued after we had finished our data collection.

Awaiting further empirical explorations, we end by reminding about other policy areas than the welfare state in which elected representatives clash with strongly held preferences among citizens. Proposals to increase taxes, to regulate lifestyles, and to site infrastructural ventures are some examples of critical events within normal politics. We maintain that researchers interested in the legitimacy of representative democracies have much to gain from taking a closer look at these recurring controversies.

To study such phenomena as they develop in real time requires data that are hard to obtain. Our suggested "fire house" approach to data collection uses the flexibility of web surveys along with auxiliary cross-sectional surveys with nationally representative samples. To develop that approach, it is important to learn more about the validity of artificial T0 measures (Todosijevic 2012). But there are many alternative ways forward. Opinion scholars have always been able to find data to study political support in relation to terrorist attacks and other extraordinary critical events. If that creativity is used to study policy controversies, we will learn important things about citizens' relationships to their elected representatives, and about what explains fluctuations in citizens' political support.

This chapter concludes Part 3 of the book in which we tried to assess what (new) explanations can account for differences in legitimacy between established democracies. The three previous chapters examined the effect of macro level, in particular institutional factors on levels and trends of support in different countries. In this chapter we examined how important specific events can be for the level and development of political support. Supplementing the previous chapters in this part of the book we found that grievances resulting from an unwelcome authoritative intervention in peoples' lives impact negatively on political support. We also find that perceptions of the fairness of the processes leading up to the intervention are an important mediator between the event and support attitudes. Overall, our results suggest that future research should acknowledge that procedural fairness assessments are at least partly endogenous to the substantial outcomes people receive.

Notes

1. The research reported in the chapter was financed by MOD (Multidisciplinary Opinion and Democracy Research Group) at University of Gothenburg and by Grant no. P10–0210:1 from Riksbankens Jubileumsfond (the Swedish Bank of Tercentenary Foundation). We thank Sofie Marien, Chris Wlezien, book editors, and other contributors to the book for valuable suggestions, and Maria Andreasson and Sebastian Lundmark for their efforts when collecting the data. Earlier versions of the text were presented at the 2012 and 2014 Annual Midwestern Meetings in Chicago.
2. It is, of course, hard to say how the results would have turned out if everyone had responded. However, comparisons between those who responded to all survey waves compared to those who did not does not show any significant differences on key variables such as gender and education.
3. Considering the small sample size (n = 50), we included parents (according to self-reports, twenty-seven of fifty respondents in the control had children in their home, of which ten reported that they were affected by the proposal). As a robustness check, we re-estimated our models deleting all parents from the control and results are substantially similar (results are available on request).
4. We refer to Appendices: Table 10.3 for detailed statistics.
5. As expected, this tendency is stronger among protesters who found the compromise decision satisfactory (see Appendices Table 10.3).
6. Formally, the model looks as follows: $SWD_{local}T2 = \alpha + \beta1SWD_{local}T1 + \beta2Decision\ viewT2 + \beta3Responsiveness\ action + \varepsilon$.
7. See also Esaiasson, Gilljam, and Persson (2016).

Part IV
Reflections and Conclusions

11

Studying Political Legitimacy

Findings, Implications, and an Uneasy Question

Rudy B. Andeweg and Kees Aarts

11.1 Introduction

In 399 BC, Socrates was found guilty of impiety and corrupting the youth of Athens, and sentenced to death by drinking hemlock. While he awaited his execution, he was visited in prison by one of his friends, Crito, who had made arrangements for Socrates to escape and go into exile. Socrates refused, not because he feared that an attempt to break out of prison would be unsuccessful or would have dire consequences for Crito and himself, nor because he agreed with the sentence, but because he regarded the laws and government under which he was convicted as legitimate. In Plato's account of the conversation, Socrates argues that the city of Athens has provided him, like all other citizens, with a "share of all the good things" the city had to offer. After reaching adulthood, every Athenian is free to "take his possessions and go wherever he pleases." However, when he stays—as Socrates did all his life—he has factually agreed to obey the city's rules. Even then, these very rules leave open the possibility of persuading the city that its decision was wrong. But after the trial has been concluded and the verdict made, as in Socrates's case, he must accept that verdict (Crito 51c–52e).

The story illustrates the importance of legitimacy: without it, a government is either limited to do only what all citizens agree with in the first place (and then government is redundant), or it is condemned to rely solely on coercion (and then even an authoritarian government is not viable). This is the reason why so many are so concerned about a perceived erosion of political legitimacy in recent decades, and why the study of legitimacy takes such a prominent place in political science.

This book aims to take stock of what that study has brought to light. It evaluates in a systematic fashion the empirical evidence for legitimacy decline in established democracies, it reappraises the validity of theories of legitimacy decline, and it explores what (new) explanations can account for differences between established democracies.

This chapter brings our findings together, to summarize what this book contributes to the already-extensive body of literature on this topic, but also to reflect on the implications of our findings for politicians and citizens who do fear a legitimacy crisis, and for political scientists planning future studies in this field.

11.2 What Have We Learned?

Political legitimacy is a complex concept. Over decades of empirical, survey-based research, legitimacy has been operationalized predominantly as political support. In order to engage with this literature, we, too, focused on political support, and operationalized it in terms of satisfaction with the working of democracy, trust in parliament, etc. As discussed in Chapter 1, we realize that political support is not identical to political legitimacy, but argue that legitimacy is the most important source of political support (we will return to this question later). The key question underlying most studies of political support is whether it has indeed declined in recent decades. This question is addressed by Van Ham and Thomassen in Chapter 2. Using various data sources (Eurobarometer, World Values Study, European Values Study) they find no evidence for a secular decline in political support across established democracies for the third of a century from the mid-1970s or early 1980s to 2015. Support for the political community is strong and growing in thirteen out of sixteen countries studied. Support for the principle of democracy is widespread and shows little variation across countries or across time. Support for the practice of democracy (satisfaction with the working of democracy), however, varies widely, both in terms of country averages and in terms of trends within countries. Yet, the overall picture is one of considerable satisfaction with an upward rather than a downward trend in eleven countries. Support for political institutions presents a less rosy picture. Here too, there is considerable variation and fluctuation, but more than half the countries studied experienced a decline of trust in parliament, especially in the most recent decade. Trust in political parties is indeed quite low, but for the relatively short period for which we have data for this variable there does not seem to be a downward trend. Finally, trust in political authorities, measured as trust in the national government, mirrors the finding for trust in parliament. In conclusion, it appears that the pattern for the political regime (support for, and satisfaction with democracy) differs from that for specific institutions and authorities. Support for the regime looks healthy, while support for institutions and authorities shows a modest decline, at least in recent years, and in most countries. The lack of a universal trend, and the considerable variation between countries and fluctuation over time, lead us to reject the hypothesis that political support is in secular decline across established democracies. This does not imply, of course, that there are no reasons for concern about political support in these countries.

That core finding set the agenda for the remainder of the book: Chapters 3 to 6 look back at what went wrong in empirical research into the causes of a legitimacy decline that did not occur, and Chapters 7 to 10 look forward at potential explanations for the variation and fluctuation that do take place. First, the lack of evidence for a universal and consistent erosion of political support prompted a reassessment of various theories that offered plausible explanations for a decline that was presumed, but that did not take place. We selected from the literature some of the strongest contenders: modernization, globalization, eroding social capital, weakening political parties, and changes in political coverage by the media. For each of these theories, potentially two explanations can account for their "failure": either the social developments that supposedly caused a decline in political support also did not take place, or they did occur but the presumptions about the underlying mechanisms linking the social development (globalization, media malaise, etc.) to declining support at the level of individual citizens were flawed.

There is evidence for both these explanations, depending on whether we are looking at modernization and globalization, or at the other three theories (social capital, political parties, media). That modernization and globalization actually have occurred is not in doubt. Modernization is a multifaceted phenomenon, and in Chapter 3, Aarts et al. focused on two of these aspects: cognitive mobilization and value change. Using the age until which respondents received full-time education, the Eurobarometers from the 1970s until 2015 show an impressive increase in the proportion of longer (thus presumably higher) educated citizens in all countries studied. Similarly, in all but a few countries, the proportion of the electorate espousing materialist values has decreased while the proportion holding post-materialist values has increased. Turning to economic globalization, they report data showing a clear increase in economic globalization in all established democracies in their sample (with the exception of Luxembourg where the standard index of economic globalization started at such a high level that there was hardly any room for a further increase).

The evidence for a decline of social capital and a weakening of parties, and a rise of negative reporting on politics in the media is less clearcut. In Chapter 4, Hooghe and Kern accept that civil society is mobilized to a lesser extent into traditional organizations based on social cleavages, but they argue that especially younger generations use new, looser types of organizations. As a result, people are differently involved, not less involved. Comparing two recent points in time, they also find no overall decline in the proportion reporting activity in voluntary or charitable organizations. In a related fashion, Andeweg and Farrell qualify reports of a decline of parties in Chapter 5. There has been a substantial decline of formal party membership between 1980 and 2008 but many parties have developed alternative opportunities to support them, and other indicators of partisanship present a more varied pattern. The linkage function of political parties in particular, does not appear to have weakened substantially. Political parties may have undergone a transformation rather than a decline. In Chapter 6, Van Aelst also casts doubt on the notion that the role of the media has fundamentally changed and that this change has led to a decline of political support. The media do not always and everywhere increasingly use a negative frame when they bring political news. To the extent that such a "media malaise" is real, it occurred before the 1990s and has leveled off since, and it was concentrated primarily in the reporting of elections. Moreover, it remains to be established to what extent negativity in political reporting was initiated by the media, or constituted an accurate account of politicians' changing communication strategies. Recently, the concern about a media malaise has shifted from negative reporting to structural changes in the media landscape that allow citizens to avoid exposure to political reporting altogether, especially in the US.

The question whether the theories explaining a decline in political support were mistaken because they supposed underlying mechanisms that did not exist presents a mirror image. Aarts et al. find no evidence for either modernization or globalization weakening political support. The two theories present rival hypotheses with regard to education levels. Modernization theory leads us to expect a growing proportion of highly educated, hence critical citizens, while globalization theory expects the lower educated to have suffered from the impact of globalization, and to feel alienated from a political regime that did not protect them from shifting production to low-wage countries and from immigration of low-wage labor. Using satisfaction with the working of democracy over a forty-year period as their dependent variable, they find no evidence for either hypothesis. Satisfaction with democracy has increased among the higher educated in all established democracies in their sample. Among the lower educated, satisfaction with democracy declined in three out of nine countries in the sample, but *increased* in all the other cases. To the extent that there is support for the globalization thesis, in most countries the increase in satisfaction with democracy has been less pronounced among the lower educated than among the higher educated, generating a widening "satisfaction gap" between the two categories of citizens.

There is more evidence for the mechanisms linking social capital, partisanship, and consuming political news to political support. Using ESS data from 2006 and 2012 Hooghe and Kern find a clear and significant correlation between social involvement on the one hand and satisfaction with the working of democracy and political trust on the other hand, which largely survives the introduction of a range of control variables. Using ESS data from 2002 to 2010 on partisanship, Andeweg and Farrell find a difference between their two independent variables—party membership and party closeness: although the contribution of both variables to the explanation of political support is unimpressive, being close to a particular party is much more important than being a member of a political party. They argue that closeness to a party should not be interpreted as a form of party attachment or even party identification, but rather as a sign that the party system as a whole facilitates citizens in making a meaningful political choice by allowing them to identify a party that is closer to them than other parties. Both these two chapters, however, also warn that it may be too easy to see the arrow of causality pointing exclusively from social involvement or partisanship to political support. Hooghe and Kern argue that social involvement may be linked to political trust by self-selection rather than by socialization. And Andeweg and Farrell mention that a loss of political support may equally well lead to a decline in party closeness as the other way around.

Reviewing a variety of experiments, Van Aelst concludes that negative political news does have a modest impact on political support once controlled for level of education, but that effect can be both positive and negative, depending on the medium, the receiver, and the indicator of political support. For example, more general indicators of political trust appear to be less affected, and actual behavior (political participation) may even be positively affected by negative news. People tune in to different media, and political support seems to cluster together with higher levels of education and a preference for public broadcasting.

Summarizing the findings so far, our evaluation of theories of legitimacy decline suggests that processes of modernization and globalization did indeed occur, but that empirical evidence for the micro-level causal link between modernization, globalization, and political support is weaker. Conversely, there is less compelling evidence that processes of eroding social capital, weakening political parties, and changes in political coverage by the media actually occurred as often presumed. There is more empirical evidence for the proposed micro-level causal mechanisms between social capital, partisanship, and media consumption, and political support, although the direction of causation is ambiguous and media effects in particular appear to be contingent on message, messenger, and receiver.

The core finding that there is variation and fluctuation in political support rather than a structural and universal decline not only led us to reassess the social developments previously assumed to be related to legitimacy, but also prompted a search for explanations of the differences in levels and trends. Here, too, we selected some of the strongest contenders: variation in political institutions, in the quality of government, in economic outcomes, and in policy controversies. All four variables appear to affect political support, but not to the same extent. Bowler, for example, warns that we should not expect too much of institutional design. While decentralization and a high number of representatives per head of the population have no significant impact, electoral systems that provide voters with more choice about candidates (rather than just parties), multiparty governments, and "responsive" legislatures (i.e. parliaments that are unicameral and have relatively short terms) do correlate positively with satisfaction with the working of democracy and trust in parliament and politicians. But the effects are modest. Perhaps institutions do affect the political support of particular groups of citizens, or perhaps institutions are further down the causal chain, affecting political support only indirectly. Anyhow, the widely held belief that political support is strongly dependent on the institutional design of representative democracy needs to be qualified.

Magalhães questions another widely held belief about the causes of political support, that "it is the economy, stupid." Relating aggregate indicators of GDP growth, inflation, unemployment, and the budget deficit to satisfaction with the working of democracy, he does find an overall effect of economic performance, but in some countries this effect is statistically insignificant, while in other countries it is significant and substantial. What sets these two categories of countries apart is the quality of government. Where this is high, the impact of economic indicators is marginal, but where the quality of government is low, political support is quite sensitive to economic outcomes. In their study of the effect of policy controversies, Esaiasson et al. find a similar interaction between outcome favorability and procedural fairness. Within the general category of "critical events," they focus on the impact of the introduction of a controversial policy on satisfaction with the working of democracy. The cross-national analysis of survey data, on which the other chapters in this volume rely, is ill-suited for the study of the effect of a critical event. Esaiasson et al. therefore use a natural experiment: a case study of the decision to close several schools by a Swedish local government—a plan that had not been mentioned during the preceding election campaign. Tracking satisfaction with local democracy over time after the decision among both the town's general population and among those protesting the policy, they find an immediate twenty percent drop in satisfaction among the protesters, and no such drop in the control group. For most of the protesters, this loss of support was still visible after half a year. However, the local government eventually offered a compromise solution, and this did repair some of the damage. Esaiasson et al. conclude that this partial recovery of political support was caused by agreement with the compromise solution, but also by the belief that the local government had been responsive in terms of listening to the protests and explaining the decision.

The importance of the quality of government for political support is further underlined by Van der Meer's analysis, correlating expert judgments of the impartiality of the bureaucracy, the independence of the judiciary, the professionalism of the bureaucracy, and lack of corruption with citizens' satisfaction with the working of democracy and trust in parliament. Of these indicators, it is the impartiality of policy implementation by the national bureaucracy that stands out as a consistently significant, robust, and strong predictor of satisfaction and trust. One of the surprising findings is that the impact of the level of corruption—generally regarded as the strongest determinant of variation in political support—is greatly reduced once impartiality of the bureaucracy is included in the analysis.

Given the different research designs, it is difficult to compare the impact of controversial policies to that of institutions, economic performance, and quality of government. A provisional conclusion is that quality of government and policy controversies appear to hold most promise for explaining the variation and fluctuation in political support.

11.3 Implications for Politics

These findings have important practical implications for the current public debate about political legitimacy, and for attempts to strengthen political legitimacy. It would not be an exaggeration to say that the focus of the current public debate is on a long-term and structural erosion of political support, and on its causes. This study, and Chapter 2 in particular, has shown that such a focus is misplaced, at least for European established democracies in the past third of a century. This should be welcome news for all who are concerned about legitimacy for at least two reasons. First, of various possible scenarios a structural and universal weakening of legitimacy would have been the most threatening for democracy. And second, most of the theories designed to explain the decline (modernization, globalization, individualization, party decline, media developments) centered on long-term social and political developments that are not easily reversed or mitigated by reform. Finding no support for the thesis of a structural weakening of political support also implies a rejection of these putative causes. True, this project also found some evidence for parts of some of these theories: satisfaction with the working of democracy increased less among the lower educated, and those who are socially involved show higher levels of democratic satisfaction and political trust, as do citizens who feel close to a specific political party. If we forget for the moment the doubts about the direction of causality for social involvement and partisanship, these findings alert us to the fact that political support is not distributed equally across all groups in society, and that some groups appear to become more easily dissatisfied with the functioning of democracy, or to lose trust in political institutions more easily than other groups.

The new diagnosis proffered in this book is that levels of political support vary across countries and fluctuate. Although this outlook is less bleak than that of a structural decline of support, it is still cause for concern. Fortunately, the most likely causes for this variation and fluctuation are not beyond repair. The hypothesized cause that would be most difficult to manipulate in today's globalized economy, economic performance, proved to be relatively unimportant, provided the quality of government is high. Quality of government, operationalized as an impartial state bureaucracy, appears to have most explanatory power. Examples are a bureaucracy in which public procurement contracts are relatively immune to kickbacks to senior officials, in which civil servants treat all groups in society fairly, in which applications for licenses are decided upon regardless of personal connections, and in which civil servants act impartially in individual cases. Another potential cause for a decrease of political support is a policy controversy. Of course, unpopular policies cannot be avoided at all times, but the good news is that investing in explaining the policy to citizens, in listening to their criticisms, and in taking some of their concerns on board do appear to mitigate the negative impact of a policy controversy on political support.

Currently, institutional reform and electoral system reform in particular are often suggested as the measure of choice to foster political legitimacy. However, the finding that institutional variation has but a modest impact on political support implies that such reforms are unlikely to provide a prime solution for countries where political support has ebbed. This is a counter-intuitive finding, even more if seen in combination with the important role played by bureaucratic impartiality. Understandably, when it comes to maintaining or improving democratic legitimacy most attention so far focused on the input side of politics, on the institutional design of political representation. This study indicates that most potential for improvement is rather to be found on the output side—in impartiality and procedural fairness.

In conclusion, both the diagnosis of variation and fluctuation rather than structural decline, and the importance of impartiality rather than representation, require a major reorientation in our thinking about the prevention or reparation of low legitimacy.

11.4 Implications for Political Science

This book aims to take stock of the state of the art in studying political legitimacy in established democracies; it does not pretend to offer the last word. As always the analyses in this book leave us with loose ends and new questions. Some conclusions in this book definitely require further research. Both Van Aelston—the effect of media reporting, and Esaiasson et al. on the effect of a policy controversy—call for more studies and for more replications. Whereas most chapters use survey data from several points in time and several countries, these two chapters rely almost exclusively on experiments, both natural and in the laboratory. It is inherent to this research strategy that more such studies are needed in order to be able to generalize. Do policy controversies have a similar effect when the contested policy decision is announced in the ruling party's election manifesto, or when it affects other policy domains, or when it is a decision taken by the national government rather than a local authority? And do we see similar patterns in other established democracies than Sweden? Van Aelst also points to relatively new developments in the media domain for which only few studies are available: does political news that is disseminated via the social media have the same effect on political support as news reporting by the "classic" media? And what is the effect of the multiplication of media outlets allowing citizens to "zap away" from being exposed to any political news?

Not surprisingly, most of the chapters that are based on survey evidence have the opposite problem. Their main concern is not generalizability, but establishing causality, as they find only correlations. Sometimes the question for future research is about the direction of causality. Hooghe and Kern, and Andeweg and Farrell question whether the correlations found between social and partisan involvement on the one hand, and political support on the other hand indicate that such involvement produces support, or whether politically supportive citizens are more inclined to become active in social organizations and political parties. The fact that involvement loses some but not all of its effect on support once other variables that are known to affect political support are included is seen as provisional evidence that both mechanisms may be at work. The question is particularly acute with regard to support for parties of the populist right: does involvement with parties that question the legitimacy of the political system lead one to share that view, or do citizens who have lost trust in the system opt to support an antiestablishment party?

In other chapters it is not so much the direction of causality that is at stake, but the underlying mechanism is not yet clear. Aarts et al. find a relationship between level of education and political support that fits neither modernization nor globalization theories. It is unclear why satisfaction with the working of democracy has increased across the board, but at a slower rate among the less educated; is it an interaction of factors pushing in opposite directions? Is it the fact that the general increase in the level of education has changed the composition of the category with low education? In his analysis of the impact of institutions on political support (direct, indirect, and spurious), Bowler calls for studying natural experiments—the effect of institutional reform on political trust and democratic satisfaction—to establish the nature of the relationship. The change of the electoral system of New Zealand from majoritarian to proportional in 1996 provides a well-studied example (Karp and Bowler 2001; Vowles et al. 2013). Magalhães suggests several possible mechanisms to explain why quality of government reduces the vulnerability of political support to economic performance. For example, does high quality of government make it more difficult for citizens to blame the government for economic adversity? Or does it prompt them to adopt a long-term perspective when evaluating democratic government? Van der Meer's puzzle seems to be the most fundamental of all: quality of government as measured by expert surveys is a strong predictor of political support (Thomassen 2014; Rohrschneider 2005), but it is not clear whether it is actually citizens' perception of that quality of government that causes them to be more or less satisfied and trustful. If the effect of bureaucratic impartiality is not mediated by perception, how can we account for this finding? Here, too, the precise causation needs to be further elaborated.

It is questions such as these that may shape the agenda for future studies of political legitimacy.

11.5 An Uneasy Question

To that agenda should be added an uneasy question: why is the belief in a legitimacy crisis so persistent despite earlier reports to the contrary by other scholars? Although the existing literature was not unanimous, studies focusing on the same time period and the same set of established democracies generally arrived at similar conclusions that there is no long-term structural decline of political support. Yet, these findings have done little to alter the belief that there is a legitimacy crisis, a democratic malaise, a *Politikverdrossenheit,* a widening confidence gap, etc. In the Netherlands, for example, surveys of both MPs and voters indicate that about two-thirds agree that a confidence gap between citizens and politics does exist. One might, of course, argue that a widely perceived confidence gap does not logically imply that a crisis of legitimacy is developing, but such nuances easily get lost in the ensuing debate. The legitimacy crisis has some of the characteristics of the Loch Ness monster: there are regular reports of sightings by villagers and tourists, but repeated scientific expeditions using the latest technology all fail to come up with solid evidence. Yet, the belief in the existence of the phenomenon is unaffected. In the words of Van der Walle et al. (2008: 61–2): "The most interesting phenomenon, however, is the strength and tenacity of the policy discourse on a decline in citizens' trust in the public sector. The indicators do not show a decline in public trust in the public sector, yet it is quite generally believed by policy-makers that there is such a decline." Is this imperviousness to empirical evidence a symptom of fact-free politics? Some of the conclusions of earlier studies as quoted by Van Ham and Thomassen in Chapter 2 seem to point in that direction: " . . . an élite discourse without any real mass basis" (Fuchs and Klingemann 1995: 435), " . . . the dangers of fact-free hyperbole" (Norris 2011: 241).

One possibility would be that it is in the interest of some people to keep the myth of a legitimacy crisis alive, just as it is for the local tourist industry in Drumnadrochit to maintain the belief in the Loch Ness monster. Politicians who advocate constitutional reform, for example, stand to lose a powerful ally if the myth is put to rest. So do populist parties who can exploit feelings of cynicism and alienation to further their own cause. And let us not forget the political scientists for whom legitimacy is a key concept of their discipline and who might have a difficult time believing that it is relatively unaffected by what goes on in the rest of the world.

A less cynical possibility is that many are genuinely concerned about developments such as declining turnout in elections, eroding party membership, the rise of populist parties, "Eurosceptic" referendum outcomes such as the 2016 "Brexit" referendum in the UK, etc., and worry that these are symptoms of an underlying legitimacy crisis. Of course, inferring attitudes from behavior is never straightforward, and for each of the developments mentioned alternative explanations are more plausible than a collapse of political support: political involvement may decline because of a general trend of individualization affecting political and non-political organizations indiscriminately; new political issues such as the negative consequences of migration and European integration may be neglected by established parties, leaving the field open for populist parties and referendum surprises. But the label of a legitimacy crisis is, in all its simplicity, more attractive than the nuanced explanation offered by empirical studies.

Both these possibilities can explain the tenacity of the belief in a legitimacy crisis, but can we exclude completely a third possibility, that those most concerned—politicians and citizens—are sensing a development that goes undetected by our studies?

Without detracting from the findings and conclusions of this book, we address that uneasy question by way of a counterfactual: imagine that we would be mistaken, what could have caused that gap between the belief in a legitimacy crisis and our findings? Or put differently, what are the vulnerabilities in the current study of political legitimacy that need to be addressed in future studies? We identify three potential blind spots in current studies.

First, one of the oldest criticisms of behavioralist studies in political science, namely that they suffer from "inputism," may also apply to the empirical study of legitimacy. In our analyses of citizens' attitudes and beliefs about democracy, we tend to prioritize the input-side over the output-side. Democratic politics is operationalized in terms of the representation of political preferences rather than policy outcomes or implementation. It is perhaps telling that one of the strongest predictors of political support proves to be the impartiality of the bureaucracy rather than the representation of partisan interests. In Chapter 2, Van Ham and Thomassen also mention the need to ask more specifically what citizens understand democracy to be. Some of them define democracy in terms completely at odds with any textbook definition. Also, it has been shown time and again since Prothro and Grigg (1960) that people do support abstract principles of popular sovereignty and the rule of law, but that this support dwindles when they are asked to apply those abstract principles to concrete cases. The 2012 edition of the European Social Survey took a major step to address these concerns by asking respondents to indicate the importance of a range of potential aspects of democracy. These did not include bureaucratic impartiality and procedural fairness yet, and the variance of the answers is small, but it is telling that the highest average importance of fourteen "principles of democracy" was attached to the principle "The courts treat everyone the same" (mean: 9.25 on an eleven-point scale) whereas the principle "Different political parties offer clear alternatives to one another" ranks near the bottom (although still quite high in absolute terms: mean 8.0) (see Chapter 7, Table 7.1; and Ferrin and Kriesi 2016). It may well be that, when confronted with a question about their satisfaction with how democracy works in their country, respondents answer that question with the quality of government rather than the quality of representation in mind. Specifically differentiating between the evaluations of democracy-as-representation and democracy-as-procedural-fairness may elicit more valid indications of the state of political support in a country at a particular time.

A second vulnerability regards the relationship between political legitimacy and political support. Legitimacy is an elusive concept, but the most usual definitions involve the normative justification of authority—that is what caused Socrates to accept the verdict and drink the hemlock (compare Friedrich 1963). However, what is most usually measured is diffuse support for the political regime—primarily satisfaction with the working of democracy and trust in political institutions such as parliament (Weatherford 1992). Legitimacy and political support are closely related, yet not identical. In their introductory chapter, Thomassen and Van Ham argue that political support is the broader of the two concepts: legitimacy is a purely normative judgment.

A positive evaluation of the regime contributes to satisfaction and trust, but political support may also derive from instrumental considerations—from a running tally of experiences with the regime. The indicators of political support that we employ are thus based on a mixture of normative and instrumental considerations. For example, in Chapter 10, Esaiasson et al. found satisfaction with the working of (local) democracy to drop sharply among the opponents of the school closures announced by the local government. It seems plausible that purely instrumental considerations can account for most of that drop, but normative judgments may also have played a role: the controversial policy had not been part of the election manifesto and was only announced after the elections, and this lack of a democratic mandate for the policy may have led some to question the authorities' justification. The conditional effect of economic performance on political support that Magalhães discussed in Chapter 9 is another example of the interaction between normative (procedural justice) and instrumental (outcome favorability) considerations. Theoretically, it is possible that the lack of a structural decline in political support can be attributed to positive instrumental considerations masking a decline in moral justification, or the other way around. It would be important to distinguish these two components of political support more clearly in future research.

These first two blind spots—the emphasis on the input side of politics and the neglect of normative evaluations as a source of legitimacy—are related to the longitudinal design of most studies of legitimacy: in order to assess whether legitimacy is in decline or not, we need to follow legitimacy beliefs over a long period of time. Hence we have to rely on surveys that have included the same questions, using the same answering categories at several points in time. It is generally recognized that some of these questions are far from ideal. For example, the question "How satisfied are you with the way democracy works in [your country"] has long been criticized as being ambiguous and tapping into very different types of support, including support for the incumbents (e.g. Canache et al. 2001; Linde and Ekman 2003). Some of the questions on trust in institutions are equally suspect. Questions about trust in political parties, or in politicians, ask respondents to evaluate entire categories, while it is likely that their evaluations will vary across items within a category. In elections, voters are explicitly asked to choose between parties or politicians and they may even base that choice wholly or partially on that candidate's or party's perceived trustworthiness. We do not know what happens when we ask indiscriminately about the trustworthiness of "parties" and of "politicians": is the question interpreted to focus on their preferred party, or on the other parties, or do voters arrive at some average somehow? Even questions about trust in a single institution, e.g. parliament, may suffer from this ambiguity.

It is not too difficult to develop indicators that take such criticisms on board, just as it is not impossible to broaden our range of indicators to include procedural justice and impartiality as well as normative evaluations. The problem here is not collective laziness (attempts at improved measurements are easily found, for example in the World Values Survey and the 2012 European Social Survey; see also Weatherford 1992, Ferrin and Kriesi 2016), but the simple fact that we cannot travel back in time. We cannot return to, say, the early 1970s and ask survey respondents of the time to answer our improved questions. Legitimacy studies are captives of indicators developed long ago. We comfort ourselves with the thought that any bias caused by the imperfections of these indicators is likely to be a constant, still allowing us to detect trends.

A third and final blind spot of the current study of legitimacy refers to the very core of the longitudinal design: the assumption that the operational meaning of the indicators used remains constant, and is not affected by political or social developments. For example, the wording of survey questions about political parties may not have changed over time, but political parties themselves may have undergone a transformation. More generally, the democratic systems of which we aim to assess the legitimacy have evolved considerably since our time series started. Most of our questions refer to domestic democracy, institutions, and political authorities at the national level. During the past third of a century, European integration has created a new layer of political decision-making. Meanwhile, many of the countries studied have embarked on a process of decentralization, in some countries even federalization. Such developments do not render questions about, for example, the way national democracy works irrelevant, but the object of such a question in 2016 is no longer identical to the object of the same question in the 1970s. The longer the time series, the bigger the risk that keeping our survey questions unchanged actually reduces comparability over time, and in that sense the availability of longitudinal data about political support over such a long time period may be a poisoned chalice.

However, the core finding of this book that legitimacy is likely to vary and fluctuate rather than to be in a structural and universal decline, considerably reduces both the need for a long time series and the path dependency of legitimacy studies. Even a single cross-sectional study in several countries using new and better indicators allows us to study the causes of variation in legitimacy beliefs across countries, and even a few such studies allow us to study the causes of short-term fluctuation in legitimacy beliefs. Thus, this volume does not only identify important new questions about political legitimacy for future studies, but it also makes it possible to address these new questions without the constraints of imperfect and incomplete indicators bequeathed by our predecessors.

Appendices

Appendices to Chapter 2

Appendices: Table 2.A Sample

Country[a]	EES (1989–2014)	Eurobarometer (1973–2015)	WVS/EVS[b] (1980–2010)	ANES (1958–2012)
Austria	X	X	X	
Belgium	X	X	X	
Denmark	X	X	X	
Finland	X	X	X	
France	X	X	X	
Germany	X	X	X	
Greece	X	X	X	
Ireland	X	X	X	
Italy	X	X	X	
Luxembourg	X	X	X	
Netherlands	X	X	X	
Portugal	X	X	X	
Spain	X	X	X	
Sweden	X	X	X	
United Kingdom	X	X	X	
United States			X	X

a. Note that several of these datasets, such as the WVS/EVS and the ESS include more countries. We only provide an overview here of the countries analyzed in this paper, i.e. 15 European democracies and the United States.

b. Note that due to similar question wording for all of the political support questions WVS and EVS were analyzed together. Since WVS waves of surveys were conducted in 1981–84 (1st wave), 1989–1993 (2nd wave), 1994–99 (3rd wave), 1999–2004 (4th wave), 2005–7 (5th wave), and 2010–14 (5th wave); and EVS waves of surveys in 1981–84 (1st wave), 1990–93 (2nd wave), 1999–2001 (3rd wave) and 2008–10 (4th wave); in the combined data the 3rd wave of EVS is recoded as 4th wave, and the last wave of EVS is recoded as 6th wave, so that the data match each other in terms of the time period in which they were collected and follow each other chronologically. In terms of years used in the graphs, we code wave 1 as 1980, wave 2 as 1990, wave 3 as 1995, wave 4 as 2000, wave 5 as 2005, and wave 6 as 2010.

Appendices: Table 2.B Question wording political support questions

Level of support Dataset	Question wording	Data coding
Political community[a]		
WVS/EVS	"How proud are you to be (nationality/a nationality citizen)?" Answer categories: very proud, quite proud, not very proud, not at all proud. (1st , 2nd, 3rd, 4th, 5th , 6th wave)	% very and quite proud
Eurobarometer	"Would you say you are very proud, quite proud, not very proud, not at all proud, to be (nationality)?" In 1982 question ends: "to be a citizen of our country?" (asked from 1982 until 2006, in 17 EBs, in 16 years, note that if there were multiple EBs in one year, we took the average score for that year)	% very and quite proud
Political regime		
Principles		
WVS/EVS	"I'm going to describe various types of political systems and ask what you think about each as a way of governing this country?. For each one, would you say it is a very good, fairly good, fairly bad or very bad way of governing this country?": "Having a democratic political system." (3rd, 4th, 5th, 6th wave)	% very good and fairly good % agree strongly and agree
	"I'm going to read off some things that people sometimes say about a democratic political system. Could you please tell me if you agree strongly, agree, disagree or disagree strongly, after I read each one of them?": "Democracy may have problems but it's better than any other form of government." (3rd, 4th, 5th, 6th wave)	
Eurobarometer[b]	"Here are three opinions about political systems. Which one comes closest to your own way of thinking?" • Democracy is the best political system in all circumstances • In certain circumstances a dictatorship could be a good thing (EB 47.1: can be preferable to democracy) • Whether we live (EB 47.1: Living) in a democracy or under a dictatorship makes no difference to people like me." (asked in 3 EBs in 1988, 1992, 1997)	% prefer democracy
Performance		
EES	"On the whole, are you very satisfied, fairly satisfied, not very satisfied, or not at all satisfied with the way democracy works in your country?" (1989, 1994, 1999)	% very and fairly satisfied
	"On the whole, how satisfied are you with the way democracy works in {country}? Are you: very satisfied, fairly satisfied, not very satisfied, or not at all satisfied?" (2004, 2009)	
Eurobarometer[c]	"On the whole, are you very satisfied, fairly satisfied, not very satisfied or not at all satisfied with the way democracy works (in your country)?" (asked from 1973 until 2014, in 73 EBs, 7 excluded from analysis, leaving 66 EBs in 38 years. Note that if there were multiple EBs in one year, we took the average score for that year)	% very and fairly satisfied

Some more notes on question wording for EBs that were included:

- ECS73: "A few more areas of interest, are you very satisfied, fairly satisfied, not very satisfied, or not at all satisfied with the way democracy is functioning in (country)?"
- EB47.1: "Would you say that you are very satisfied…"
- EB49, EB51.0, EB52.0, EB53.0, EB54.1, EB56.1, EB56.2: Wording without question following.

Political institutions

Parliament

WVS/EVS	"I am going to name a number of organizations. For each one, could you tell me how much confidence you have in them: is it a great deal of confidence, quite a lot of confidence, not very much confidence or none at all?" · "Parliament". · (all waves: 1st , 2nd, 3rd, 4th, 5th , 6th wave)	% a great deal and quite a lot of confidence
Eurobarometer[d]	(asked from 1997 until 2014, in 30 EBs for national parliament; we leave 3 EBs out, leaving: 32 EBs, covering 17 years. Note that if there were multiple EBs in one year, we took the average score for that year) "I would like to ask you a question about how much trust you have in certain institutions. For each of the following institutions, please tell me if you tend to trust it or tend not to trust it." "The national Parliament (use proper name)"	% tend to trust

Political parties

WVS/EVS	I am going to name a number of organizations. For each one, could you tell me how much confidence you have in them: is it a great deal of confidence, quite a lot of confidence, not very much confidence or none at all?" "Political parties" (all waves except the first waves) . "The government in [Your Capital]" .	% a great deal and quite a lot of confidence
Eurobarometer[e]	(Asked from 1997 until 2014, in 34 EBs for political parties, we exclude 5 EBs, leaving 31 EBs for political parties, covering 17 years. Note that if there were multiple EBs in one year, we took the average score for that year.) "I would like to ask you a question about how much trust you have in certain institutions. For each of the following institutions, please tell me if you tend to trust it or tend not to trust it." "Political parties"	% tend to trust

Political authorities

National government

Eurobarometer[e]	(Asked from 1997 until 2014, in 37 EBs for national government, we exclude 5 EBs, leaving 32 EBs for national government, covering 16 years. Note that if there were multiple EBs in one year, we took the average score for that year.) "I would like to ask you a question about how much trust you have in certain institutions. For each of the following institutions, please tell me if you tend to trust it or tend not to trust it." "The (national) government"	% tend to trust

(continued)

Appendices: Table 2.B Continued

Level of support Dataset	Question wording	Data coding
WVS/EVS	"I am going to name a number of organizations. For each one, could you tell me how much confidence you have in them: is it a great deal of confidence, quite a lot of confidence, not very much confidence or none at all?"	% a great deal and quite a lot of confidence
EES	"The government in [Your Capital]." (all waves, except the first wave) "Let us now come back to {country}. Do you approve or disapprove (of) the government's record to date?" (1989, 1999, 2004, 2009, 2014)	% approve
ANES	"How much of the time do you think you can trust the government in Washington to do what is right—just about always, most of the time, or only some of the time?"	% most of the time and just about always

a. In the EES, this question was only asked in the 1989 and 1994 surveys. Not asked in ESS.

b. In the EES, this question was only asked in the 1989 survey. Not asked in ESS.

c. Note that in EB 3, 5, and part of 6, satisfaction with democracy was asked on an 11-point scale. Note also that in EB 30, satisfaction with democracy was asked on a 10-point scale. Finally, in EB 31A this question was asked in a split ballot as follows: Split in EB31A: split ballot A: Standard-Version; split ballot B: "Some people are for the present government (of your country). Others are against it. Putting aside whether you are for or against the present government, on the whole, are you . . . ". Since in all but 1 of these 5 surveys, there were other EBs in the same year in which satisfaction with democracy was asked along the 4-point scale, these 5 surveys were left out of the analyses. Note that if there were multiple EBs in one year, we took the average score for that year. For two other EBs, i.e. EB14 and EB 37.0, while indicated in the data-guide that satisfaction with democracy was asked, the data are not available online, so these were excluded as well.

d. In EB71.3, 72.1, and 74.1, the answer categories varied on a 10-point scale. Since in all these 3 surveys, there were other EBs in the same year in which trust was asked with a dichotomous answering scale, these 3 surveys were left out of the analyses.

e. In EB24 (1985) a different question about trust in the national government was asked in Germany, France, Italy, Great Britain, and Spain. "How much do you trust the (national government) to do what is right? Do you trust it about always, most of the time, only some of the time, or almost never?" In EB50.1 (1998) the following question was asked: "Please tell me how much you trust each of the following: a) your local (city, town, village) government; b) your regional government; c) your national government; d) the European Union. Answer categories: a lot/a great deal of trust, some/a little trust, not very much trust, no trust at all. " Since in both these EBs, not only the answer scale but also the question was phrased differently, these surveys were left out of the analysis. Finally, in EB71.3, 72.1, and 74.1, the answer categories varied on a 10-point scale. Since in all these 3 surveys, there were other EBs in the same year in which trust was asked with a dichotomous answering scale, these 3 surveys were left out of the analyses.

Appendices: Table 2.C Significance time trends

Country / Dataset	National price	Period	T	Satisfaction democracy	Period	T	Trust in parliament	Period	T	Trust in parties	Period	T	Trust in government	Period	T
Austria															
Eurobarometer	0.706+	1997–2006	9	0.473*	1995–2015	19	−0.038	1997–2015	18	0.802**	1997–2014	17	0.053	1997–2015	17
WVS/EVS	−0.183+	1990–2010	3				−0.565	1990–2010	3						
EES				−1.075	1999–2009	3							−1.045	1999–2014	4
Belgium															
Eurobarometer	0.665*	1982–2006	15	0.303*	1973–2015	39	0.527	1997–2015	18	0.682**	1997–2014	17	0.635	1997–2015	17
WVS/EVS	0. 97	1980–2010	4				0.095	1980–2010	4						
EES				0.212	1989–2009	5							0.115	1989–2014	5
Denmark															
Eurobarometer	0.391***	1982–2006	15	0.830***	1973–2015	39	0.040	1997–2015	18	0.431	1997–2014	17	−0.565	1997–2015	17
WVS/EVS	0.537	1980–2010	4				1.076+	1980–2010	4						
EES				1.111*	1989–2009	5							0.831+	1989–2014	5
Finland															
Eurobarometer	0.701**	1997–2006	9	1.121***	1993–2015	21	0.525*	1997–2015	18	1.000***	1997–2014	17	0.232	1997–2015	17
WVS/EVS	0.388*	1980–2010	6				−0.324	1980–2010	6	0.316	1995–2010	3	1.027	1995–2010	3
EES				−0.408	1999–2009	3							−1.047	1999–2014	4
France															
Eurobarometer	0.365*	1982–2006	16	0.246**	1973–2015	39	−0.997**	1997–2015	18	−0.143	1997–2014	17	−0.981**	1997–2015	17
WVS/EVS	0.328*	1980–2010	5				−0.331	1980–2010	5						
EES				0.281	1989–2009	5							−1.465	1989–2014	5
Germany															
Eurobarometer	0.373	1982–2006	16	−0.491**	1973–2015	39	0.317	1997–2015	18	0.423*	1997–2014	17	0.423	1997–2015	17
WVS/EVS	0.317	1980–2010	6				−0.746	1980–2010	6	0.013	1995–2010	3	0.424	1995–2010	3
EES				−0.386	1989–2009	5							0.311	1989–2014	5
Greece															
Eurobarometer	0.244***	1982–2006	15	−0.842***	1981–2015	33	−2.748***	1997–2015	18	−0.999**	1997–2014	17	−2.032**	1997–2015	17
WVS/EVS															
EES				−0.715	1989–2009	5							−0.882	1989–2014	5
Ireland															
Eurobarometer	0.365***	1982–2006	15	0.226+	1973–2015	39	−1.531***	1997–2015	18	−0.789***	1997–2014	17	−1.569***	1997–2015	17
WVS/EVS	0.141	1980–2010	4				−0.261	1980–2010	4						
EES				0.063	1989–2009	5							−1.159	1989–2014	5

(continued)

Appendices: Table 2.C Continued

Country Dataset	National pride	Period	T	Satisfaction democracy	Period	T	Trust in parliament	Period	T	Trust in parties	Period	T	Trust in government	Period	T
Italy															
Eurobarometer	0.295*	1982–2006	16	0.538***	1973–2015	39	-1.551***	1997–2015	18	-0.373	1997–2014	17	-1.242***	1997–2015	17
WVS/EVS	0.251	1980–2010	5				0.135*	1980–2010	5				0.559	1989–2014	5
EES				1.188*	1989–2009	5									
Luxembourg															
Eurobarometer	-0.066	1982–2006	15	0.430***	1973–2015	39	-0.718**	1997–2015	18	-0.074	1997–2014	17	-0.602+	1997–2015	17
WVS/EVS															
EES				0.310	1989–2009	5							-0.604	1989–2014	5
Netherlands															
Eurobarometer	0.307**	1982–2006	16	0.421***	1973–2015	39	-0.696*	1997–2015	18	-0.339	1997–2014	17	-0.949*	1997–2015	17
WVS/EVS	0.692**	1980–2010	5				-0.209	1980–2010	5						
EES				0.199	1989–2009	5							-0.223	1989–2014	5
Portugal															
Eurobarometer	0.158	1985–2006	13	-1.481***	1985–2015	29	-2.497***	1997–2015	18	-0.510**	1997–2014	17	-2.584***	1997–2015	17
WVS/EVS	0.206	1990–2010	3				0.066	1980–2010	3						
EES				-1.636**	1989–2009	5							-2.004*	1989–2014	5
Spain															
Eurobarometer	0.122	1985–2006	13	-0.317	1985–2015	29	-2.889***	1997–2015	18	-1.110*	1997–2014	17	-2.617***	1997–2015	17
WVS/EVS	0.244*	1980–2010	6				0.228	1980–2010	6	-1.536	1990–2010	5	0.555	1990–2010	5
EES				0.964	1989–2009	5							-1.625	1989–2014	5
Sweden															
Eurobarometer	0.710**	1997–2006	9	1.486***	1995–2015	19	1.182***	1997–2015	18	1.271***	1997–2014	17	0.992*	1997–2015	17
WVS/EVS	0.457*	1980–2010	6				0.443*	1980–2010	6	0.026	1995–2010	3	0.642	1995–2010	3
EES				0.527	1999–2009	3									
United Kingdom															
Eurobarometer	0.174*	1982–2006	16	0.240**	1973–2015	39	-0.987**	1997–2015	18	-0.295*	1997–2014	17	-0.930**	1997–2015	17
WVS/EVS	0.120*	1980–2010	5				-0.503	1980–2010	5						
EES				-0.546	1989–2009	5							-0.367	1989–2014	5
United States															
WVS/EVS	-0.175+	1980–2010	6				-1.142**	1980–2010	6	-0.762+	1995–2010	6	0.091	1995–2010	4
ANES													-0.676**	1958–2012	24

Appendices to Chapter 7

Appendices: Table 7.1A Coding of variables

Dependent variables	
Satisfaction with democracy	Ordinal 0–10, 0 = extremely dissatisfied, 10 = extremely satisfied
Trust in parliament	Ordinal 0–10, 0 = no trust at all, 10 = complete trust
Trust in politicians	Ordinal 0–10, 0 = no trust at all, 10 = complete trust

Independent variables	
Individual-level variables	
Close to party in government	Dummy 0–1, 1= close to party in government
Ideological left–right position	Ordinal from 0 to 10, 0 = left, 10 = right
No ideological position	Dummy 0–1, 1 = replied "don't know" to left/right placement
Political interest	Ordinal 0–4, 1 = very interested, 4 = not at all interested
Political participation	Count 0–6, count of number of political activities engaged in including worked for a party; worked for another organization; worn/displayed campaign badge; signed petition, taken part in lawful demonstration; boycotted certain products
Subjective social class	Ordinal 0–10, respondents self-report of "place in society", 0 = 0 Bottom of our society, 10 = Top of our society
Discrimination	Dummy 0–1, 1 = Personally experienced discrimination
Religiosity	Ordinal 1–7, how often attend religious services apart from special occasions: 1 = every day, 7 = never
Age of respondent	Continuous, age in years
Education of respondent	Ordinal 0–7, highest level of education ES–ISCED, 1 = less than lower secondary education, 7 = higher tertiary education
Gender	Dummy variable 0–1, 1 = Female
Institutional variables	
Closed electoral system	Dummy variable 0–1, 1 = Closed electoral system. Coded by author (see Table 7.1B)
Gallagher Index of proportionality of most recent election	Gallagher, source: <http://www.tcd.ie/Political_Science/staff/michael_gallagher/ElSystems/Docts/ElectionIndices.pdf>
Multi-party government	Dummy variable 0–1, 1 = 3 or more parties in government coalition. Coded by author (see Table 7.1B)
Single-party government	Dummy variable 0–1, 1 = 1 party in government. Coded by author (see Table 7.1B)
Legislative responsiveness	Categorical -1 - +1, 1 = unicameral + 4 year term, -1 = bicameral +5-year term; 0 = else. Coded by author (see Table 7.1B)
Seats in legislature per million population	Calculated by author (see Table 7.1B)
Regionalization index	From Marks et al. 2008, minimum = 0 (Iceland), maximum = 28.1 (Belgium)
Performance variables	
Unemployment in 2012	World Bank Development Indicators: national level aggregate data, source: <http://data.worldbank.org/data-catalog/world-development-indicators>
Economic growth in 2012	World Bank Development Indicators: national level aggregate data, source: <http://data.worldbank.org/data-catalog/world-development-indicators>
Corruption in 2012	Transparency International Corruption Perceptions Index, 0–100, 0 = corrupt government, 100 = clean government. Source: <http://www.transparency.org/research/cpi>

Appendices: Table 7.1B Categorization of countries on main institutional measures

Country	Closed electoral system	Multiparty government	Legislative responsiveness unicameral + short term	Regionalism index
Belgium		Y		28.1
Denmark		Y	Y	10.2
Finland		Y	Y	7.1
France		Y		16
Germany				29.3
Iceland			Y	0
Ireland				6
Italy	Y			22.7
Netherlands		Y		14.5
Norway		Y	Y	10
Portugal	Y		Y	3.6
Spain	Y			22.1
Sweden		Y	Y	10
Switzerland		Y		7
UK				9.5

Source: Author's own coding and Marks et al. 2008.

Appendices: Table 7.2A Satisfaction with democracy

	(1)	(2)	(3)	(4)	(5)
Individual-level variables					
Close to governing party		0.527**	0.526**	0.527**	0.526**
		(0.032)	(0.032)	(0.032)	(0.032)
Left–right self-placement		0.042**	0.042**	0.042**	0.042**
		(0.006)	(0.006)	(0.006)	(0.006)
Don't know left–right self-placement		−0.348**	−0.347**	−0.346**	−0.348**
		(0.060)	(0.060)	(0.059)	(0.060)
Political interest		−0.164**	−0.164**	−0.164**	−0.164**
		(0.016)	(0.016)	(0.016)	(0.016)
Participation score		−0.058**	−0.058**	−0.059**	−0.058**
		(0.012)	(0.012)	(0.012)	(0.012)
Subjective social class		0.191**	0.191**	0.191**	0.190**
		(0.008)	(0.008)	(0.008)	(0.008)
Personally experienced discrimination		−0.850**	−0.850**	−0.852**	−0.853**
		(0.050)	(0.051)	(0.051)	(0.051)
How often attend religious services		−0.115**	−0.116**	−0.116**	−0.116**
		(0.009)	(0.009)	(0.009)	(0.009)
Age		−0.004**	−0.004**	−0.004**	−0.004**
		(0.001)	(0.001)	(0.001)	(0.001)
Education		0.062**	0.062**	0.062**	0.062**
		(0.007)	(0.007)	(0.007)	(0.007)
Gender		−0.105**	−0.105**	−0.105**	−0.106**
		(0.026)	(0.026)	(0.026)	(0.026)

Institutional variables

	(1)	(2)	(3)	(4)	(5)
Closed electoral system				−1.447**	0.035
				(0.226)	(0.779)
Gallagher Index				−0.022	−0.032+
				(0.026)	(0.019)
Multiparty (3+) government				0.463*	0.202
				(0.206)	(0.157)
One-party government				−0.398	−0.289
				(0.372)	(0.693)
Legislature "responsive"				0.468**	−0.068
				(0.173)	(0.248)
Seats in legislature per capita				−0.003	−0.004+
				(0.002)	(0.002)
Regionalism Index				0.003	−0.016
				(0.015)	(0.013)

Performance variables

	(1)	(2)	(3)	(4)	(5)
Unemployment				−0.059**	−0.037
				(0.018)	(0.031)
Economic growth				0.104*	0.136**
				(0.053)	(0.049)
Corruption				0.047**	0.045+
				(0.007)	(0.027)
Constant	5.847**	5.567**	5.797**	2.573**	2.921
	(0.281)	(0.261)	(0.406)	(0.608)	(2.346)
Var (cons)	1.250	0.890	0.084	0.083	0.038
Var (residual)	4.440	4.075	4.075	4.075	4.075
N level 1 (respondents)	25909	25909	25909	25909	25909
N level 2 (countries)	16	16	16	16	16

Standard errors in parentheses, + p < 0.10, * p < 0.05, ** p < 0.01. Dependent variable: How satisfied are you with the way democracy works in your country?

Appendices: Table 7.2B Trust in parliament

	(1)	(2)	(3)	(4)	(5)
Individual level variables					
Close to governing party		0.582**	0.582**	0.582**	0.583**
		(0.033)	(0.033)	(0.033)	(0.033)
Left–right self-placement		0.004	0.004	0.004	0.004
		(0.007)	(0.007)	(0.007)	(0.007)
Don't know left–right self-placement		−0.354**	−0.352**	−0.355**	−0.352**
		(0.065)	(0.065)	(0.065)	(0.065)
Political interest		−0.416**	−0.416**	−0.416**	−0.415**
		(0.017)	(0.017)	(0.017)	(0.017)
Participation score		−0.059**	−0.059**	−0.059**	−0.058**
		(0.012)	(0.012)	(0.012)	(0.012)
Subjective social class		0.229**	0.229**	0.229**	0.228**
		(0.009)	(0.009)	(0.009)	(0.009)
Personally experienced discrimination		−0.773**	−0.774**	−0.774**	−0.776**
		(0.053)	(0.053)	(0.053)	(0.053)

(continued)

Appendices: Table 7.2B Continued

	(1)	(2)	(3)	(4)	(5)
How often attend religious services		−0.166** (0.010)	−0.166** (0.010)	−0.166** (0.010)	−0.167** (0.010)
Age		−0.010** (0.001)	−0.010** (0.001)	−0.010** (0.001)	−0.010** (0.001)
Education		0.098** (0.008)	0.097** (0.008)	0.098** (0.008)	0.098** (0.008)
Gender		−0.021 (0.027)	−0.022 (0.027)	−0.022 (0.027)	−0.0221 (0.027)
Institutional variables					
Closed electoral system			−1.479** (0.220)		−1.371 (0.876)
Gallagher Index			−0.004 (0.026)		−0.001 (0.021)
Multiparty (3+) government			0.646** (0.200)		0.567** (0.177)
One-party government			0.380 (0.362)		1.896* (0.779)
Legislature "responsive"			0.525** (0.168)		0.446 (0.279)
Seats in legislature per capita			−0.003 (0.002)		−0.004* (0.002)
Regionalism Index			0.016 (0.014)		−0.006 (0.015)
Performance variables					
Unemployment				−0.049+ (0.025)	−0.101** (0.035)
Economic growth				−0.001 (0.072)	−0.090 (0.055)
Corruption				0.053** (0.009)	−0.005 (0.030)
Constant	4.690** (0.284)	5.403** (0.258)	5.215** (0.397)	1.879* (0.817)	6.816** (2.636)
Var (cons)	1.280	0.840	0.790	0.150	0.049
Var (residual)	5.130	4.500	4.500	4.500	4.500
N level 1 (respondents)	25662	25662	25662	25662	25662
N level 2 (countries)	16	16	16	16	16

Standard errors in parentheses, + $p < 0.10$, * $p < 0.05$, ** $p < 0.01$. Dependent variable: How much do you personally trust parliament in your country?

Appendices: Table 7.2C Trust in Politicians

	(1)	(2)	(3)	(4)	(5)
Individual-level variables					
Close to governing party		0.511**	0.512**	0.512**	0.512**
		(0.031)	(0.031)	(0.031)	(0.031)
Left–right self-placement		0.008	0.008	0.008	0.008
		(0.006)	(0.006)	(0.006)	(0.006)
Don't know left–right self-placement		−0.200**	−0.197**	−0.202**	−0.195**
		(0.059)	(0.059)	(0.059)	(0.059)
Political interest		−0.396**	−0.396**	−0.395**	−0.393**
		(0.016)	(0.016)	(0.016)	(0.016)
Participation score		−0.067**	−0.067**	−0.068**	−0.066**
		(0.011)	(0.011)	(0.011)	(0.011)
Subjective social class		0.194**	0.194**	0.195**	0.193**
		(0.008)	(0.008)	(0.008)	(0.008)
Personally experienced discrimination		−0.746**	−0.745**	−0.745**	−0.750**
		(0.049)	(0.049)	(0.049)	(0.049)
How often attend religious services		−0.158**	−0.158**	−0.159**	−0.158**
		(0.009)	(0.009)	(0.009)	(0.009)
Age		−0.008**	−0.008**	−0.008**	−0.008**
		(0.001)	(0.001)	(0.001)	(0.001)
Education		0.029**	0.028**	0.029**	0.028**
		(0.007)	(0.007)	(0.007)	(0.007)
Gender		0.170**	0.170**	0.170**	0.169**
		(0.025)	(0.025)	(0.025)	(0.025)
Institutional variables					
Closed electoral system			−1.683**		0.053
			(0.186)		(0.328)
Gallagher Index			−0.045*		−0.039**
			(0.021)		(0.008)
Multiparty (3+) government			0.662**		0.456**
			(0.169)		(0.062)
One-party government			0.066		0.950**
			(0.306)		(0.290)
Legislature "responsive"			0.192		−0.363**
			(0.142)		(0.103)
Seats in legislature per capita			−0.001		−0.001
			(0.002)		(0.001)
Regionalism Index			−0.005		−0.029**
			(0.012)		(0.005)
Performance variables					
Unemployment				−0.079**	−0.105**
				(0.016)	(0.012)
Economic growth				−0.029	−0.040+
				(0.044)	(0.021)
Corruption				0.057**	0.050**
				(0.006)	(0.012)
Constant	3.801**	4.683**	5.055**	1.13*	2.238*
	(0.291)	(0.273)	(0.338)	(0.514)	(1.016)
Var (cons)	1.390	1.000	0.050	0.058	0.004
Var (residual)	4.360	3.910	3.910	3.910	3.910
N level 1 (respondents)	25785	25785	25785	25785	25785
N level 2 (countries)	16	16	16	16	16

Standard errors in parentheses, $+ p < 0.10$, $* p < 0.05$, $** p < 0.01$. Dependent variable: How much do you personally trust politicians in your country?

Appendices to Chapter 8

Appendices: Table 8.A Perturbation analyses: satisfaction with democracy

	Max. errorterm	% significant p<.05 (2-sided)	mean p-value	% same direction as model 1
Impartiality executive	0.5	94%	0.04 **	100%
Rule of law	0.4	15%	0.37	95%
Lack of corruption	0.5	14%	0.42	92%
GDP/Capita	10.000	13%	0.33	100%
Professionalism	0.6	0%	0.60	86%

Appendices: Table 8.B Perturbation analyses: trust in parliament

	Max. errorterm	% significant p<.05 (2-sided)	mean p-value	% same direction as model 1
Impartiality executive	0.5	87%	0.04 **	100%
Rule of law	0.4	11%	0.28	100%
Lack of corruption	0.5	26%	0.24	100%
GDP/Capita	10.000	44%	0.16	100%
Professionalism	0.6	0%	0.51	99%

Appendices to Chapter 9

Appendices: Table 9.1 Countries and surveys in the ESS1-6 Cumulative Data File and included in the analyses

Countries	Number of surveys	QoG (min–max)	Impartiality	ENPP	GDP per capita thousands(min–max)	Age of democracy (min–max)	EPI (min–max)	Gini Index Net (min–max)
Austria	3	1.82–1.84	.87	3.48	35.7–39.5	57–61	91.3–96.2	26.7–26.9
Belgium	6	1.34–1.54	.78	6.40	34.5–36.6	58–68	85.6–92.9	25.3–26.9
Bulgaria	4	.01–08	–.46	3.40	4.0–4.6	16–22	84.0–92.0	29.5–34.6
Cyprus	4	1.13–1.26	–	3.77	21.8–24.3	31–37	76.2–96.4	–
Czech Republic	5	.75–.79	–.18	3.75	10.9–14.2	12–22	82.4–91.0	24.3–26.1
Denmark	6	1.98–2.16	1.21	4.86	45.6–49.0	57–67	89.2–102.8	22.6–27.8
Estonia	5	.98–1.07	.79	4.85	9.3–11.8	5–13	76.8–102.4	31.8–34.7
Finland	6	1.97–2.13	1.02	5.05	34.4–40.6	58–68	86.3–99.6	25.2–26.3
France	6	1.35–1.51	.69	2.69	32.8–34.8	34–43	83.1–89.5	27.0–30.3
Germany	6	1.56–1.69	.54	3.58	33.0–38.2	53–63	85.1–93.2	27.4–28.7
Greece	4	.41–.84	–.40	2.39	19.3–22.7	27–31	62.3–84.4	32.7–33.6
Hungary	6	.55–.91	–.21	2.52	9.6–11.5	12–22	79.6–85.4	26.7–28.1
Iceland	2	1.62–1.97	–	3.74	53.2–54.9	61–68	85.7–103.2	24.6–25.8
Ireland	6	1.47–1.61	.99	2.84	44.9–51.0	70	73.2–98.8	29.0–31.0
Israel	4	.87–1.00	.36	7.02	18.3–23.1	54–64	79.1–92.5	34.8–37.9
Italy	3	.70–.77	–.18	5.59	28.3–30.7	54–65	81.6–87.9	33.8–34.0
Lithuania	2	.64	–.05	5.15	8.6–10.0	20–22	81.0–88.0	34.5
Luxembourg	2	1.73–1.83	–	3.92	75.9–78.1	59–60	95.1–95.9	26.8–26.9
Netherlands	6	1.78–1.90	1.03	5.50	37.8–42.5	57–67	86.6–97.8	25.5–27.0
Norway	6	1.81–1.96	1.33	4.58	62.2–67.0	57–67	105.7–114.9	22.9–25.6
Poland	6	.43–.76	.23	3.41	7.0–10.6	11–21	74.5–90.1	29.3–31.5
Portugal	6	1.00–1.27	–.15	2.72	17.9–18.9	26–36	71.8–88.0	33.7–36.4
Slovakia	5	.58–.69	–.12	4.92	10.7–14.9	11–21	76.8–90.2	25.3–26.9
Slovenia	6	.92–1.02	–.20	4.66	16.0–20.7	11–21	81.8–96.9	22.1–25.2
Spain	6	1.06–1.42	.21	2.51	24.7–26.7	24–34	60.6–94.4	31.1–33.7
Sweden	6	1.85–2.00	1.07	4.22	37.7–43.8	70	91.4–98.0	23.0–24.1
Switzerland	6	1.85–1.97	1.25	5.04	50.2–55.4	70	96.0–99.8	26.8–30.7
Turkey	2	–.01–.09	–.14	2.25	6.7–7.7	21–25	77.5–84.1	38.9–40.9
United Kingdom	6	1.54–1.77	1.06	2.32	35.3–39.6	70	80.6–93.8	34.0–35.7

Appendices: Table 9.2 Economic performance, quality of governance, and satisfaction with democracy

	Model 3	Model 4	Model 5	Model 6
EPI	.08 (.02)***	–	–	.11 (.02)***
QoG	3.88 (1.52)**	.74 (.29)**	.49 (.24)*	4.65 (.98)***
QoG*EPI	-.04 (.02)**	–	–	-.05 (.01)***
GDP growth	–	.10 (.03)***	–	–
QoG*GDP growth	–	-.04 (.03)	–	–
EPI centered	–	–	.10 (.02)***	–
QoG*EPI centered	–	–	-.05 (.01)***	–
Contextual controls				
ENPP	-.01 (.09)	.06 (.08)	.08 (.08)	.04 (.10)
GDP per capita	.02 (.01)*	.03 (.01)**	.02 (.00)**	.02 (.01)*
Age of democracy	-.01 (.04)	-.007 (.008)	-.001 (.008)	-.01 (.01)
Income inequality	-.01 (.02)	-.004 (.02)	-.01 (.02)	-.04 (.03)
Age of democracy*EPI	.0001 (.0004)	–	–	–
Individual controls				
Female	-.20 (.01)***	-.20 (.009)***	-.20 (.009)***	-.23 (.01)***
Age of respondent	-.005 (.0003)***	-.005 (.0002)***	-.005 (.0003)***	-.004 (.0003)***
Years of education	.01 (.001)***	.01 (.001)***	.01 (.001)***	.01 (.001)***
Religiosity	.05 (.002)***	.05 (.002)***	.05 (.002)***	.06 (.002)***
Social trust	.30 (.003)***	.30 (.003)***	.30 (.003)***	.30 (.003)***
Political interest	.18 (.006)***	.18 (.006)***	.18 (.006)***	.20 (.007)***
LRSP	.22 (.007)***	.22 (.007)***	.22 (.007)***	.24 (.008)***
LRSP squared	-.01 (.0007)***	-.01 (.0007)***	-.01 (.0007)***	-.02 (.0008)***
Constant	-5.12 (1.72)***	1.03 (.82)	1.39 (.88)	-5.55 (1.66)***
Variance components				
Country-year intercept	.14	.18	.14	.11
EPI/cEPI/GDP growth	.00	.00	.00	.00
Country intercept	.28	.21	.20	.23
Countries	29	29	29	21
Country-years	130	130	130	98
Respondents	207,919	207,919	220,263	163,585

*p<.10; **p<.05; ***p<.01 (two-tailed tests).

Appendices to Chapter 10

1. *Question wordings*

Satisfaction with [local] [national] democracy:

"Generally speaking, how satisfied are you with the way democracy works in [your local commune] [Sweden]? Response alternatives: Very satisfied; rather satisfied; rather unsatisfied; very unsatisfied.

Process preference:

"Two individuals, A and B, disagree over the best way of organizing democracy. Do you agree mostly with person A or person B?"

Person A: Citizens should primarily influence politics through voting on parties and candidates. Because of that, it is important, particularly before elections, that voters are well informed about the positions of parties. Between elections it is primarily up to the elected representatives to make decisions. Politicians shall, of course, listen to citizens also between elections, but to public opinion as a whole, not exclusively on those who speak with high voices and who call attention to their own problems only.

Person B: Citizens should vote for parties and candidates in elections. But citizens should be active in politics also between elections. Therefore, it is preferable to hold frequent referenda. Furthermore, it is important that a multitude of citizen groups systematically voice opinion through petitions, actions, and demonstrations.
Do you agree mostly with Person A; agree with both but mostly with person A; agree with both but mostly with person B; agree mostly with person B?

Views on the proposal:

What is your view on the decision [T1: proposal] regarding changes in the school system and pre-school system in Suburbia that was recently [T0: that has recently been suggested] made by the politicians in the local government?

"Very positive; somewhat positive; neither positive nor negative; somewhat negative; very negative; don't know about the proposal"?

Perceived responsiveness:

"If you think about the issue of changes and savings within school and childcare in Suburbia, would you say that politicians in the majority have been trying to find out about citizen wishes; explained their politics to citizens; and tried to accommodate citizen wishes?"

Response scale 0–10 for each item with designated endpoints "very little so"; "very much so".

Appendices: Table 10.1 Satisfaction with democracy in own municipality (0–1)

	T0A Simulated from national SOM	T0B Observed	T1	T2	T3	p-value T0–T1	p-value T1–T2	p-value T2–T3	p-value T0–T3	n
Protesting Citizens										
Protesting citizens – Satisfied with decision	0.589 (0.006)	—	0.418 (0.030)	0.482 (0.026)	0.511 (0.022)	.000((A)	.010	.134	.002((A)	90 observed T1–T3 75 simulated
Protesting citizens – Dissatisfied with decision	0.596 (0.004)	—	0.380 (0.026)	0.368 (0.026)	0.347 (0.023)	.000((A)	.601	.330	.000((A)	109 observed T1–T3 88 simulated
Citizens in Suburbia (Control group)	0.574 (0.010)	0.666 (0.049)	0.706 (0.036)	0.591 (0.038)	0.589 (0.038)	.042((A) .161(B)	.001	.937	.649((A) .102(B)	50 observed T1–T3 34 simulated

Appendices: Table 10.2 Satisfaction with national democracy (0–1)

	T0A Simulated from national SOM	T0B Observed	T1	T2	T3	p-value T0–T1	p-value T1–T2	p-value T2–T3	p-value T0–T3	n
Protesting citizens										
Protesting citizens – Satisfied with decision	0.671 (0.010)	–	0.722 (0.020)	0.676 (0.019)	0.684 (0.020)	.020((A)	.008	.646	.797((A)	90 observed T1–T3 72 simulated
Protesting citizens – Dissatisfied with decision	0.683 (0.007)	–	0.691 (0.014)	0.711 (0.017)	0.668 (0.015)	.360((A)	.245	.009	.468((A)	109 observed T1–T3 88 simulated
Citizens in Suburbia (Control group)	0.647 (0.016)	0.742 (0.040)	0.743 (0.027)	0.696 (0.030)	0.672 (0.027)	.090((A) .326(B)	.009	.295	.774((A) .003(B)	50 observed T1–T3 34 simulated

Appendices: Table 10.3 Process preference (0 = electoral democracy; 1 = participatory democracy)

	T0A Simulated from national SOM	T1	T2	T3	p-value T0–T1	p-value T1–T2	p-value T2–T3	p-value T0–T3	n
Protesting citizens									
Protesting citizens – Satisfied with decision	0.356 (0.011)	0.514 (0.028)	0.426 (0.029)	0.399 (0.026)	.000	.003	.372	.122	90 observed T1–T3 72 simulated
Protesting citizens – Dissatisfied with decision	0.365 (0.010)	0.597 (0.025)	0.479 (0.024)	0.482 (0.024)	.000	.000	.901	.000	109 observed T1–T3 88 simulated
Citizens in suburbia (Control group)	0.382 (0.020)	0.340 (0.046)	0.342 (0.044)	0.344 (0.041)	.850	.966	.951	.711	50 observed T1–T3 34 simulated

Bibliography

Aalberg, T., Van Aelst, P., and Curran, J. (2010). "Media systems and the political information environment. Supply and demand of news and current affairs across countries and time." *International Journal of Press/Politics* 15 (3): 255–71.

Aarts, K., Fladmoe, A., and Strömbäck, J. (2012). "Media, Political Trust, and Political Knowledge," in T. Aalberg and J. Curran (eds), *How Media Inform Democracy: A Comparative Approach* (New York: Routledge).

Aarts, K. and Semetko, H. A. (2003). "The divided electorate: Media use and political involvement." *Journal of Politics* 65 (3): 759–84.

Aarts, K. and Thomassen, J. (2008). "Satisfaction with democracy: Do institutions matter?" *Electoral Studies* 27 (1): 5–18.

Aarts, K., Thomassen, J., and Van Ham, C. (2014). "Globalization, representation, and attitudes towards democracy," in J. Thomassen (ed.), *Elections and Democracy. Representation and Accountability* (Oxford: Oxford University Press).

Abramson, P. R. (2014). "Value Change over a Third of a Century: The Evidence for Generational Replacement," in R. J. Dalton and C. Welzel (eds), *The Civic Culture Transformed: From Allegiant to Assertive Citizens* (New York: Cambridge University Press) 19–34.

Acemoglu, D. and Robinson, J. (2012). *Why Nations Fail. The Origins of Power, Prosperity and Property* (New York: Crown Business).

Achen, C. H. (2005). "Let's Put Garbage-Can Regressions and Garbage-Can Probits Where They Belong." *Conflict Management and Peace Science* 22: 327–39.

Adriaansen, M. L., Van Praag, P., and De Vreese, C. H. (2010). "Substance Matters: How News Content can Reduce Political Cynicism." *International Journal of Public Opinion Research* 22 (4): 433–57.

Almond, G. A. (1960). "Introduction: A functional approach to comparative politics," in G. Almond and J. Coleman (eds), *The Politics of Developing Areas* (Princeton, NJ: Princeton University Press).

Almond, G. A. and Verba, S. (1965). *The civic culture: political attitudes and democracy in five nations* (Princeton, NJ: Princeton University Press).

Alonso, S. (2013). "The growing economic and ideological breach between Northern and Southern EU countries is pushing Europe towards a perfect storm." EUROPP: LSE blog on European Politics and Policy. <http://blogs.lse.ac.uk/europpblog/2013/07/22/the-growing-economic-and-ideological-breach-between-northern-and-southern-eu-countries-is-pushing-europe-towards-a-perfect-storm/> accessed October 2014.

American National Election Studies (1948–2008). "American National Election Studies (ANES) Cumulative Data File, 1948–2008." ICPSR08475-v14: 2011–12–05 edn (Ann Arbor, MI: Inter-university Consortium for Political and Social Research).

Andersen, R. (2012). "Support for democracy in cross-national perspective: The detrimental effect of economic inequality." *Research in Social Stratification and Mobility* 30 (4): 389–402.

Anderson, C. J. (1998). "Political satisfaction in old and new democracies." *Working Paper* 98.4, Institute for European Studies, Cornell University.

Anderson, C. J., Blais, A., Bowler, S., Donovan, T., and Listhaug, O. (2005). *Losers' consent: elections and democratic legitimacy* (Oxford: Oxford University Press).

Anderson, C. J. and Guillory, C. A. (1997). "Political institutions and satisfaction with democracy: A cross-national analysis of consensus and majoritarian systems." *American Political Science Review* 91 (1): 66–81.

Anderson, C. J. and Just, A. (2013). "Legitimacy from Above: the partisan foundations of support for the political system in democracies." *European Political Science Review* 5 (3): 335–62.

Anderson, C. J. and Singer, M. M. (2008). "The sensitive left and the impervious right— Multilevel models and the politics of inequality, ideology, and legitimacy in Europe." *Comparative Political Studies* 41 (4–5): 564–99.

Anderson, C. J. and Tverdova, Y. V. (2003). "Corruption, political allegiances, and attitudes toward government in contemporary democracies." *American Journal of Political Science* 47 (1): 91–109.

Andeweg, R. B. (2003). "Beyond Representativeness? Trends in Political Representation." *European Review* 11 (2): 147–61.

Andeweg, R. B. (2014). "A growing confidence gap in politics? Data versus discourse," in J. W. Van Prooijen and P. A. M. Van Lange (eds), *Power, Politics, and Paranoia; Why people are suspicious of their leaders* (Cambridge: Cambridge University Press) 176–96.

Ansolabehere, S. and Iyengar, S. (1995). *Going Negative: How Political Advertisements Shrink and Polarize the Electorate* (New York: Free Press).

Arceneaux, K. (2006). "The Federal Face of Voting: Are Elected Officials Held Accountable for the Functions Relevant to Their Office?" *Political Psychology* 27: 731–54.

Arceneaux, K. and Stein, R. (2006). "Who is Held Responsible When Disaster Strikes? The Attribution of Responsibility for a Natural Disaster in an Urban Election." *Journal of Urban Affairs* 28: 43–53.

Armingeon, K. and Guthmann, K. (2014). "Democracy in crisis? The declining support for national democracy in European countries, 2007–2011." *European Journal of Political Research* 53 (3): 423–42.

Atkeson, L. and Maestas, C. (2012). *Catastrophic Politics. How Extraordinary Events Redefine Perceptions of Government* (Cambridge: Cambridge University Press).

Avery, J. M. (2009). "Videomalaise or Virtuous Circle? The Influence of the News Media on Political Trust." *International Journal of Press-Politics* 14 (4): 410–33.

Banducci, S. A., Donovan, T., and Karp, J. A. (1999). "Proportional representation and attitudes about politics: results from New Zealand." *Electoral Studies* 18 (4): 533–55.

Barber, B. (1984). *Strong Democracy* (Berkeley, CA: University of California Press).

Barnes, S. H., and Kaase, M. (eds) (1979). *Political action: mass participation in five Western democracies* (Beverly Hills, CA: Sage).

Bartle, J. and Bellucci, P. (2009). "Introduction: Partisanship, social identity and individual attitudes," in J. Bartle and P. Bellucci (eds), *Political Parties and Partisanship; social identity and individual attitudes* (London: Routledge) 1–25.

Beetham, David. (1991). *The legitimation of power* (Basingstoke: Macmillan).

Bélanger, E. (2004). "Antipartyism and third-party choice: a comparison of Canada, Britain and Australia." *Comparative Political Studies* 37: 1054–78.

Bélanger, E. and Aarts, K. (2006). "Explaining the Rise of the LPF: Issues, Discontent, and the 2002 Dutch Election." *Acta Politica* 41 (1): 4–20.

Bell, Daniel. (1960). *The End of Ideology* (Glencoe: Free Press).

Belsley, D. A. (1991). *Conditioning diagnostics, collinearity and weak data in regression* (New York: John Wiley and Sons).

Bengtsson, Å. and Christensen, H. (2016). "Ideals and Actions: Do Citizens' Patterns of Political Participation Correspond to their Conceptions of Democracy?" *Government and Opposition* 51 (2): 234–60.

Bennett, L. and Entman, R. (2001). *Mediated Politics: Communication in the Future of Democracy* (Cambridge: Cambridge University Press).

Bennett, L. and Iyengar, S. (2008). "A New Era of Minimal Effects? The Changing Foundations of Political Communication." *Journal of Communication* 58: 707–31.

Bennett, S. E. et al. (1999). "'Video malaise' revisited—Public trust in the media and government." *Harvard International Journal of Press-Politics* 4 (4): 8–23.

Benoit, K. and Laver, M. (2006). *Party Policy in Modern Democracies* (London/New York: Routledge).

Benoit, W. L., Stein, K. A., and Hansen, G. J. (2005). "*New York Times* Coverage of Presidential Campaigns." *Journalism & Mass Communication Quarterly* 82 (2): 356–76.

Berman, S. (1997). "Civil Society and the Collapse of the Weimar Republic." *World Politics* 49 (3): 401–29.

Bernauer, J. and Vatter, A. (2012). "Can't get no satisfaction with the Westminster model? Winners, losers and the effects of consensual and direct democratic institutions on satisfaction with democracy." *European Journal of Political Research* 51 (4): 435–68.

Blais, A., Gidengil, E., Nevitte, N., and Nadeau, R. (2004). "Where does turnout decline come from?" *European Journal of Political Research* 43: 221–36.

Boda, Z. and Medve-Bálint, G. (2014). "The Poorer You Are, the More You Trust? The Effect of Inequality and Income on Institutional Trust in East-Central Europe." *Sociologický časopis/Czech Sociological Review* 3: 419–53.

Booth, J. A. and Seligson, M. A. (2009). *The Legitimacy Puzzle in Latin America: Political Support and Democracy in Eight Nations* (New York: Cambridge University Press).

Borre, O. and Scarbrough, E. (1995). *The scope of government*, vol. 3 (Oxford: Oxford University Press).

Boukes, M. and Boomgaarden, H. G. (2014). "Soft News With Hard Consequences? Introducing a Nuanced Measure of Soft Versus Hard News Exposure and Its Relationship With Political Cynicism." *Communication Research* 42 (5): 701–31.

Boulianne, S. (2015). "Social media use and participation: a meta-analysis of current research." *Information, Communication & Society* 18 (5): 524–38.

Bovens, M. and Wille, A. (2009). *Diploma democracy: On the tensions between meritocracy and democracy* (Utrecht/Leiden: NOW).

Bowler, S. and Donovan, T. (2013). *The Limits of Electoral Reform* (Oxford: Oxford University Press).

Bowler, S. and Karp, J. A. (2004). "Politicians, scandals, and trust in government." *Political Behavior* 26 (3): 271–87.

Brå (2012). "Politikernas trygghetsundersökning 2012. Förtroendevaldas utsatthet och oro för hot, våld och trakasserier." Rapport 2012:14, Stockholm.

Brants, K. and Van Kempen, H. (2002). "The ambivalent watchdog: the changing culture of political journalism and its effects," in R. Kuhn and E. Neveu (eds), *Political Journalism. New challenges, new practices* (London: Routledge) 168–86.

Brittan, S. (1975). "The economic contradictions of democracy." *British Journal of Political Science* 5: 129–59.

Brockner, J. (2002). "Making sense of procedural fairness: How high procedural fairness can reduce or heighten the influence of outcome favorability." *Academy of Management Review* 27 (1): 58–76.

Brockner, J., Fishman, A. Y., Reb, J., Goldman, B., Spiegel, S., and Garden, C. (2007). "Procedural fairness, outcome favorability, and judgments of an authority's responsibility." *Journal of Applied Psychology* 92 (6): 1657–571.

Brockner, J. and Wiesenfeld, B. M. (1996). "An integrative framework for explaining reactions to decisions: interactive effects of outcomes and procedures." *Psychological Bulletin* 120 (2): 189–208.

Brockner, J. and Wiesenfeld, B. M. (2005). "How, When, and Why Does Outcome Favorability Interact with Procedural Fairness?" in J. Greenberg and J. A. Colquitt (eds), *Handbook of Organizational Justice* (Mahwah, NJ: Lawrence Erlbaum Associates) 525–53.

Brody, R. (1991). *Assessing the President: The Media, Elite Opinion, and Public Support* (Stanford, CA: Stanford University Press).

Budge, I. and Newton, K. et al. (1997). *The Politics of the New Europe. Atlantic to Urals* (London: Addison Wesley Longman).

Burstein, P. (1998). "Bringing the Public Back In: Should Sociologists Consider the Impact of Public Opinion on Public Policy?" *Social Forces* 77: 27–62.

Cain, B. E., Dalton, R. J., and Scarrow, S. E. (2003). *Democracy Transformed? Expanding Political Opportunities in Advanced Industrial Democracies* (Oxford: Oxford University Press).

Campbell, R. (2011). "Social Capital and Political Support: A Reassessment of the Putnam Thesis in East and West Germany." *German Politics* 20 (4): 568–90.

Canache, D., Mondak, J. J., and Seligson, M. A. (2001). "Meaning and measurement in cross-national research on satisfaction with democracy." *Public Opinion Quarterly* 65 (4): 506–28.

Capella, J. and Jamieson, K. H. (1997). *Spyral of cynism. The press and the public good* (New York: Oxford University Press).

Carman, Chr. (2010). "The Process is the Reality: Perceptions of Procedural Fairness and Participatory Democracy." *Political Studies* 58 (4): 731–51.

Castles, F. (1982). "The impact of parties on public expenditure," in F. Castles (ed.), *The Impact of Parties: Politics and Policies in Democratic Capitalist States* (Beverly Hills, CA: Sage Publications).

Castles, F. and Wildenmann, R. (1986). *Visions and Realities of Party Government* (Berlin: de Gruyter).

Castles, F. G. (1994). "The policy consequences of proportional representation: A sceptical commentary." *Political Science* 46: 161–71.

Catterberg, G. and Moreno, A. (2006). "The individual bases of political trust: Trends in new and established democracies." *International Journal of Public Opinion Research* 18 (1): 31–48.

Ceron, A. (2015). "Internet, News, and Political Trust: The Difference Between Social Media and Online Media Outlets." *Journal of Computer-Mediated Communication* 20 (5): 487–503.

Chanley, V. A., Rudolph, T. J., and Rahn, W. M. (2000). "The origins and consequences of public trust in government—A time series analysis." *Public Opinion Quarterly* 64 (3): 239–56.

Chu, Y., Diamond, L., Nathan, A. J., and Shin, D. C. (2008). *How East Asians view democracy* (New York: Columbia University Press).

Chu, Y., et al. (2008). "Public opinion and democratic legitimacy." *Journal of Democracy* 19 (2): 74–87.

Clarke, H. D., Dutt, N., and Kornberg, A. (1993). "The political economy of attitudes toward polity and society in Western European democracies." *Journal of Politics* 55 (4): 998–1021.

Crewe, I., Sarlvik, B., and Alt, J. (1977). "Partisan Dealignment in Britain 1964-1974." *British Journal of Political Science* 7 (2): 129–90.

Criado, H. and Herreros, F. (2007). "Political support taking into account the institutional context." *Comparative Political Studies* 40 (12): 1511–32.

Crotty, W. and Jacobson, G. (1980). *American Parties in Decline* (Boston, MA: Little, Brown and Co).

Crozier, M. J., Huntington, S. P., and Watanuki, J. (1975). *The crisis of democracy. Report on the governability of democracies to the trilateral commission* (New York: New York University Press).

Curini, L., Jou, W., and Memoli, V. (2012). "Satisfaction with Democracy and the Winner/Loser Debate: The Role of Policy Preferences and Past Experience." *British Journal of Political Science* FirstView, 1–21.

Curran, J., Coen, S., Soroka, S., Aalberg, T., Hayashi, K., Hichy, Z., and Tiffen, R. (2014). "Reconsidering 'virtuous circle' and 'media malaise' theories of the media: An 11-nation study." *Journalism* 15 (7): 815–33.

Dahl, R. (1956). *A preface to democratic theory* (Chicago, IL: University of Chicago Press).

Dahl, R. A. (1967). "The city in the future of democracy." *American Political Science Review* 61 (4): 953–70.

Dahl, R. A. (1971). *Polyarchy: participation and opposition* (New Haven, CT: Yale University Press).

Dahl, R. A. (1989). *Democracy and its critics* (New Haven, CT: Yale University Press).

229

Dahlberg, S., Dahlström, C., Sundin, P., and Teorell, J. (2013). "The QoG Expert Survey 2008–2011: A Report."

Dahlberg, S., Svensson, R., and Sundin, P. (2012). "The QoG Expert-Survey: Codebook." August 31, 2012: University of Gothenburg.

Dahlberg, S. and Holmberg, S. (2014). "Democracy and Bureaucracy: How their Quality Matters for Popular Satisfaction." *West European Politics* 37 (3): 515–37.

Dalton, R. and Welzel, C. (2014). *The Civic Culture Transformed. From Allegiant to Assertive Citizenship* (Cambridge: Cambridge University Press).

Dalton, R. J. (1999). "Political Support in Advanced Industrial Democracies," in P. Norris (ed.), *Critical citizens: global support for democratic government* (New York: Oxford University Press) 57–77.

Dalton, R. J. (2000). "The Decline of Party Identifications," in R. J. Dalton and M. P. Wattenberg (eds), *Parties Without Partisans: Political change in advanced industrial democracies* (Oxford: Oxford University Press) 19–36.

Dalton, R. J. (2004). *Democratic challenges democratic choices. The erosion of political support in advanced industrial democracies* (New York: Oxford University Press).

Dalton, R. J. (2005). "The social transformation of trust in government." *International Review of Sociology* 15 (1): 133–54.

Dalton, R. J. (2009). *The Good Citizen: How a Younger Generation is Reshaping American Politics*, 2nd edn (Washington DC: Congressional Quarterly Press).

Dalton, R. J. (2012). "Tracking Political Support: Can Trust Decline (and not) at the Same Time?." *Expert Meeting about the (presumed) legitimacy crisis of representative democracy in advanced industrial democracies*, Netherlands Royal Academy of Sciences, Amsterdam.

Dalton, R. J., Farrell, D. M., and McAllister, I. (2011). *Political Parties and Democratic Linkage: How Parties Organize Democracy* (Oxford: Oxford University Press).

Dalton, R. J., Scarrow, S., and Cain, B. (2003). "New Forms of Democracy? Reform and Transformation of Democratic Institutions," in R. J. Dalton, D. Scarrow, B. Cain (eds), *Democracy Transformed? Expanding Political Opportunities in Advanced Industrial Democracies* (Oxford: Oxford University Press) 1–20.

Dalton, R. J., Shin, D. C., and Jou, W. (2007). "Popular Conceptions of the Meaning of Democracy: Democratic Understanding in Unlikely Places." UC Irvine: Center for the Study of Democracy.

Dalton, R. J. and Wattenberg, M. P. (2000). *Parties Without Partisans: Political change in advanced industrial democracies* (Oxford: Oxford University Press).

Dancey, L. (2012). "The Consequences of Political Cynicism: How Cynicism Shapes Citizens' Reactions to Political Scandals." *Political Behavior* 34: 411–23.

De Vreese, C. and Boomgaarden, H. (2006). "News, Political Knowledge and Participation: The Differential Effects of News Media Exposure on Political Knowledge and Participation." *Acta Politica* 41: 317–41.

De Vreese, C. and Tobiasen, M. (2007). "Conflict and identity: explaining turnout and anti-integrationist voting in the Danish 2004 elections for the European Parliament." *Scandinavian Political Studies* 30 (1): 87–114.

De Vreese, C. H. (2005). "The spiral of cynicism reconsidered." *European Journal of Communication* 20 (3): 283–301.

De Vreese, C. H. and Elenbaas, M. (2008). "Media in the game of politics: Effects of strategic metacoverage on political cynicism." *International Journal of Press-Politics* 13 (3): 285–309.

Della Porta, D. (2000). "Social capital, beliefs in government and political corruption," in S. J. Pharr and R. D. Putnam (eds), *Disaffected Democracies: What's Troubling the Trilateral Countries?* (Princeton, NJ: Princeton University Press) 202–29.

Della Porta, D. (2004). "Political Parties and Corruption: Ten Hypotheses on Five Vicious Circles." *Crime, Law and Social Change* 42: 35–60.

Denemark, D. and Bowler, S. (2002). "Minor Parties and Protest Votes in Australia and New Zealand: locating populist politics." *Electoral Studies* 21 (1): 46–67.

Diamond, L. and Plattner, M. F. (2008). *How people view democracy* (Baltimore, MD: Johns Hopkins University Press).

Dimitrova-Grajzl, V. and Simon, E. (2010). "Political Trust and Historical Legacy: The Effect of Varieties of Socialism." *East European Politics and Societies* 24 (2): 206–28.

Dinesen, P. T. and Jæger, M. M. (2013). "The Effect of Terror on Institutional Trust: New Evidence from the 3/11 Madrid Terrorist Attack." *Political Psychology* 34: 917–26.

Dogan, M. (1994). "Testing the Concepts of Legitimacy and Trust," in M. Dogan and A. Kazancigil (eds), *Comparing Nations: concepts, strategies, substance* (Oxford: Blackwell) 297–313.

Downs, W. (1999). "Accountability Payoffs in Federal Systems? Competing Logics and Evidence from Europe's Newest Federation." *Publius: The Journal of Federalism* 29: 87–110.

Dreher, Axel. (2006). "Does globalization affect growth? Evidence from a new index of globalization." *Applied Economics* 38 (10): 1091–110.

Duch, R. M. and Taylor, M. A. (1993). "Postmaterialism and the economic condition." *American Journal of Political Science* 37 (3): 747–79.

Duverger, M. (1964). *Political Parties* (London: Methuen and Co.).

Easton, D. (1965). *A Systems Analysis of Political Life* (New York: Wiley).

Easton, D. (1975). "A Re-assessment of the Concept of Political Support." *British Journal of Political Science* 5 (4): 435–57.

Elenbaas, M. and De Vreese, C. H. (2008). "The Effects of Strategic News on Political Cynicism and Vote Choice Among Young Voters." *Journal of Communication* 58 (3): 550–67.

Eliasoph, N. (1998). *Avoiding Politics. How Americans Produce Apathy in Everyday Life* (Cambridge: Cambridge University Press).

Erber, R. and Lau, R. R. (1990). "Political cynicism revisited—an information-processing reconciliation of policy-based and incumbency-based interpretations of changes in trust in government." *American Journal of Political Science* 34 (1): 236–53.

Erikson, R. S. (1989). "Economic Conditions and the Presidential Vote." *American Political Science Review* 83: 567–83.

Erlingsson, G. O., Linde, J., and Öhrvall, R. (2016). "Distrust in Utopia? Public Perceptions of Corruption and Political Support in Iceland before and after the Financial Crisis of 2008" *Government and Opposition* 51 (4): 553–79.

Esaiasson, P. (2010). "Will citizens take no for an answer? What government officials can do to enhance decision acceptance." *European Political Science Review* 2 (3): 351–71.

Esaiasson, P., Kölln, A., and Turper, S. (2015). "External Efficacy and Perceived Responsiveness—Similar but Distinct Concepts." *International Journal of Public Opinion Research* 27: 432–45.

Esaiasson, P. R., Gilljam, M., and Persson, M. (2010). "Medborgarnas demokratiuppfattningar," in L. Weibull and H. Oscarsson Sören Holmberg (eds), *Lycksalighetens ö* (Göteborg: SOM-institutet).

Esaiasson, P. R., Gilljam, M., and Persson, M. (2013). "Communicative responsiveness and other concepts in between-election democracy," in Peter Esaiasson and Hanne-Marthe Narud (eds.), *Between-Election Democracy. The Representative Relationship Between Elections* (Colchester: ECPR Press).

Esaiasson, P. R., Gilljam, M., and Persson, M. (2016). "Responsiveness Beyond Policy Satisfaction: Does It Matter to Citizens?." *Comparative Political Studies*.

Esser, F., De Vreese, C. H., Strömbäck, J., Van Aelst, P., Aalberg, T., Stanyer, J., Reinemann, C., Lengauer, G., Berganza, R., Legnante, G., Papathanassopoulos S., Salgado, S., and Sheafer, T. (2012). "Political Information Opportunities in Europe: A Longitudinal and Comparative Study of Thirteen Television Systems." *International Journal of Press/Politics* 17 (3): 247–74.

Esser, F., Engesser, S., Matthes, J., and Berganza, R. (2016). "Negativity," in F. Esser, D. Hopmann, and C. H. De Vreese (eds), *Where's the Good News? Comparing Political Journalism in 16 Countries* (London: Routledge) 111–39.

Ezrow, L. and Xezonakis, G. (2011). "Citizen Satisfaction With Democracy and Parties' Policy Offerings." *Comparative Political Studies* 44 (9): 1152–78.

Fails, M. D. and Pierce, H. N. (2010). "Changing Mass Attitudes and Democratic Deepening." *Political Research Quarterly* 63 (1): 174–87.

Falk, A. and Fischbacher, U. (2006). "A theory of reciprocity." *Games and Economic Behavior* 54: 293–315.

Fallows, J. M. (1996). *Breaking the news: How the media undermine American democracy* (New York: Pantheon Books).

Farnsworth, S. J. and Lichter, S. R. (2007). *The nightly news nightmare: Television's coverage of US presidential elections 1988–2004* (Rowman & Littlefield).

Farrell, D. M. (2006). "Political Parties in a Changing Campaign Environment," in R. S. Katz and W. Crotty (eds), *Handbook of Party Politics* (London: Sage) 122–33.

Farrell, D. M. and McAllister, I. (2006). "Voter satisfaction and electoral systems: Does preferential voting in candidate-centred systems make a difference?." *European Journal of Political Research* 45 (5): 723–49.

Farrell, D. M. and Schmitt-Beck, R. (2008). *Non-Party Actors in Electoral Politics: The Role of Interest Groups and Independent Citizens in Contemporary Election Campaign* (Baden-Baden: Nomos).

Ferrin, M. and Kriesi, H. (eds) (2016). *How Europeans View and Evaluate Democracy* (Oxford: Oxford University Press).

Fieschi, C. and Heywood, P. (2004). "Trust, cynicism and populist anti-politics," *Journal of Political Ideologies* 9 (3): 289–309.

Fisher, R., Ury, W., and Patton, B. (1997). *Getting to Yes: Negotiating an Agreement Without Giving In*, 2nd edn (London: Arrow Business Books).

Fitzgerald, J. and Wolak, J. (2016). "The roots of trust in local government in western Europe." *International Political Science Review* 37 (1): 130–46.

Flanagan, C. (2013). *Teenage citizens: The political theories of the young* (Cambridge, MA: Harvard University Press).

Flavin, P. (2013). "Policy Representation and Evaluations of State Government." *State and Local Government Review* 45 (3): 139–52.

Folger, R. (1986). "Rethinking equity theory," in R. L. Cohen, J. Greenberg, and H. W. Bierhoff (eds), *Justice in social relations* (New York: Plenum Press) 145–62.

Folger, R. and Cropanzano, R. (1998). *Organizational justice and human resource management* (Thousand Oaks, CA: Sage).

Folger, R. and Greenberg, J. (1985). "Procedural justice: An interpretive analysis of personnel systems." *Research in personnel and human resources management* 3: 141–83.

Franklin, M. (2004). *Voter Turnout and the Dynamics of Electoral Competition in Established Democracies* (Cambridge: Cambridge University Press).

Fraser, J. (1974). "Validating a measure of national political legitimacy." *American Journal of Political Science* 18 (1): 117–34.

Freitag, M. and Ackermann, M. (2016). "The impact of associational life on trust in local institutions: a comparison of 57 Swiss municipalities." *Local Government Studies* 42 (4): 616–36.

Friedrich, C. J. (1963). *Man and his Government; An Empirical Theory of Politics* (New York: McGraw-Hill).

Fuchs, D. (1989). *Die Unterstützung des politischen Systems der Bundesrepublik Deutschland* (Opladen: Westdeutscher Verlag).

Fuchs, D. and Klingemann, H. D. (1995). "Citizens and the State: A Relationship Transformed," in D. Fuchs. and H. D. Klingemann (eds), *Citizens and the State* (Oxford: Oxford University Press) 419–43.

Fukuyama, F. (1992). *The end of history and the last man* (New York: Free Press).

Gallagher, M., Laver, M., and Mair, P. (2011). *Representative Government in Modern Europe*, 5th edn (New York: McGraw-Hill).

Gallagher, M. (2014). Election indices dataset at <http://www.tcd.ie/Political_Science/staff/michael_gallagher/ElSystems/index.php> accessed October 2014.

Gallego, A. (2007). "Unequal political participation in Europe." *International Journal of Sociology* 37 (4): 10–25.

Gangl, A. (2003). "Procedural justice theory and evaluations of the lawmaking process." *Political Behavior* 25 (2): 119–49.

Gil de Zúñiga, H., Jung, N., and Valenzuela, S. (2012). "Social Media Use for News and Individuals' Social Capital, Civic Engagement and Political Participation." *Journal of Computer-Mediated Communication* 17 (3): 319–36.

Gilley, B. (2006). "The meaning and measure of state legitimacy: Results for 72 countries." *European Journal of Political Research* 45 (3): 499–525.

Gilljam, M. and Jodal, O. (2002). "Medborgarnas demokratiuppfattningar," in S. Holmberg and L. Weibull (eds), *Det våras för politiken* (Gothenburg: SOM-institute).

Goddard, P., Scammell, M., and Semetko, H. (1998). "Too much of a good thing? Television in the 1997 election campaign,.." in B. Gosschalk and J. Bartle I. Crewe (eds), *Political communications: Why Labour Won the General Election of 1997* (London: Frank Cass Publishers) 149–75.

Goul Andersen, J. and Hoff, J. (2001). *Democracy and Citizenship in Scandinavia* (Houndsmills: Palgrave Macmillan).

Grasso, M. T. (2014). "Age, period and cohort analysis in a comparative context: Political generations and political participation repertoires in Western Europe." *Electoral Studies* 33: 63–76.

Grimes, M. (2006). "Organizing consent: The role of procedural fairness in political trust and compliance." *European Journal of Political Research* 45 (2): 285–315.

Grimes, M. (2016). "Procedural justice and political trust," in S. Zmerli and T. W. G. van der Meer (eds), *Handbook on Political Trust* (Cheltenham: Edward Elgar Publishing).

Gross, K., Aday, S., and Brewer, P. R. (2004). "A panel study of media effects on political and social trust after September 11, 2001." *Harvard International Journal of Press-Politics* 9 (4): 49–73.

Habermas, J. (1973). *Legitimationsprobleme im Spätkapitalismus* (Frankfurt am Main: Suhrkamp).

Hague, R. and Harrop, M. (2001). *Comparative Government and Politics,* 6th edn (New York: Palgrave Macmillan).

Hakhverdian, A. and Mayne, Q. (2012). "Institutional trust, education, and corruption: A micro-macro interactive approach." *Journal of Politics* 74 (3): 739–50.

Hardin, R. (2000). "Do we want trust in government?," in M. E. Warren (ed.), *Democracy and trust* (Cambridge: Cambridge University Press) 22–41.

Hardin, R. (2002). *Trust and trustworthiness* (New York: Sage).

Hasisi, B. and Weisburd, D. (2011). "Going beyond ascribed identities: the importance of procedural justice in airport security screening in Israel." *Law and society review* 45 (4): 867–92.

Hay, C. (2007). *Why we hate politics* (Cambridge, MA: Polity Press).

Hazan, R. Y. and Rahat, G. (2010). *Democracy Within Parties: Candidate Selection Methods and their Political Consequences* (Oxford: Oxford University Press).

Heijstek-Ziemann, K. (2014). "Democratic Reforms and Legitimacy in Established Western Democracies," Leiden University.

Hendriks, F., Van Ostaaijen, J., and Boogers, M. (2011). "Legitimiteitsmonitor Democratisch Bestuur," Den Haag.

Hetherington, M. and Husser, J. (2012). "How Trust Matters: The Changing Political Relevance of Political Trust." *American Journal of Political Science* 56: 312–25.

Hetherington, M. and Nelson, M. (2003). "Anatomy of a Rally Effect: George W. Bush and the War on Terrorism." *PS Politics & Society* 36: 37–42.

Hibbing, J. R. and Theiss-Morse, E. (2002). *Stealth Democracy; Americans' beliefs about how government should work* (New York: Cambridge University Press).

Holmberg, S. (1999). "Down and down we go: Political Trust in Sweden," in P. Norris (ed.), *Critical citizens: global support for democratic government* (New York: Oxford University Press) 103–22.

Holmberg, S. (2014). "Feeling Policy Represented," in J. Thomassen (ed.), *Elections and Representative Democracy. Representation and Accountability* (Oxford: Oxford University Press) 132–52.

Holmberg, S., Rothstein, B., and Nasiritousi, N. (2009). "Quality of government: What you get." *Annual Review of Political Science* 12: 135–61.

Holz-Bacha, C. and Norris, P. (2001). "To entertain, inform, and educate: Still the role of public television?" *Political communication* 18: 123–40.

Hooghe, M. (2002). "Watching television and civic engagement. Disentangling the effects of time, programs, and stations." *Harvard International Journal of Press/Politics* 7 (2): 84–104.

Hooghe, M. and Kern, A. (2015). "Party membership and closeness and the development of trust in political institutions: an analysis of the European Social Survey, 2002–2010." *Party Politics* 21 (6): 944–56.

Hooghe, M. and Quintelier, E. (2013). "Do All Associations Lead to Lower Levels of Ethnocentrism? A Two-Year Longitudinal Test of the Selection and Adaptation Model." *Political Behavior* 35 (2): 289–309.

Hooghe, M. and Stolle, D. (2003). *Generating Social Capital: Civil Society and Institutions in Comparative Perspective* (New York: Palgrave).

Huber, J. and Powell, G. B. (1994). "Congruence between citizens and policymakers in two visions of liberal democracy." *World Politics* 46: 291–326.

Inglehart, R. (1971). "The silent revolution in Europe: Intergenerational Change in Post-Industrial Societies." *American Political Science Review* 65 (4): 991–1017.

Inglehart, R. (1977). *The silent revolution: changing values and political styles among Western publics* (Princeton, NJ: Princeton University Press).

Inglehart, R. (1990). *Culture shift in advanced industrial society* (Princeton, NJ: Princeton University Press).

Inglehart, R. (1997). *Modernization and Postmodernization. Cultural, Economic, and Political Change in 43 Societies* (Princeton, NJ: Princeton University Press).

Inglehart, R. and Welzel, C. (2005). *Modernization, Cultural Change and Democracy. The Human Development Sequence* (Cambridge: Cambridge University Press).

Jackson, D. (2011). "Strategic Media, Cynical Public? Examining the Contingent Effects of Strategic News Frames on Political Cynicism in the United Kingdom." *International Journal of Press-Politics* 16 (1): 75–101.

Jennings, M. K. and Van Deth, J. W. et al. (1990). *Continuities in political action: a longitudinal study of political orientations in three western democracies* (New York: de Gruyter).

Johnson, T. J. and Kaye, B. K. (2015). "Site Effects: How Reliance on Social Media Influences Confidence in the Government and News Media." *Social Science Computer Review* 33 (2): 127–44.

Kaase, M. and Newton, K. (1995). *Beliefs in Government* (Oxford: Oxford University Press).

Kahn, K. F. and Kenney, P. J. (1999). "Do Negative Campaigns Mobilize or Suppress Turnout? Clarifying the Relationship between Negativity and Participation." *American Political Science Review* 93 (4): 877–89.

Kahneman, D. and Tversky, A. (1982). "The simulation heuristic," in P. Slovic, D. Kahneman, and A. Tversky (eds), *Judgment under uncertainty: Heuristics and biases* (New York: Cambridge University Press) 201–8.

Karp, J. and Banducci, S. (2011). "The influence of party and electoral systems on campaign engagement," in R. J. Dalton and C. Anderson (eds), *Citizens, Context and Choice* (Oxford: Oxford University Press).

Karp, J., Banducci, S., and Bowler, S. (2008). "Getting out the vote: Party mobilization in comparative perspective." *British Journal of Political Science* 38: 91–112.

Karp, J. A. and Bowler, S. (2001). "Coalition government and satisfaction with democracy: An analysis of New Zealand's reaction to proportional representation." *European Journal of Political Research* 40 (1): 57–79.

Kasperson, R., Golding, D., and Tuler, S. (1992). "Social distrust as a factor in siting hazardous facilities and communicating risks." *Journal of Social Issues* 48 (4): 161–87.

Katz, R. (2013). "Should we Believe that Improved Intra-Party Democracy Would Arrest Party Decline?," in R. Cross and R. Katz (eds), *The Challenges of Intra-Party Democracy* (Oxford: Oxford University Press) 49–64.

Katz, R. and Mair, P. (1995). "Changing models of party organization and party democracy. The emergence of the cartel party." *Party Politics* 1 (1): 17–21.

Kaufmann, D., Kraay, A., and M. Mastruzzi (2010). "The worldwide governance indicators: methodology and analytical issues," World Bank.

Kennedy, P. (2008). *A Guide to Econometrics* (Malden, MA: Blackwell Publishers).

Kenski, K. and Stroud, N. J. (2006). "Connections between Internet use and political efficacy, knowledge, and participation." *Journal of Broadcasting & Electronic Media* 50 (2): 173–92.

Keohane, R.O. and Nye, J. S. (2000). "Globalization: What's new? What's not? (And so what?)," *Foreign Policy* 118 (118): 104–120.

Kepplinger, H. M. (2000). "The Declining Image of the German Political Elite." *Harvard International Journal of Press/Politics* 5 (4): 71–80.

Kern, A., Marien, S., and Hooghe, M. (2015). "Economic Crisis and Levels of Political Participation in Europe, 2002–2010: The Role of Resources and Grievances." *West European Politics* 38 (3): 464–89.

Khramov, V. and Lee, J. R. (2013). "The Economic Performance Index (EPI): an Intuitive Indicator for Assessing a Country's Economic Performance Dynamics in an Historical Perspective." *Working Paper No. 13/214*, IMF.

Kirkpatrick, J. (1978). *Dismantling the Parties: Reflections on Party Reform and Party Decomposition* (Washington, DC: American Enterprise Institute).

Klingemann, H. (1999). "Mapping political support in the 1990s: a global analysis," in P. Norris (ed.), *Critical citizens: global support for democratic government* (New York: Oxford University Press) 31–56.

Klingemann, H. and Fuchs, D. (1995). *Citizens and the State* (Oxford: Oxford University Press).

Klingemann, H-D. (2009). *The Comparative Study of Electoral Systems* (Oxford: Oxford University Press).

Klingemann, H-D. (2014). "Dissatisfied democrats: Democratic maturation in old and new democracies," in R. J. Dalton and C. Welzel (eds), *The Civic Culture Revisited: From Allegiant to Assertive Citizens* (Cambridge: Cambridge University Press) 116–57.

Klingemann, H-D. Hofferbert, R., and Budge, I. (1994). *Parties, Policies and Democracy* (Boulder, CO: Westview Press).

Klosko, G. (2000). *Democratic procedures and liberal consensus* (Oxford: Oxford University Press).

Kölln, A-K. (2014). "Party Decline and Response: The Effects of Membership Decline on Party Organisations in Western Europe, 1960–2010." University of Twente.

Kotzian, P. (2011). "Public support for liberal democracy." *International Political Science Review* 32 (1): 23–41.

Kriesi, H. et al. (2008). *West European Politics in the Age of Globalization* (Cambridge: Cambridge University Press).

Kumlin, S. (2004). *The Personal and the Political: How Personal Welfare State Experiences Affect Political Trust and Ideology* (New York: Palgrave Macmillan).

Kumlin, S. (2009). "The Welfare State: Values, Policy Preferences, and Performance Evaluations," in R. Dalton and H-D. Klingemann (eds), *The Oxford Handbook of Political Behavior* (Oxford: Oxford University Press) 362–83.

Kumlin, S. (2011). "Dissatisfied Democrats, Policy Feedback and European Welfare States, 1976–2001," in S. and Hooghe Zmerli, M. (eds), *Political trust: Why context matters* (Colchester: ECPR Press) 163–86.

Kumlin, S. and Esaiasson, P. (2012). "Scandal Fatigue? Scandal Elections and Satisfaction with Democracy in Western Europe, 1977–2007." *British Journal of Political Science* 42 (2): 263–82.

Lane, R. E. (1996). "Losing touch in a democracy: demands versus needs," in J. Hayward (ed.), *Elitism, Populism and European politics* (Oxford: Clarendon Press).

Lang, K. and Lang, G. E. (1959). "The mass media and voting," in E. Burdick and A. J. Brodbeck (eds), *American voting behavior* (New York: Free Press).

Lau, R. R. (1985). "Two Explanations for Negativity Effects in Political Behavior." *American Journal of Political Science* 29 (1): 119–38.

Lawson, K. (1980). "Political parties and linkage," in K. Lawson (ed.), *Political Parties and Linkage: A Comparative Perspective* (New Haven, CT: Yale University Press).

Lawson, K. and Merkl, P. (1988). *When Parties Fail: Emerging Alternative Organizations* (Princeton, NJ: Princeton University Press).

Lengauer, G., Esser, F., amd Berganza, R. (2012). "Negativity in political news: A review of concepts, operationalizations and key findings." *Journalism* 13 (2): 179–202.

Lengauer, G. and Holler, I. (2012). "Turning voters on? Effects of news frame exposure on voter mobilization in the 2008 Austrian elections." *Journal of Mass Communication & Journalism* 2 (11).

Leventhal, G. S. (1980). "What should be done with equity theory? New Approaches to the Study of Fairness in Social Relationships," in M. S. Greenberg, R. H. Willies, and K. J. Gergen (eds), *Social Exchange: Advances in Theory and Research* (New York: Plenum Press) 27–55.

Levi, M., Sacks, A., Tyler, T. (2009). "Conceptualizing Legitimacy, Measuring Legitimating Beliefs." *American Behavioral Scientist* 53 (3): 354–75.

Levi, M. and Stoker, L. (2000). "Political trust and trustworthiness." *Annual Review of Political Science* 3: 475–507.

Lichter, R. and Noyes, R. (1996). *Good intentions make bad news. Why Americans hate campaign journalism* (Lanham: Rowman & Littlefield).

Lichterman, P. and Eliasoph, N. (2014). "Civic Action." *American Journal of Sociology* 120 (3): 798–863.

Lijphart, A. (1999). *Patterns of democracy: Government forms and performance in thirty-six countries* (New Haven, CT: Yale University Press).

Lijphart, A. (2012). *Patterns of democracy: Government forms and performance in thirty-six countries*, 2nd edn (New Haven, CT: Yale University Press).

Lind, E. A. (2001). "Fairness heuristic theory: Justice judgments as pivotal cognitions in organizational relations," in R. Greenberg, and J. Cropanzano, (eds), *Advances in organizational justice* (Stanford, CA: Stanford University Press) 56–88.

Lind, E. A. and Tyler, T. R. (1988). *The social psychology of procedural justice* (New York: Plenum Press).

Linde, J. and Ekman, J. (2003). "Satisfaction with democracy: A note on a frequently used indicator in comparative politics." *European Journal of Political Research* 42 (3): 391–408.

Linde, J. and Erlingsson, G. Ó. (2013). "The eroding effect of corruption on system support in Sweden." *Governance* 26 (4): 585–603.

Lipset, S. M. (1959). "Some social requisites of democracy—economic development and political legitimacy." *American Political Science Review* 53 (1): 69–105.

Lipset, S. M. (1960). *Political Man: The Social Bases of Politics* (New York: Doubleday).

Listhaug, O. (1995). "The dynamics of trust in politicians," in H-D. Klingemann and D. Fuchs (eds), *Citizens and the State* (Oxford: Oxford University Press) 261–97.

MacCoun, R. (2005). "Voice, Control and Belonging: The Double-Edged Sword of Procedural Fairness." *Annual Review of Law and Social Science* 1: 171–201.

Magalhães, P. C. (2016). "Economic evaluations, procedural fairness, and satisfaction with democracy." *Political Research Quarterly* 69 (3): 522–34.

Magin, M. (2015). "Shades of Mediatization: Components of Media Logic in German and Austrian Elite Newspapers (1949–2009)." *International Journal of Press/Politics* 20 (4): 415–37.

Maier, J. (2011). "The impact of political scandals on political support: An experimental test of two theories." *International Political Science Review* 32 (3): 283–302.

Mair, P. (2002). "Populist Democracy vs Party Democracy," in Y. Mény and Y. Surel (eds), *Democracies and the Populist Challenge* (Houndmills: Palgrave) 81–98.

Mair, P. (2009). "Representative versus Responsible Government." *MPIfG Working Paper 09/8*, Cologne: Max Planck Institute for the Study of Societies.

Mair, P. (2013). *Ruling the void. The hollowing out of Western democracy* (London: Verso).

Majone, G. (2001). "Nonmajoritarian Institutions and the Limits of Democratic Governance: A Political Transaction-Cost Approach." *Journal of Theoretical and Institutional Economics* 157: 57–78.

Mansbridge, J. (1997). "Taking Coercion Seriously." *Constellation* 3 (3): 407–16.

Marien, S. (2011a). "Measuring political trust across time and space," in S. Marien, M. Hooghe, and M. Zmerli (eds), *Political trust: Why context matters* (Colchester: ECPR Press) 13–46.

Marien, S. (2011b). "The effect of electoral outcomes on political trust: A multi-level analysis of 23 countries." *Electoral Studies* 30 (4): 712–26.

Marien, S., Hooghe, M., and Quintelier, E. (2010). "Inequalities in Non-Institutionalized Forms of Political Participation. A Multilevel Analysis for 26 countries." *Political Studies* 58 (1): 187–213.

Markoff, J. (2011). "A moving target: Democracy," *European Journal of Sociology* 52 (2): 239–76.

Marks, G., Hooghe, L., and Schakel, A. H. (2008). "Measuring regional authority." *Regional and Federal Studies* 18 (2): 111–21.

McAllister, I. (1999). "The economic performance of governments," in P. Norris (ed.), *Critical citizens: Global support for democratic government* (Oxford: Oxford University Press) 188–203.

McNair, B. (2002). "Journalism and democracy in contemporary Britain," in R. Kuhn and E. Neveu (eds), *Political Journalism. New challenges, new practices* (London: Routledge) 189–202.

McQuail, D. (1993). *Mass communication theory, An introduction* (London: Sage).

Mény, Y. and Surel, Y. (2002). "The Constitutive Ambiguity of Populism ," in Y. Mény and Y. Surel (eds), *Democracies and the Populist Challenge* (Houndmills: Palgrave) 1–21.

Miller, A. and Listhaug, O. (1999). "Political performance and institutional trust," in P. Norris (ed.), *Critical Citizens: Global Support for Democratic Government* (Oxford: Oxford University Press) 204–16.

Miller, A. H. and Listhaug, O. (1998). "Policy preferences and political distrust: A comparison of Norway, Sweden and the United States." *Scandinavian Political Studies* 21 (2): 161–87.

Mishler, W. and Rose, R. (2001a). "Political support for incomplete democracies: Realist vs. idealist theories and measures." *International Political Science Review* 22 (4): 303–20.

Mishler, W. and Rose, R. (2001b). "What Are the Origins of Political Trust?" *Comparative Political Studies* 34 (1): 30–62.

Moy, P. and Hussain, M. M. (2011). "Media influences on political trust and engagement," in R. Y. Shapiro and L. R. Jacobs (eds), *Oxford Handbook of American Public Opinion and the Media* (Oxford: Oxford University Press) 220–35.

Moy, P., Pfau, M., and Kahlor, L. (1999). "Media use and public confidence in democratic institutions," *Journal of Broadcasting & Electronic Media* 43 (2): 137–58.

Moy, P. and Scheufele, D. A. (2000). "Media effects on political and social trust." *Journalism & Mass Communication Quarterly* 77 (4): 744–59.

Mudde, C. (2004). "The Populist Zeitgeist." *Government and Opposition* 39 (4): 542–63.

Mueller, J. (1973). *War, Presidents and Public Opinion* (New York: John Wiley & Sons).

Mutz, D. C. and Reeves, B. (2005). "The new videomalaise: Effects of televised incivility on political trust." *American Political Science Review* 99 (1): 1–15.

Mutz, D. C. and Young, L. (2011). "Communication and Public Opinion Plus Ça Change?" *Public Opinion Quarterly* 75 (5): 1018–44.

Neblo, M., Esterling, K., Kennedy, R., Lazer, D., and Sokhey, A. (2010). "Who Wants To Deliberate—And Why?" *American Political Science Review* 104 (3): 566–83.

Newton, K. (1999). "Mass media effects: mobilization or media malaise?" *British Journal of Political Science* 29 (4): 577–99.

Newton, K. (2001). "Trust, social capital, civil society, and democracy." *International Political Science Review* 22 (2): 201–14.

Newton, K. (2006a). "May the weak force be with you: The power of the mass media in modern politics." *European Journal of Political Research* 45 (2): 209–34.

Newton, K. (2006b). "Political support: Social capital, civil society and political and economic performance." *Political Studies* 54 (4): 846–64.

Newton, K. (2007). "Social and Political Trust," in R. J. Dalton and H-D. Klingemann (eds), *The Oxford Handbook of Political Behavior* (Oxford: Oxford University Press) 342–61.

Newton, K. and Norris, P. (2000). "Confidence in Public Institutions: Faith, Culture, or Performance?," in S. Pharr and R. Putnam (eds), *Disaffected Democracies: What's troubling the trilateral countries?* (Princeton, NJ: Princeton University Press) 52–73.

Niedermayer, O. and Sinnott, R. (1995). *Public opinion and internationalized governance*, 2 (Oxford: Oxford University Press).

Norris, P. (1999a). *Critical Citizens: Global Support for Democratic Governance* (Oxford: Oxford University Press).

Norris, P. (1999b). "Institutional explanations for political support," in P. Norris (ed.), *Critical Citizens: Global Support for Democratic Government* (Oxford: Oxford University Press) 217–35.

Norris, P. (1999c). "Introduction: the growth of critical citizens?," in P. Norris (ed), *Critical Citizens: Global Support for Democratic Government* (Oxford: Oxford University Press) 1–27.

Norris, P. (2000). *A Virtuous Circle. Political communications in Postindustrial societies* (Cambridge: Cambridge University Press).

Norris, P. (2001). "Global Governance and Cosmopolitan Citizens," in J. S. Nye and J. Donahue (eds), *Governance in a Globalizing World* (Washington, DC: Brookings Institution Press) 155–77.

Norris, P. (2011). *Democratic deficit. Critical Citizens Revisited* (New York: Cambridge University Press).

Norris, P. (2012). "Trust in Government: The US and Europe." *Expert Meeting about the (presumed) legitimacy crisis of representative democracy in advanced industrial democracies*, Netherlands Royal Academy of Sciences, Amsterdam.

Nye Jr., J. S., Zelikow, P. D., and King, D. C. (1997). *Why people don't trust government* (Cambridge, MA: Harvard University Press).

O'Connor, J. (1973). *The fiscal crisis of the state* (New York: St. Martin's Press).

Offe, C. and Keane, J. (eds.) (1984). *Contradictions of the welfare state* (London: Hutchinson).

Oskarsson, S. (2010). "Generalized trust and political support: A cross-national investigation." *Acta Politica* 45 (4): 423–43.

Ostrom, E. (1990). *Governing the Commons* (Cambridge: Cambridge University Press).

Pariser, E. (2011). *The filter bubble: What the Internet is hiding from you* (London: Penguin).

Parker, S. (1995). "Toward an Understanding of 'Rally Effects': Public Opinion in the Persian Gulf War." *Public Opinion Quarterly* 59 (4): 526–46.

Parker, S. L. and Parker, G. R. (1993). "Why do we trust our Congressman." *Journal of Politics* 55 (2): 442–53.

Paskeviciute, A. (2009). "Partisanship and system support in established and new democracies," in J. Bartle and P. Bellucci (eds), *Political Parties and Partisanship; social identity and individual attitudes* (London: Routledge) 121–41.

Pateman, C. (1970). *Participation and Democratic Theory* (London: Cambridge University Press).

Patterson, T. (1980). *The mass media election. How Americans choose their president* (New York: Praeger).

Patterson, T. (1993). *Out of order* (New York: Knopf).

Patterson, T. (1996). "Bad news, bad governance," in K. H. Jamieson (ed.), *The media and politics, The annals of the American academy of political and social science,* 546 (New York: Sage Periodical Press) 99–108.

Patterson, T. (2000). "Doing Well and Doing Good". KSG Working Paper No. 01–001. Available at SSRN: <https://ssrn.com/abstract=257395 orhttp://dx.doi.org/10.2139/ssrn.257395>.

Patterson, T. (2002). *The vanishing voter* (New York: Knopf).

Pedersen, R. T. (2012). "The game frame and political efficacy: Beyond the spiral of cynicism." *European Journal of Communication* 27 (3): 225–40.

Peffley, M. and Rohrschneider, R. (2003). "Democratization and political tolerance in seventeen countries: A multi-level model of democratic learning." *Political Research Quarterly* 56 (3): 243–57.

Peffley, M. and Rohrschneider, R. (2014). "The multiple bases of democratic support: procedural representation and governmental outputs," in J. Thomassen (ed.), *Elections and Representative Democracy. Representation and Accountability* (Oxford: Oxford University Press) 181–200.

Pharr, S. J. and Putnam, R. D. (2000). *Disaffected democracies: what's troubling the trilateral countries?* (Princeton, NJ: Princeton University Press).

Pharr, S. J., Putnam, R. D., and Dalton, R. J. (2000). "A Quarter-Century of Declining Confidence." *Journal of Democracy* 11 (2): 5–25.

Philippa, M. et al. (2009). *Etymologisch woordenboek van het Nederlands,* 4 (Amsterdam: Amsterdam University Press).

Pickup, M. and Evans, G. (2013). "Addressing the Endogeneity of Economic Evaluations in Models of Political Choice." *Public Opinion Quarterly* 77 (3): 735–54.

Pitkin, H. F. (1967). *The Concept of Representation* (Berkeley, CA: University of California Press).

Poguntke, T., Scarrow, S., and Webb, P. (2015). "Party rules, party resources, and the politics of parliamentary democracies: How parties organize in the 21st century." *Annual Conference of the American Political Science Association,* San Francisco, CA.

Poguntke, T. and Webb, P. (2005). *The Presidentialization of Politics: A Comparative Study of Modern Democracies* (Oxford: Oxford University Press).

Powell Jr, Bingham, G. and Whitten, Guy D. (1993). "A Cross-National Analysis of Economic Voting: Taking Account of the Political Context." *American Journal of Political Science* 37 (2): 391–414.

Powell, G. B. (2000). *Elections as instruments of democracy: Majoritarian and proportional visions* (New Haven, CT: Yale University Press).

Powell, G. B. (2004). "The Quality of Democracy: The Chain of Responsiveness." *Journal of Democracy* 15 (4): 91–105.

Prior, M. (2007). *Post-broadcast democracy: How media choice increases inequality in political involvement and polarizes elections* (Cambridge: Cambridge University Press).

Prothro, J. W. and Grigg, C. M. (1960). "Fundamental Principles of Democracy: Bases of Agreement and Disagreement." *Journal of Politics* 22 (2): 276–94.

Przeworski, A., Stokes, S., and Manin, B. (1999). *Democracy, Accountability, and Representation* (Cambridge: Cambridge University Press).

Putnam, R. (1993). *Making Democracy Work. Civic Traditions in Modern Italy* (Princeton, NJ: Princeton University Press).

Putnam, R. (2000). *Bowling Alone: The Collapse and Revival of American Community* (New York: Simon & Schuster).

Putnam, R. (2002a). *Democracies in Flux* (Oxford: Oxford University Press).

Putnam, R. (2002b). "Bowling Together." *American Prospect* 13 (3): 20–3.

Rabash, J., Steele, F., Browne, W., and Goldstein, H. (2012). "A user's guide to MLwiN, v2.29," Bristol: University of Bristol, Centre for Multilevel Modelling.

Rauch, J. E. and Evans, P. B. (2000). "Bureaucratic structure and bureaucratic performance in developing countries." *Journal of Public Economics* 75 (1): 49–71.

Reinemann, C. and Wilke, J. (2007). "It's the debates, stupid! How the introduction of televised debates changed the portrayal of chancellor candidates in the German press, 1949–2005." *Harvard International Journal of Press/Politics* 12 (4): 92–111.

Reiter, H. (1989). "Party Decline in the West: A Skeptic's View." *Journal of Theoretical Politics* 1 (3): 325–48.

Robinson, M. J. (1976). "Public affairs televison and the growth of political malaise: The case of 'the selling of the Pentagon." *American Political Science Review* 70 (2): 409–32.

Rohrschneider, R. (2005). "Institutional Quality and Perceptions of Representation in Advanced Industrial Democracies." *Comparative Political Studies* 38 (7): 850–74.

Rosanvallon, P. (2008). *Counter-Democracy. Politics in an Age of Distrust* (Cambridge: Cambridge University Press).

Rose, R. and McAllister, I. (1986). *Voters Begin to Choose; From Closed-Class to Open Elections in Britain* (London: Sage).

Rose, R. and Mishler, W. (2011). "Political Trust and Distrust In Post-Authoritarian Contexts," in S. Zmerli and M. Hooghe (eds), *Political trust: Why context matters* (Colchester: ECPR Press) 117–40.

Rose, R., Mishler, W., and Haerpfer, C. (1998). *Democracy and its alternatives: Understanding post-communist societies* (Baltimore, MD: Johns Hopkins University Press).

Rothstein, B. (2009). "Creating Political Legitimacy: Electoral Democracy versus Quality of Government." *American Behavioral Scientist* 53 (3): 311–30.

Rothstein, B. (2011). *The Quality of Government. Corruption, Social Trust, and Inequality in International Perspective* (Chicago, IL: University of Chicago Press).

Rothstein, B. and Stolle, D. (2008). "The State and Social Capital: An Institutional Theory of Generalized Trust." *Comparative Politics* 40 (4): 441–59.

Rothstein, B. and Teorell, J. (2008). "What is Quality of Government? A theory of impartial government institutions." *Governance* 21 (2): 165–90.

Rudolph, T. J. (2009). "Political Trust, Ideology, and Public Support for Tax Cuts." *Public Opinion Quarterly* 73 (1): 144–58.

Sander, T. and Putnam, R. (2010). "Still Bowling Alone? The Post-9/11 Split." *Journal of Democracy* 21 (1): 9–16.

Sanders, D. H. C., Stewart, M., and Whiteley, P. (2014). "Output-oriented Legitimacy: Individual- and System-level Influences on Democracy Satisfaction," in Jacques Thomassen (ed.), *Elections and representative democracy. Representation and Accountability* (Oxford: Oxford University Press) 153–80.

Saward, M. (2010). *The Representative Claim* (Oxford: Oxford University Press).

Scarrow, S. E. (2015). *Beyond Party Members: Changing Approaches to Partisan Mobilization* (Oxford: Oxford University Press).

Schade, J. and Baum, M. (2007). "Reactance or Acceptance? Reactions towards the introduction of road pricing," *Transportation Research* 41 (1): 41–8.

Schäfer, A. (2012). "Consequences of social inequality for democracy in Western Europe." *Zeitschrift für vergleichende Politikwissenschaft* 6 (2): 23–45.

Scharpf, F. W. (1997). *Games real actors play: Actor-centered institutionalism in policy research* (Boulder, CO: Westview).

Scharpf, F. W. (1999). *Governing in Europe: effective and democratic?* (New York: Oxford University Press).

Scharpf, F. W. (2009). "Legitimacy in the multilevel European polity." *European Political Science Review* 1 (2): 173–204.

Schattschneider, E. E. (1960). *The Semi-Sovereign People* (New York: Holt).

Schattschneider, E. E. (1977). *Party Government* (Westport, CT: Greenwood Press).

Schedler, A. and Sarsfield, R. (2007). "Democrats with adjectives: Linking direct and indirect measures of democratic support." *European Journal of Political Research* 46 (5): 637–59.

Schmitt, H. (2009). "Partisanship in nine western democracies: causes and consequences," in J. Bartle and P. Bellucci (eds), *Political Parties and Partisanship; social identity and individual attitudes* (London: Routledge) 75–87.

Schmitt, H., Scholz, E., Leim, I., and Moschner, M. (2008). "The Mannheim Eurobarometer Trend File 1970–2002 (ed 2.00)." Cologne: GESIS Data Archive.

Schmitt-Beck, R. and Wolsing, A. (2010). "European TV environments and citizens' social trust. Evidence from multilevel analyses." *Communications* 35 (4): 461–83.

Schmitter, P. (2001). "Parties are not what they once were," in L. Diamond and R. Gunther (eds), *Political Parties and Democracy* (Baltimore, MD: Johns Hopkins University Press).

Schmitter, P. C. and Trechsel, A. H. (2004). *The future of democracy in Europe: trends, analyses and reforms* (Strasbourg: Council of Europe Publishing).

Schoon, I. and H. Cheng (2011). "Determinants of political trust: A lifetime learning model." *Developmental Psychology* 47 (3): 619–31.

Schuck, A. R. T., Boomgaarden, H. G., and De Vreese, C. H. (2013). "Cynics All Around? The Impact of Election News on Political Cynicism in Comparative Perspective." *Journal of Communication* 63 (2): 287–311.

Schuck, A. R. T., Vliegenthart, R., and De Vreese, C. H. (2016). "Who's Afraid of Conflict? The Mobilizing Effect of Conflict Framing in Campaign News." *British Journal of Political Science* 46 (1): 177–94.

Schudson, M. (1995). *The power of news* (Cambridge, MA: Harvard University Press).

Seligson, M. A. (2002). "The impact of corruption on regime legitimacy: A comparative study of four Latin American countries." *Journal of Politics* 64 (2): 408–33.

Semetko, H. A., Blumler, J. G., Gurevitch, M., and Weaver, D. H. (1991). *The Formation of Campaign Agendas: A Comparative Analysis of Party and Media Roles in Recent American and British Elections* (Hillsdale, NJ: Lawrence Erlbaum Associates Publishers).

Shehata, A. (2014). "Game Frames, Issue Frames, and Mobilization: Disentangling the Effects of Frame Exposure and Motivated News Attention on Political Cynicism and Engagement." *International Journal of Public Opinion Research* 26 (2): 157–77.

Shehata, A. and Strömbäck, J. (2014). "Mediation of Political Realities: Media as Crucial Sources of Information," in F. Esser, and Strömbäck, J. (eds), *Mediatization of Politics. Understanding the Transformation of Western Democracies* (Houndmills: Palgrave Macmillan) 93–113.

Sinnott, R. (1998). "Party Attachment in Europe: Methodological Critique and Substantive Implications." *British Journal of Political Science* 28 (4): 627–50.

Sloam, J. (2014). "New Voice, Less Equal. The Civic and Political Engagement of Young People in the United States and Europe." *Comparative Political Studies* 47 (5): 663–88.

Snijders, T. A. B. and Bosker, R. J. (1999). *Multilevel Analysis: An Introduction to Basic and Advanced Multilevel Modeling.* (London: Sage).

Solt, F. (2009). "Standardizing the World Income Inequality Database." *Social Science Quarterly* 90 (2): 231–42.

Soroka, S., Andrew, B., Aalberg, T., Iyengar, S., Curran, J., Coen, S., Tiffen, R. O. D. (2013). "Auntie Knows Best? Public Broadcasters and Current Affairs Knowledge." *British Journal of Political Science* 43 (4): 719–39.

Soroka, S. N. (2014). *Negativity in democratic politics: Causes and consequences* (Cambridge: Cambridge University Press).

Sperling, J. (2004). *Germany at Fifty-five* (Manchester: Manchester University Press).

Steenbergen, M. (2012). "Hierarchical Linear Models for Electoral Research: A worked example in Stata mimeo Zurich."

Strömbäck, J. (2005). "In Search of a Standard: four models of democracy and their normative implications for journalism." *Journalism Studies* 6 (3): 331–45.

Strömbäck, J., Djerf-Pierre, M., and Shehata, A. (2015). "A Question of Time? A Longitudinal Analysis of the Relationship between News Media Consumption and Political Trust." *International Journal of Press/Politics* 21 (1): 88–110.

Strömbäck, J. and Shehata, A. (2010). "Media malaise or a virtuous circle? Exploring the causal relationships between news media exposure, political news attention and political interest." *European Journal of Political Research* 49 (5): 575–97.

Sunstein, C. R. (2007). *Republic.com 2.0* (Princeton, NJ: Princeton University Press).

Takens, J., van Atteveldt, W., van Hoof, A., and Kleinnijenhuis, J. (2013). "Media logic in election campaign coverage." *European Journal of Communication* 28 (3): 277–93.

Taylor, M. A. (2000). "Channeling frustrations: Institutions, economic fluctuations, and political behavior." *European Journal of Political Research* 38 (1): 95–134.

Teorell, J., Charron, N., Dahlberg, S., Holmberg, S., Rothstein, B., Sundin, P., and Svensson, R. (2013). "The Quality of Government Dataset."

Teorell, J., Dahlberg, S., Holmberg, S., Rothstein, B., Khomenko, A., and Svensson, R. (2016). "The Quality of Government Standard Dataset," Jan 16 edn.

Thibaut, J. W. and L. Walker. (1975). *Procedural justice: A psychological analysis* (Hillsdale, NJ/New York: L. Erlbaum Associates).

Thomassen, J. (ed.) (2014). *Elections and Representative Democracy. Representation and Accountability* (Oxford: Oxford University Press).

Thomassen, J. (2015). "What's gone wrong with democracy, or with theories explaining why it has?" in T. Poguntke, S. Roßteutscher, R. Schmitt-Beck, and S. Zmerli (eds), *Citizenship and Democracy in an Era of Crisis* (Abingdon: Routledge) 34–52.

Thomassen, J. and van der Kolk, H. (2009). "Effectiveness and political support in old and new democracies," in H-D. Klingemann (ed.), *The Comparative Study of Electoral Systems* (Oxford: Oxford University Press) 333–46.

Thomassen, J., Van Ham, C., and Andeweg, R. (2014). *De wankele democratie. Heeft de democratie zijn beste tijd gehad?* (Amsterdam: Prometheus/Bert Bakker).

Thomassen, J. J. A. (2007). "Democratic values," in R. J. Dalton and H-D. Klingemann, (eds), *Oxford Handbook of Political Behavior* (New York: Oxford University Press).

Thomassen, J. J. A. (2010). "De permanente crisis van de democratie." *Valedictory address,* University of Twente.

Thomassen, J. J. A., Andeweg, R. B., and Van Ham, C. (2017). "Political Trust and the Decline of Legitimacy Debate," in S. Zmerli and T. W. G. van der Meer (eds), *Handbook on Political Trust* (Cheltenham: Edward Elgar Publishing).

Thomassen, J. J. A. and Schmitt, H. (1999). "Introduction: political representation and legitimacy in the European Union," in J. J. A. Thomassen and H. Schmitt (eds), *Political representation and legitimacy in the European Union* (New York: Oxford University Press) 3–24.

Tiemeijer, W. (2010). "'t Is maar wat je democratie noemt…," in H. Dijstelbloem et al. (eds), *Het gezicht van de publieke zaak. WRR* (Amsterdam: Amsterdam University Press).

Todosijevic, B. (2012). "Transfer of Variables between Different Data Sets, or Taking 'Previous Research' Seriously," *Bulletin de Méthodologie Sociologique* 113 (1): 20–39.

Torcal, M. (2014). "The Decline of Political trust in Spain and Portugal: Economic Performance or Political Responsiveness?" *American Behavioral Scientist* 58 (12): 1542–67.

Tsebelis, G. (1995). "Decision-making in political systems: Veto players in presidentialism, parliamentarism, multicameralism and multipartyism." *British Journal of Political Science* 25 (3): 289–325.

Tyler, T. R. (1984). "Justice in the political arena," in R. Folger (ed.), *The sense of injustice* (New York: Plenum Press: 189–225).

Tyler, T. R. (1990). *Why People Obey the Law* (New Haven, CT: Yale University Press).

Tyler, T. R. (2001). "The psychology of public dissatisfaction with government," in J. R. Hibbing and E. Theiss-Morse (eds), *What is it about government that Americans dislike?* (New York: Cambridge University Press) 227–42.

Tyler, T. R. (2006). "Psychological perspectives on legitimacy and legitimation." *Annual Review of Psychology* 57: 375–400.

Tyler, T. R. and Lind, A. (1992). "A Relational Model of Authority in Groups," in M. Zanna (ed.), *Advances in Experimental Social Psychology* 25 (San Diego, CA: Academic Press Inc) 115–91.

Uba, K. (2010). "'Save our school!' What kinds of impact have protests against school closures in Swedish local politics?." *Statsvetenskaplig Tidskrift* 112 (1): 96–104.

245

Ulbig, S. G. (2002). "Policies, procedures, and people: Sources of support for government?" *Social Science Quarterly* 83 (3): 789–809.

Uslaner, E. M. (2008). *Corruption, Inequality, and the Rule of law. The bulging pocket makes the easy life* (Cambridge: Cambridge University Press).

Valentino, N. A., Beckmann, M. N., and Buhr, T. A. (2001). "A spiral of cynicism for some: The contingent effects of campaign news frames on participation and confidence in government." *Political Communication* 18 (4): 347–67.

Van Aelst, P. (2007). *Toeschouwer, speler of scheidsrechter? Een studie naar de rol van de media in de verkiezingscampagne van 2003* (Brugge: Vanden Broele).

Van Aelst, P. and De Swert, K. (2009). "Politics in the news. Do campaigns matter? A comparison between political news during campaign periods and routine periods in Flanders (Belgium)." *Communications* 34 (2): 149–68.

Van Biezen, I., Mair, P., and Poguntke, T. (2012). "Going, going, . . . gone? The decline of party membership in contemporary Europe." *European Journal of Political Research* 51 (1): 24–56.

Van de Walle, S., Van Roosbroek, S., and Bouckaert, G. (2008). "Trust in the public sector: Is there any evidence for a long-term decline?" *International Review of Administrative Sciences* 74 (1): 47–64.

Van der Brug, W. (2003). "How the LPF Fuelled Discontent: Empirical tests of explanations of LPF support." *Acta Politica* 38 (1): 89–106.

Van der Brug, W. (2004). "Voting for the LPF: Some Clarifications." *Acta Politica* 39 (1): 84–91.

Van der Brug, W., Van der Eijk, C., and Franklin, M. (2007). *The Economy and the Vote: Economic Conditions and Elections in Fifteen Countries* (Cambridge: Cambridge University Press).

Van der Meer, T. W. G. and Van Ingen, E. J. (2009). "Schools of democracy? Disentangling the relationship between civic participation and political action in 17 European countries." *European Journal of Political Research* 48: 281–308.

Van der Meer, T. and Dekker, P. (2011). "Trustworthy States, Trusting Citizens? A Multilevel Study into Objective and Subjective Determinants of Political Trust," in S. Zmerli and M. Hooghe (eds), *Political Trust: Why Context Matters* (Colchester: ECPR Press) 95–116.

Van der Meer, T. W. G. (2010). "In what we trust? A multi-level study into trust in parliament as an evaluation of state characteristics." *International Review of Administrative Sciences* 76 (3): 517–36.

Van der Meer, T. W. G. (2016). "Democratic input, macro-economic output, and political trust," in S. Zmerli and T. W. G. van der Meer (eds), *Handbook on Political Trust* (Cheltenham: Edward Elgar Publishing).

Van der Meer, T. W. G. and Hakhverdian, A. (2017). "Political trust as the evaluation of process and performance: A cross-national study of forty-two European democracies." *Political Studies* 65 (1): 81–102.

Van der Zwan, A. (2004). "How the LPF Fuelled Discontent: A Comment." *Acta Politica* 39 (1): 79–83.

Van Deth, J., Montero, J. R., and Westholm, A. (2007). *Citizenship and Involvement in European Democracies: A Comparative Analysis* (Abingdon: Routledge).

Van Deth, J. W. and Scarbrough, E. (1995). *The Impact of Values* 4 (Oxford: Oxford University Press).

Van Deth, J. W. and Zmerli, S. (2010). "Introduction: Civicness, Equality, and Democracy—A "Dark Side" of Social Capital?" *American Behavioural Scientist* 53 (5): 631–9.

Van Erkel, P. and Van der Meer, T. W. G. (2016). "Macro-economic performance, Political trust, and the Great Recession: A multilevel analysis of the effects of within-country fluctuations in macro-economic performance on political trust in fifteen EU countries, 1999–2011." *European Journal of Political Research* 55 (1): 177–97.

Van Ham, C. and Thomassen, J. (2012). "A legitimacy crisis of representative democracy?" *Expert Meeting about the (presumed) legitimacy crisis of representative democracy in advanced industrial democracies* (Netherlands Royal Academy of Sciences, Amsterdam).

Van Ingen, E. and Van der Meer, T. (2016). "Schools or Pools of Democracy? A Longitudinal Test of the Relation Between Civic Participation and Political Socialization." *Political Behavior* 38 (1): 83–103.

Van Kessel, S. (2015). *Populist Parties in Europe: Agents of Discontent?* (Houndmills: Palgrave Macmillan).

Van Kersbergen, K. and Waarden, F. V. (2004). "'Governance' as a bridge between disciplines: Cross-disciplinary inspiration regarding shifts in governance and problems of governability, accountability and legitimacy." *European Journal of Political Research*, 43: 143–71.

Vatter, A., Flinders, M., and Bernauer, J. (2014). "A Global Trend Toward Democratic Convergence? A Lijphartian Analysis of Advanced Democracies." *Comparative Political Studies* 47 (6) a: 903–29.

Vliegenthart, R., Boomgaarden, H. G., and Boumans, J. (2010). "Changes in political news coverage: Personalization, conflict and negativity in British and Dutch newspapers," in K. Brants and K. Voltmer (eds), *Political Communication in Postmodern Democracy* (Houndmills: Palgrave Macmillan) 92–110.

Voicu, M. and Bartolome Peral, E. (2014). "Support for democracy and early socialization in a non-democratic country: does the regime matter?" *Democratization* 21 (3): 554–73.

Vowles, J., Aimer, P., Catt, H., Lamare, and J., Miller, R. (2013). *Towards Consensus? The 1993 Election and Referendum in New Zealand and the Transition to Proportional Representation* (Auckland: Auckland University Press).

Wagner, A. F., Schneider, F., and Halla, M. (2009). "The quality of institutions and satisfaction with democracy in Western Europe–A panel analysis." *European Journal of Political Economy* 25 (1): 30–41.

Warren, M. A. (1999). *Democracy and Trust* (New York: Cambridge University Press).

Warren, M. E. (2004). "What does corruption mean in a democracy?" *American Journal of Political Science* 48 (2): 328–43.

Wattenberg, M. P. (1991). *The Rise of Candidate-Centered Politics: Presidential Elections of the 1980s* (Harvard, MA: Harvard University Press).

Wattenberg, M. P. (1998). *The Decline of American Political Parties, 1952–1996* (Harvard, MA: Harvard University Press).

Weatherford, M. S. (1992). "Measuring Political Legitimacy." *American Political Science Review* 86 (1): 149–66.

Wells, J. M. and Krieckhaus, J. (2006). "Does national context influence democratic satisfaction? A multi-level analysis." *Political Research Quarterly* 59 (4): 569–78.

Wessels, B. and Schmitt, H. (2014). "Meaningful Choices: Does Parties' Supply Matter?" in J. Thomassen (ed.), *Elections and Democracy; Representation and Accountability* (Oxford: Oxford University Press) 38–59.

Wollebaek, D., Enjolras, B., Steen-Johnsen, K., and Ødegård, G. (2012). "After Utøya: How a High-Trust Society Reacts to Terror—Trust and Civic Engagement in the Aftermath of July 22." *PS Political Science & Politics* 45 (1): 32–7.

Wollebaek, D. and Selle, P. (2002). "Does Participation in Voluntary Associations Contribute to Social Capital? The Impact of Intensity, Scope, and Type." *Nonprofit and Voluntary Sector Quarterly* 31 (1): 32–61.

Wroe, A., Allen, N., and Birch, S. (2013). "The Role of Political Trust in Conditioning Perceptions of Corruption." *European Political Science Review* 5 (2): 175–95.

Zakaria, F. (1997). "The rise of illiberal democracy." *Foreign Affairs* 76 (6): 22–43.

Zaller, J. (1992). *The Nature and Origins of Mass Opinion* (Cambridge: Cambridge University Press).

Zaller, J. (1999). *A theory of media politics. How the interests of politicians, journalists, and citizens shape the news* (Chicago, IL: University of Chicago Press).

Zeh, R. and Hopmann, D. N. (2013). "Indicating mediatization? Two decades of election campaign television coverage." *European Journal of Communication* 28 (3): 225–40.

Zittel, T. and Fuchs, D. (2007). *Participatory Democracy and Political Participation; Can participatory engineering bring citizens back in?* (Abingdon: Routledge).

Zmerli, S. and Hooghe, M. (2011). *Political Trust. Why Context Matters* (Colchester: ECPR Press).

Zmerli, S. and Newton, K. (2011). "Winners, Losers and Three Types of Trust," in S. Zmerli and M. Hooghe (eds), *Political Trust: Why Context Matters* (Colchester: ECPR Press) 67–94.

Zmerli, S. and Newton, K. (2016). "The interdependency of political and social trust," in S. Zmerli and T. W. G. van der Meer (eds), *Handbook on Political Trust* (Cheltenham: Edward Elgar Publishing).

Zmerli, S., Newton, K., and Montero, J. R. (2007). "Trust in people, confidence in political institutions, and satisfaction with democracy," in J. R. Montero, A. Westholm, and J. W. van Deth (eds), *Citizenship and Involvement in European Democracies* (Abingdon: Routledge) 35–65.

Author Index

Subject Index

Tables, figures, and boxes are indicated by an italic *t*, *f* and *b* following the page number.

Printed and bound by CPI Group (UK) Ltd, Croydon, CR0 4YY